"This powerful volume, in the hands of students, researchers and educators, will be wonderfully dangerous – it will help to change the world. Featuring outstanding contributions by established and upcoming scholars writing on gender, sexuality, and feminist activism, the book advances ideas about how we can work toward more equitable futures in the context of leisure research, theory, and practice. *Feminisms in Leisure Studies: Advancing a Fourth Wave* represents a big wave indeed."

Brett Lashua, Reader in Leisure and Culture at Leeds Beckett University, UK

"Using the framework of the 4th Wave, Parry brings together an array of researchers to provide a theoretically sophisticated and yet accessible approach to contemporary feminist perspectives on leisure. This book is long overdue in our field and marks a turning point for current and future researchers who want to move beyond gender based discussions grounded in individual markers of identities and in binaries, toward institutional and structural level analyses. This book is a must read for those interested in doing research that allows for direct and ongoing gender-related critiques while also providing the theoretical underpinnings to support advocacy for social change and social justice. Regardless of one's area of research or interest in leisure studies, this book is a must read for everyone."

Dana Kivel, Professor of Recreation, Parks & Tourism Administration and Director of the Community Engagement Center, California State University, USA

Feminisms in Leisure Studies

Feminisms in Leisure Studies acknowledges and advances the contribution of feminist theories to leisure knowledge and research. Building upon the strong history of feminist leisure scholarship, the book reviews key feminist theories and offers an overview of a fourth wave of feminism and its relevance to leisure.

Written by a team of leading international feminist scholars, each chapter addresses a particular theoretical perspective, using examples from each author's research to unpack methodological and substantive issues essential to leisure studies. Critically, this book moves beyond women, the emphasis of much gender scholarship to date, to focus on issues of feminism as connected to leisure scholarship more broadly.

This book is an important and engaging read for students and scholars of diversity, women's studies, multiculturalism, social justice, gender studies, leisure studies, LGBTQQ studies, and feminist research.

Diana C. Parry is Associate Vice-President of Human Rights, Equity and Inclusion and Professor in Applied Health Sciences at the University of Waterloo, Canada. Utilizing a feminist lens to explore the personal and political links between women's leisure and women's health, Dr. Parry's research privileges women's standpoints and aims to create social change and enact social justice by challenging the medical model of scholarship.

Routledge Critical Leisure Studies

Series Editor: Tony Blackshaw, Sheffield Hallam University

The modern world is one that holds an intense fascination with the activities we place under the heading 'leisure'. Rather than simply being the opposite of 'work', 'leisure' today can be seen as a form of social and cultural life in which 'work' and 'leisure' intersect and mutually inform one another.

This series is a forum for agenda-setting research that examines our contemporary world of leisure. It places a strong emphasis not only on mapping current developments in individual and collective leisure activities, but also on challenging our understanding of these from different perspectives. Providing detailed empirical and theoretical accounts, this series explores the critical issues that underpin people's leisure lives at the beginning of the twenty-first century.

While this series is devoted to leisure, many of its books touch on other subject fields, contributing to interdisciplinary studies and appealing to readers from across the social sciences and the humanities.

Available in this series

1 **Re-Imagining Leisure Studies**
Tony Blackshaw

2 **Philosophy of Leisure**
Foundations of the good life
Johan Bouwer and Marco van Leeuwen

3 **Feminisms in Leisure Studies**
Advancing a Fourth Wave
Edited by Diana C. Parry

4 **Whatever Happened to the Leisure Society?**
A. J. Veal

Feminisms in Leisure Studies

Advancing a Fourth Wave

Edited by Diana C. Parry

LONDON AND NEW YORK

First published 2019 by Routledge

2 Park Square, Milton Park, Abingdon, Oxfordshire OX14 4RN
52 anderbilt Avenue, New York, NY 10017

Routledge is an imprint of the Taylor & Francis Group, an informa business

First issued in paperback 2020

British Library Cataloguing-in-Publication Data
A catalogue record for this book is available from the British Library

Library of Congress Cataloging-in-Publication Data
A catalog record has been requested for this book

ISBN: 978-1-138-09076-7 (hbk)
ISBN: 978-0-367-49911-2 (pbk)

Typeset in Goudy
by Wearset Ltd, Boldon, Tyne and Wear

For my daughters, Claire and Charlotte, who inspire me to be a better feminist every day

Contents

List of contributors xi
Acknowledgements xiv

1 **Fourth wave feminism: theoretical underpinnings and future directions for leisure research** 1
DIANA C. PARRY, COREY W. JOHNSON, AND FAITH-ANNE WAGLER

2 **Into new modes of unbecomings: engaging poststructural feminism towards alternative theorizations of gender in leisure research** 13
LISBETH A. BERBARY

3 **Feminist theories after the poststructuralist turn** 34
SIMONE FULLAGAR, ADELE PAVLIDIS, AND JESSICA FRANCOMBE-WEBB

4 **Thinking intersectionally: fourth wave feminism and feminist leisure scholarship** 58
BECCY WATSON

5 **Queering leisure: teasing out queer theory's legacies** 79
JUDY DAVIDSON

6 **"We danced around the circle": feminist standpoint theories and turning old stories into something new** 102
FELICE YUEN

7 **Manning up and manning on: masculinities, hegemonic masculinity, and leisure studies** 126
COREY W. JOHNSON AND LUC S. COUSINEAU

8 **The fourth wave: what #MeToo can teach us about millennial mobilization, intersectionality, and men's accountability** 149
STEPHEN M. A. SOUCIE, DIANA C. PARRY, AND LUC S. COUSINEAU

Index 165

Contributors

Lisbeth A. Berbary is an Associate Professor in Recreation and Leisure Studies at the University of Waterloo. She holds a PhD in Leisure Studies with graduate certificates in women's studies and interdisciplinary qualitative research. Lisbeth is committed to qualitative inquiry informed by both critical and deconstructive theories, and the postmodern, narrative, and ontological turns. She has particular interest in representing her findings through accessible and collaborative creative analytic practices, such as ethno-screenplay, slam poetry, and composite narrative. Currently, Lisbeth is co-constructing zines, comics, and graphic novels to represent her work with bisexual/pansexual-identified individuals concerning their navigation of biphobia and bisexual erasure.

Luc S. Cousineau is a PhD candidate in the department of Recreation & Leisure Studies, at the University of Waterloo. Luc's research is focused on gender and power relations in work and leisure spaces, with a particular focus on anonymized online leisure and the effects of this leisure participation on masculinity. Using feminist theory, leisure theory, and new media/internet studies to ground his work, Luc's primary focus is men's involvement in men's rights activism – its roots, propagation, and transition from anonymous participation to identifiable personal ideology.

Judy Davidson is Associate Professor in the Faculty of Kinesiology, Sport, and Recreation at the University of Alberta. Her research interests include feminist and queer approaches to sport and leisure phenomena. She has published on homonationalism and the international lesbigay sport movement.

Jessica Francombe-Webb is a lecturer at the University of Bath. Her research explores the contested politics of the (in)active body in relation to health practices, physical and digital cultures, and issues of power, gender, social class, (dis)ability. Her work has been published in a variety of interdisciplinary journals.

Simone Fullagar is Professor and Head of the Physical Culture, Sport and Health research group at the University of Bath, UK, and Adjunct Professor at Griffith University, Australia. As an interdisciplinary sociologist, Simone undertakes qualitative research across a broad range of research projects related to leisure, sport, and tourism, as well as embodied health and well-being. Her work draws upon poststructural and new materialist theories.

Corey W. Johnson is a Professor in the Department of Recreation and Leisure Studies at the University of Waterloo. His theorizing and qualitative inquiry focuses its attention on the power relations between dominant and non-dominant populations in the cultural contexts of leisure.

Diana C. Parry is Associate Vice-President of Human Rights, Equity and Inclusion and Professor in Applied Health Sciences at the University of Waterloo, Canada. Utilizing a feminist lens to explore the personal and political links between women's leisure and women's health, Dr. Parry's research privileges women's standpoints and aims to create social change and enact social justice by challenging the medical model of scholarship.

Adele Pavlidis is a Postdoctoral Fellow at Griffith University. Her current work is primarily concerned with decoupling sport and masculinity, and supporting women and girls' sustainable participation in sport and leisure. Focusing on women's contact sports in particular, Dr. Pavlidis is examining the spatiality and materiality of sport cultures as a way through current impasses in cultural sociological theorizations of sport as a site of belonging identity, and wellbeing.

Stephen M. A. Soucie is a PhD student in the Recreation and Leisure Studies program at the University of Waterloo. For the past eight years, he has been actively involved in organizing around issues such as men's violence against women. Previously, Stephen was the coordinator of Male Allies, a public education program run by the Sexual Assault Support Centre of Waterloo Region (SASC). In this position, he worked to create conversations with men and boys around issues of healthy relationships, consent, and masculinity. Stephen holds an MA in Sociology from Brock University. His thesis was a qualitative analysis of the links between sport and rape culture.

Faith-Anne Wagler is a PhD candidate in the Department of Recreation and Leisure Studies, Faculty of Applied Health Sciences, at the University of Waterloo. Faith-Anne is a feminist researcher who focuses on women's leisure and its relationship to gender ideologies, with particular attention to leisure being used as ideological resistance. Regardless of the subject of her research, she aims to conduct research that helps create change and gender equity through knowledge and awareness.

Beccy Watson is a Reader in the Carnegie School of Sport, Leeds Beckett University, UK. Her research focuses on interrelationships between gender, 'race' and class and informs work on leisure, identities and intersectional approaches across the critical, social analysis of leisure and sport. Beccy is the Academic Lead for the Graduate School at Leeds Beckett. She teaches across undergraduate and postgraduate modules, focusing on issues of diversity, equity, and inclusion. Beccy was a managing editor for the journal *Leisure Studies* between 2007 and 2014.

Felice Yuen is an Associate Professor at Concordia University in Montreal, Canada, in the Department of Applied Human Sciences. Her research encompasses healing, social justice, and community development. She often employs arts-based approaches in her research (e.g., body mapping, photographs, collage, poetry). Indigenous methodologies and participatory action research guide the epistemological lenses she brings to her work. Her work with the Native Sisterhood, an Indigenous women's group in a federal prison, and Journey Women, a group of women dedicated to exploring and advocating for Indigenous women's healing, has led to publications in journals such as *Critical Criminology*, *Arts in Psychotherapy*, *Leisure Sciences*, and the *Journal of Leisure Research*, and presentations in academic, community-based, and government sectors.

Acknowledgements

Editing a book is never a solo endeavour. In this case, many people contributed to the final product, and as a result I have many thanks to express. To begin, thank you to all the authors for contributing such thoughtful chapters that make up this book. There are many others who contributed in big and small ways to bringing this book to fruition, including Faith-Anne Wagler, Stephen Soucie, Luc Cousineau, and Joanne Adair (who has a PhD in life that comes in handy when helping with a book). A special thank you to Corey Johnson, my bae, for all the behind-scenes help and always being willing to go above and beyond to help me. Most importantly, thank you to my husband, Troy Glover, whose feminism ensures I have time to work on books like this one as he covers things on the home front without question, complaint, or expectation of special recognition. For this, and many other reasons, I will forever be grateful.

Chapter 1

Fourth wave feminism

Theoretical underpinnings and future directions for leisure research

Diana C. Parry, Corey W. Johnson, and Faith-Anne Wagler

In June 2015, Sir Tim Hunt, a Nobel Laureate scientist, gave an impromptu speech at the World Conference of Science Journalists (WCSJ) in South Korea. Through tweets from Connie St Louis, a member of the audience and then Director of the Science Journalism MA at City University, London, parts of this address were made public; including the lines: "let me tell you about my trouble with girls. Three things happen when they are in the lab: you fall in love with them, they fall in love with you, and when you criticize them they cry." Hunt went on to suggest that it might be best to build separate labs for men and women to avoid emotional entanglements. In response to his problematic and paternalistic labelling of women as girls, as objects of the male gaze, and as emotionally weak, #TimHunt quickly went viral on Twitter. Taking up the broader issue of sexism in science, female scientists from around the world then started using the hashtag #distractinglysexy to post pictures of themselves in their lab gear working to poke fun of the notion that they made it through the workday without crying.

Women using social media as a platform to provide an immediate, unforgiving, global, and humour-fuelled response to Hunt's sexist remarks is just one example of the thousands, encountered daily, that illustrate some of the basic tenets of fourth wave feminism. Contemporary technological innovations such as social media now allow feminists in the fourth wave to take up the micropolitics of the third wave while situating their individual lived experiences within broader global discourses. Hence, in recent years, we have seen a rise in the number of collective movements based on social, economic, and political agendas (e.g., sexual violence, equal pay, and reproductive rights) – a distinctly second wave organizing tactic. The result, then, is a new wave that is ushering in innovative conversations and actions around feminism that are a worthy consideration for leisure scholars.

Within the leisure literature, feminist scholarship has an established history of providing critical insight, correcting androcentric biases, identifying future areas of research, advancing innovative methodologies, and addressing key gaps in knowledge – specifically around issues of equity and social justice. For over three decades, feminist scholars have educated the field about the gendered nature of leisure experiences, activities, and choices. Honouring this tradition, contemporary feminists continue to deepen understandings of the ways in which *leisure* influences gender and *gender* influences leisure (Berbary, 2013; Johnson, 2008; Parry, 2014). This scholarship takes up multiple ways of knowing and has resulted in a more nuanced and robust understanding of the complex phenomena of leisure – including how it can be studied and represented.

Without question, feminist insights have pushed the field into important directions that serve to illustrate the complexities of the leisure landscape, expand the body of knowledge, complicate other identities through intersectionality, and emphasize the politics of its practice. Continuing this storied legacy, the purpose of this book is to explore the possibilities, opportunities, and challenges of fourth wave feminism in advancing leisure studies. To set the stage for the chapters that follow, this introductory chapter will review the history, ideological underpinnings, and main tenets of fourth wave feminism. Our historical examination begins with an inquiry into the wave metaphor most frequently used to describe key moments in feminist thinking.

The wave metaphor: possibilities and limitations

Within feminist scholarship, there have been various moments or periods that are conceptualized as waves. Parry and Fullagar (2013) review and critique the wave metaphor elsewhere, but it bears repeating to contextualize this book. To begin, the wave metaphor organizes the feminist movement and shows similarities amongst research and action produced during various timeframes. The visual of a large wave coming in and hitting the shore represents the impact of feminist scholarship. After arriving ashore, this wave then rolls out, collects more water, and rolls back in – symbolizing the way in which new ideas and suggestions are incorporated with previous contributions. This is possible because regardless of the cultural context or moment in time, feminism is "fundamentally about transforming patriarchal culture and society" (Snyder-Hall, 2010, p. 256). Even so, there are as many feminisms as there are feminists. In this context, the wave metaphor can help synthesize the immense number of feminist contributions that centre around various time periods, including the first, second, and third wave.

We recognize the implication that feminism has distinct moments, which have come and gone, can be troublesome. When issues and actions are viewed in sequential order, there is a tendency to view earlier stances as *lesser than*. At the same time, categorizing research within one wave or another can be difficult when work is neither, or when it may take inspiration from different waves. Finally, classifying research into waves can simplify complicated and nuanced histories and "create a grand feminist narrative of leisure studies" (Parry & Fullagar, 2013, p. 574), which may become too powerful and/or exclusionary to alternative possibilities. To address these critiques, Parry and Fullagar (2013) suggest a ripple metaphor might be more beneficial in examining patterns of feminist research in leisure studies. Ripples represent the notion that feminist research can make a big splash while also creating movement and action in many directions. These feminist ideas then ripple through and interconnect, rather than only moving in one, linear direction (Parry & Fullagar, 2013).

Taken together, the possibilities and problematics of the wave metaphor demonstrate its strengths and weaknesses. To be sure, our decision to use the wave metaphor in this discussion is intentional. Aided by contemporary technological innovations like social media, feminism has returned to the realm of public discourse. The fourth wave of feminism is an everyday feminism. As the #TimHunt incident demonstrates, it is not a feminism accessible only to those in academia. To those on the frontlines, the wave metaphor remains the dominant conceptual tool for characterizing distinct moments in feminist thinking. In the spirit of this particular moment, then, we have chosen to appeal to the sensibilities of those on the frontlines and adopt the wave metaphor.

History: from the first wave to contemporary conceptualizations of feminisms

The first wave of feminism largely focused on women's suffrage. At the turn of the twentieth century, citizenship was gendered in most Western nation-states (Ramirez, Soysal, & Shanahan, 1997). In response, the women's suffrage movement emerged with the aim of legally extending the category of personhood beyond men. In Canada, as similar to the US, following the protracted and disparate struggle to franchise groups of women across various racial (e.g., Indigenous, Asian) and geographic boundaries (e.g., Northwest Territories, Quebec), the collective movement re-emerged in the early 1960s when feminists began to rally around issues of abortion, sexuality, motherhood, and labour rights (Shugart, 2001). During this period, Gloria Steinem and Betty Friedan were key feminist leaders in North America, and their visibility helped define what is known as the second wave of feminist action.

While the second wave worked to highlight many inequities, the knowledge generated during this period was not representative of all women's lived experiences. As noted by hooks (2000), the second wave of feminism was a largely liberalist movement focused on advocating issues mostly relevant to the lives of White, middle-class, heterosexual women. In this context, second wave scholarship often overlooked difference and excluded women of diverse ages, ethnic identities, sexualities, socio-economic status, as well as men (Dean, 2009). Based on its exclusions, the second wave is viewed by some as judgemental, inflexible, and divisive (Braithwaite, 2002; Snyder, 2008; Snyder-Hall, 2010).

Unlike the second wave, there is considerable debate as to when the third wave of feminism began. Contemporary feminists recognize an important moment when Rebecca Walker wrote an article for *Ms* magazine in 1992, which criticized the appointment of Clarence Thomas to the Supreme Court of the United States[1] and introduced the concept of third wave feminism:

> To be a feminist is to integrate an ideology of equality and female empowerment into the very fiber of life. It is to search for personal clarity in the midst of systemic destruction, to join in sisterhood with women when often we are divided, to understand power structures with the intention of challenging them.
>
> (pp. 39–41)

Walker ended this article with the bold proclamation: "I am the Third Wave." Regardless of its arrival date, the third wave of feminism is firmly located in the socio-political culture of the late 1980s and early 1990s, and is overwhelmingly grassroots-oriented, individualistic, radical, diverse, and informal (Shugart, 2001). With a wariness for unifying conceptualizations of womanhood and subjectivity, third wave feminism embraced a multiplicity of feminist ideologies and praxes (Kinser, 2004). Despite the fractal nature of this wave, Parry and Fullagar (2013) call attention to five dominant tendencies that hold it together as a collective movement: (i) plurality and inclusivity, (ii) personal narrative, (iii) self-determination, (iv) gender equality and sexual freedom, and (v) popular culture (p. 572). While not everyone agrees that this wave of feminism is generational, many scholars are currently challenged with creating a space for their work between previous waves and emergent postfeminist rhetoric.

"Postfeminism" is a term that suggests the work of feminism is complete and no longer relevant or necessary (Braithwaite, 2002). This right-wing populist and gendered discourse works to promote hostile reactions to earlier forms of feminist action and research and negatively construct feminism and feminists as undesirable, restricting, controlling, and dogmatic (Braithwaite, 2002; Kinser, 2004). Hence, a key challenge of third wave feminism is clearly communicating its continued relevance and difference from postfeminism – especially given the emergence of postmodern and poststructural critique (see Gillis & Munford, 2004; MacCormack, 2009). The inconsistent use of postfeminism and confusion about its meaning functions to perpetuate misunderstandings about feminist perspectives on gender difference, agency/subjectivity, structure/discourse, activism, and the roles of theory as explanatory or analytic.

In addition to responding to postfeminist rhetoric perpetuated by those on the political right, third wavers have also been forced to respond to pointed critiques from those within the contemporary feminist movement. Most notably, contemporary feminists point to the economic and racial privilege of third wavers, and argue their programs are outwardly focused and unaware of historical context (Dean, 2009; Fixmer & Wood, 2005; Gillis & Munford, 2004). At the same time, some scholars note the projects taken up by third wavers are individualistic in their pursuit of change and lack a solid political agenda (Braithwaite, 2002; Gillis & Munford, 2004). Perhaps the biggest critique of third wave feminism, then, is its lack of focus on collective action. Snyder-Hall (2010) notes that third wave feminists do not prioritize forming uniform movements, and instead focus on taking up shared concerns and forming smaller coalitions to work towards contextualized and local change. Consequently, third wavers are often critiqued for focusing too much on individuality and difference – to the exclusion of forming a cohesive group or identity. In this context, Tong (2007) suggests feminist projects should aspire to reimagine conceptions of "sameness" and universality. For some contemporary feminists, this type of critique suggests the time has come to start exploring a fourth wave of feminism, which is where we turn next.

Fourth wave feminism: an emergent and dynamic wave

Discussions around the fourth wave are so new that some question its mere existence. To those who question it, Baumgardner (2011) responds, "I believe that the fourth wave exists because it says that it exists" (p. 250). Through examining the era of "terror" produced by the 9/11 attacks, Kaplan (2003) was among the first to imagine the possibilities of fourth wave feminist action and research. To Kaplan (2003), fourth wave feminist projects need to be able to articulate the violence and extremism experienced by women, both at home and abroad, brought on by imperialism in the form of global capitalism. Hence, Kaplan (2003) suggests,

> the fourth wave will be distinguished by bringing second and third wave feminists together to confront a new and devastating reality that involves us all, if not equally, then at least at once. This new reality ideally cuts across racial, ethnic, and national divides.
>
> (p. 55)

In response to the unique possibilities and limitations of this new interconnected reality, fourth wave feminists have begun to use technology to blur boundaries and rapidly globalize local women's agendas – specifically in relation to sexual harassment and violence against women (Simões & Matos, 2006, p. 95). While this wave has made great progress in raising awareness about sexual violence, there has also been a shift away from feminist scholarship focusing on more material concerns such as women's paid employment and wages (Benn, 2013).

At this point in the wave, conversations seem to cluster around four dominant tendencies: (i) blurred boundaries across waves; (ii) technological mobilization; (iii) interconnectedness through globalization; and (iv) a rapid, multivocal (i.e., humorous, angry, sad, reflexive) response to sexual violence.

Blurred boundaries

One of the main tenets associated with fourth wave feminism is the way it uniquely builds upon the second and third waves. In contrast to previous waves,

Maclaran (2015) conceptualizes the fourth wave as having less clear boundaries – folding the micropolitics of the third wave into the political, social, and economic agenda of the second wave. In the fourth wave, boundaries are further blurred because of the ever-changing geographies of digital culture, communication, work, sexuality, and the commodification of femininity. Within this shifting landscape, feminists must continuously negotiate new ways of taking action within a global society dominated by Western popular culture. This far into the fourth wave, feminist action has largely been facilitated by technological mobilization.

Technological mobilization

Technological mobilization is a key element of fourth wave feminist projects. Youth are increasingly taking up multiple and contradictory online identities through interactions with others on Instagram, Twitter, Snapchat, Tinder, and other social media outlets. The ability and desire to live online is facilitated by our technology-centred culture (Baumgardner, 2011). For some, especially women on the margins, the internet has become a space to "call out" everyday forms of sexism and misogyny. While potentially liberating, these projects are often overwhelming individual and disconnected from any larger political programs. Recognizing the need to mobilize isolated expressions of online resistance, feminist projects have begun to use the internet to politicize local programs on a global scale.

An example of the internet as a feminist mobilization tool in the fourth wave is the *hollaback!* campaign, which allows users from across the world to map their local experiences with street harassment on a global platform. This online tool was developed to aid a growing grassroots "movement to end harassment in public spaces powered by local activists" (hollaback.com). There are now country-specific versions of the website from around the world (e.g., Canada, Australia, Korea, and Italy), where local *hollaback!* users can read and share stories about sexist encounters they have had on the street. Each incident is uploaded either through the *hollaback!* mobile application or website and linked with the location where it happened, creating a visual map of everyday sexism and harassment. The focus of this campaign, then, is to highlight the continued prevalence of sexual violence and provide a forum for women and men to share their local experiences and feel empowered to incite change globally.

It should be noted that the digital environment is also a challenging space, since many feminists using the internet as a tool for change face backlash and harassment. Anita Sarkeesian, a Canadian-American blogger famous for her video series exploring sexism in gaming, *Tropes vs. Women*, has faced repeated death and rape threats (McDonald, 2014). Brianna Wu of the #GamerGate controversy has also faced similar backlash in recent years (McDonald, 2014). In this context, important questions remain as to whether internet campaigns that confront sexism bring about any real social change and/or are connected to real-world conflicts. Whether the current digital landscape demarcates a shift from third wave feminism is still being discussed, but contemporary technological innovations have unquestionably enabled the emergence of numerous online feminist communities (Munro, 2013).

Interconnectedness through globalization

Intersectionality is undoubtedly another hallmark of the fourth turn in feminist thought. Within the fourth wave, Crenshaw's (1988) foundational concept is being taken up in unique ways. Most significantly, notions of intersectionality taken up in the fourth wave are grounded in a globalized lens that focuses feminists around the world on shared gender equity issues. As Cochrane (2014) argues:

> No person is free until we're all free. I am not free if a black woman is still oppressed. I am not free if women are still being discriminated against because of their mental health, I am not free until transgender women are recognised legally and socially as women, and do not get harassed and murdered violently, regularly, on the streets – because it's not just them who are not safe, it's also me who is not safe, because they are women too.
>
> (p. 63)

Corroborating this ethos, Phillips and Cree (2014) suggest their social work students are now able to better articulate an awareness of global gender inequalities. From their perspective, contemporary students, educated at the time of an emergent fourth wave, appear to have a more heightened awareness of the interconnectedness of the global inequalities.

A recent fourth wave feminist intervention demonstrating an awareness of global gender inequalities is Fashion Revolution, which describes itself as a "global movement calling for a fairer, safer, cleaner, more transparent fashion industry" (fashionrevolution.org). This campaign started as a reaction to the collapse of the Rana Plaza building in Bangladesh that housed five garment factories, which killed 1138 people and injured 2500. The clothes manufactured there were distributed globally, and the victims were mainly local young working women, making this a global feminist issue. Through Fashion Revolution, people across the world began to ask #whomademyclothes on various social media platforms. Those participating in the production of clothing were also encouraged to participate by writing their stories and sharing them using the hashtag #imadeyourclothes. This action resulted in several retailers disclosing some of the nations, places, and people involved in the highly exploitative fashion industry. Here, then, is an example of how feminists in the fourth wave have utilized technology to organize and take action locally against global experiences of gender inequalities.

The issues raised by feminists in the fourth wave also call attention to an interconnectedness facilitated by globalization. Every wave of feminism has certain social justice issues that define the social and cultural context of that era. The social justice issues that define the fourth wave of feminism, so far, are ones that reflect global concerns. One such issue is the misrepresentation of women (Benn, 2013). Fourth wavers are particularly concerned with how women are removed from representation, represented poorly, or represented in distorted ways (such as oversexualization of girls) in various forms of media. Benn (2013) believes that young feminists' re-engagement with gender equity issues could translate into "reanimating these vital issues and creating new alliances" (p. 225). Calling attention to the focus on intersectionality, Benn (2013) notes that fourth wavers should work to deploy "their current media profile and fresh-minted sense of injustice to press for greater economic fairness" (p. 227). In this way, many feminists have become more engaged in caring about collective action and working together towards broader equity. Alongside this shift comes greater focus on how women are doing globally.

Rapid, multivocal response to sexual violence

Historically, Western feminists have faced restrictive legislative changes and violent counter-activism in response to their actions (Faludi, 1991). In recent years, backlash has most often taken the form of comments and threats made online by misogynists and/or non-feminists. More than simply a new site for men's domination of women, these spaces provide a forum for fourth wave feminists to resist and respond immediately (Chamberlain, 2016). Perhaps one of the hallmarks of fourth wave feminism, then, is the rapid, multivocal response to particular forms of sexual violence, primarily through social media platforms such as Twitter and Facebook (Chamberlain, 2016). Through these platforms, women are taking to heart the iconic feminist slogan "the personal is political" and exposing everyday encounters with sexism. In this sense, fourth wavers are less forgiving against enlightened sexism and are more public about their struggles (Chamberlain, 2016). The result is a strong sense of public support and an organized feminist community in which there is collective action based on individual incidences of sexism or harassment. Women's rapid, multivocal response to the comments made by Tim Hunt highlight the ways in which feminists in the fourth wave employ humour, wit, and sarcasm to communicate their thoughts and feelings.

Although a rapid, multivocal response can result in quick and collective action on a large scale, feminists like Martin and Valenti (2013) suggest the fourth wave is inherently unsustainable due to its reliance on technology. This is a critique we will address directly in the conclusion of this book through an examination of the #MeToo movement that emerged in the fall of 2017. For now, it is important to note that technology can still have remarkable effects, including its ability to link individual efforts to larger organizational efforts (Martin & Valenti, 2013). When there was a threat to pull funding from Planned Parenthood because of their provision of abortions alongside other women's and reproductive health services, as an example, Deanna Zandt, a media strategist, created *Planned Parenthood Saved Me*, a Tumblr account that enabled working-poor women to share stories about how Planned Parenthood saved their lives (Martin & Valenti, 2013). This fourth wave feminist intervention between an individual woman and a multinational non-governmental agency (NGO) helped convince a major funder, Susan G. Komen, to continue their financial support of Planned Parenthood.

Another event that models the rapid, multivocal response of fourth wave feminists is SlutWalk, a movement created to call out everyday forms of sexism and rape culture. On January 24, 2011, a Toronto Police Service officer addressed a group of York University students about sexual violence prevention and made a statement that, to prevent rape, women should "avoid dressing like sluts" (slutwalktoronto.com). While the officer later issued an apology, Sonya Barnett and Heather Jarvis decided that more needed to be done to reclaim and redefine the word *slut* to push back against misogynistic victim-blaming. The initial SlutWalk was a march past the Toronto police headquarters, and quickly morphed into a transnational phenomenon taken up in different ways in different places. Without question, the way that these women mobilized others to fight against sexism in their community, igniting a larger global discussion on victim-blaming, shows the emancipatory potential of the fourth wave of feminist action.

Fourth wave feminism and leisure studies

Noticeably absent from the discussion of existing literature on fourth wave feminism thus far are the voices and research contributions of leisure scholars. This lack of leisure scholarship is disconcerting given the strong history of feminist leisure literature, in addition to the links between the basic tenets of a fourth wave with leisure practices, actions, and behaviours. Indeed, the scope and impact of a fourth wave is limited without the inclusion of a full range of scholarship, including leisure studies. Interestingly, the research and commentary about fourth wave feminism is emerging from a range of discipline-specific journals; and, as such, appears to be missing in-depth analysis of how fourth wave feminism is being taken up in diverse topical, theoretical, substantive, and methodological approaches. This book addresses that gap from a leisure studies perspective. In other words, the goal of this book is to contribute toward the emergence of fourth wave feminism and provide a collection of key scholars from leisure studies to explore how they are engaging with the ideas of a fourth wave of feminism.

The structure of this book

This book offers a hopeful collection of views about how key feminist scholars in our field are engaging with fourth wave feminism. Following this introduction,

Lisbeth Berbary engages with poststructural feminist thought to expand spaces that feminist leisure research can advance. Berbary suggests poststructural feminist theory can act as another way to move towards feminist social justice in leisure research based on its ability to challenge the status quo and create alternative understandings of gender. Utilizing a historical approach, Simone Fullagar, Adele Pavlidis, and Jessica Francombe-Webb situate current feminist leisure research in relation to the poststructuralist turn while also examining the resulting (post)feminist theories that have built gendered leisure understandings. Using specific examples of feminist research, Fullagar, Pavlidis, and Francombe-Webb also explore the role that posthumanist feminisms can have in shifting the feminist research agenda. Beccy Watson writes about the importance of intersectionality in bringing together feminist leisure scholarship and draws on her own intersectional work to highlight the potential for leisure to counter postfeminist discussions.

Next, Judy Davidson highlights similar concerns about leisure's potential to reconsolidate privilege in certain versions of queer leisure and leisure research. Broadening the understanding of the role of diverse gender representations in leisure research, Davidson further discusses the presence and absence of queer theory in leisure studies. Based on her research with Indigenous women, Felice Yuen advocates for the use of feminist standpoint theory in leisure research to understand groups that would benefit from a sensitivity to the role research can play in further colonization. Yuen also discusses how leisure can be used as a space of reconciliation and social justice. This is followed by Corey W. Johnson and Luc S. Cousineau, who discuss their work on masculinity in the digital era. In this chapter, fourth wave feminism is explored topically through linkages between constructions of hegemonic masculinity, performances of masculinity, and gendered leisure practices. Finally, this book concludes with a discussion about feminist praxes in the fourth wave and uses the #MeToo movement as an heuristic tool to help leisure scholars think critically about their own activism, research, and teaching.

Note

1 In 1991, Thomas was accused of sexual harassment by Anita Hill, an attorney he supervised during his time at the Department of Education.

References

Baumgardner, J. (2011). Is there a fourth wave? If so, does it matter? In J. Baumgardner (Ed.), *F'em! Goo goo, Gaga, and some thoughts on balls* (pp. 243–250). Berkeley, CA: Seal Press.

Benn, M. (2013). After post-feminism: Pursuing material equality in a digital age. *Juncture, 20*(3), 223–227.

Berbary, L. A. (2013). Reflections of culture: A diary of a sorority girl. *Creative Approaches to Research, 6*(1), 6.

Braithwaite, A. (2002). The personal, the political, third-wave and postfeminisms. *Feminist Theory*, *3*(3), 335–344.

Chamberlain, P. (2016). Affective temporality: Towards a fourth wave. *Gender and Education*, *28*(3), 458–464.

Cochrane, K. (2013). *All the rebel women: The rise of the fourth wave of feminism*. Guardian Shorts, 8 (Kindle edition).

Crenshaw, K. W. (1988). Race, reform, and retrenchment: Transformation and legitimation in antidiscrimination law. *Harvard Law Review*, *101*(7), 1331–1387.

Dean, J. (2009). Who's afraid of third wave feminism? On the uses of the 'third wave' in British feminist politics. *International Feminist Journal of Politics*, *11*(3), 334–352.

Faludi, S. (1991). *Backlash: The undeclared war against women*. London, UK: Vintage.

Fixmer, N., & Wood, J. T. (2005). The personal is still political: Embodied politics in third wave feminism. *Women's Studies in Communication*, *28*(2), 235–257.

Gillis, S., & Munford, R. (2004). Genealogies and generations: The politics and praxis of third wave feminism. *Women's History Review*, *13*(2), 165–182.

hooks, b. (2000). *Feminist theory: From margin to center*. London: Pluto Press.

Johnson, C. W. (2008). "Don't call him a cowboy": Masculinity, cowboy drag, and a costume change. *Journal of Leisure Research*, *40*(3), 385–403.

Kaplan, E. A. (2003). Feminist futures: Trauma, the post-9/11 world and a fourth feminism? *Journal of International Women's Studies*, *4*(2), 46–59.

Kinser, A. E. (2004). Negotiating spaces for/through third-wave feminism. *National Women's Studies Association Journal*, *16*(3), 124–153.

MacCormack, P. (2009). Feminist becomings: Hybrid feminism and haecceitic (re)production. *Australian Feminist Studies*, *24*(59), 85–97.

Maclaran, P. (2015). Feminism's fourth wave: A research agenda for marketing and consumer research. *Journal of Marketing Management*, *31*(15–16), 1732–1738.

Martin, C. E., & Valenti, V. (2013, April 15). Introduction. In C. E. Martin and V. Valenti (Eds.), *#FemFuture: Online revolution* (pp. 3–5). Barnard Center for Research on Women, New Feminist Solutions, Volume 8.

McDonald, S. N. (2014, October 15). 'Gamergate': Feminist video game critic Anita Sarkeesian cancels Utah lecture after threat. *Washington Post*. Retrieved from www.washingtonpost.com/news/morning-mix/wp/2014/10/15/gamergate-feminist-video-game-critic-anita-sarkeesian-cancels-utah-lecture-after-threat-citing-police-inability-to-prevent-concealed-weapons-at-event/?utm_term=.33edcb5cf5e6

Munro, E. (2013). Feminism: A fourth wave? *Political Insight*, *4*(2), 22–25.

Parry, D. C. (2014). The gendered politics of leisure. In G. Walker, D. Scott, and M. Stodolska, *Leisure Matters: The State and Future of Leisure Studies*. Urbana, IL: State College/Venture Publishing, 209–216.

Parry, D. C., & Fullagar, S. (2013). Feminist leisure research in the contemporary era. *Journal of Leisure Research*, *45*(5), 571–582.

Phillips, R., & Cree, V. E. (2014). What does the 'fourth wave' mean for teaching feminism in twenty-first century social work? *Social Work Education*, *33*(7), 930–943.

Ramirez, F. O., Soysal, Y., & Shanahan, S. (1997). The changing logic of political citizenship: Cross-national acquisition of women's suffrage rights, 1890 to 1990. *American Sociological Review*, *62*(5), 735–745.

Shugart, H. A. (2001). Isn't it ironic?: The intersection of third-wave feminism and generation X. *Women's Studies in Communication*, *24*(2), 131–168.

Simões, S., & Matos, M. (2008). Modern ideas, traditional behaviors, and the persistence of gender inequality in Brazil. *International Journal of Sociology*, 38(4), 94–110.
Snyder, R. C. (2008). What is third-wave feminism? A new directions essay. *Signs: Journal of Women in Culture and Society*, 34(1), 175–196.
Snyder-Hall, R. C. (2010). Third-wave feminism and the defense of 'choice'. *Perspectives on Politics*, 8(1), 255–261.
Tong, R. (2007). Feminist thought in transition: Never a dull moment. *Social Science Journal*, 44, 23–39.
Walker, R. (1992). Becoming the third wave. Ms, 2(4), 39–41.

Chapter 2

Into new modes of unbecomings

Engaging poststructural feminism towards alternative theorizations of gender in leisure research

Lisbeth A. Berbary

In my experience, poststructural feminist theory is one of the more misunderstood theories or philosophies because it lacks clear boundaries, is often inaccessible, and is less thoroughly read than many other theories (Berbary & Johnson, 2012). A friend of mine joked that she never took the time to really read poststructural feminist theory because it always came as the last chapter in her books on theory. Perhaps that is why it is so misunderstood and why many people do not take the time to read it, sometimes even those who vehemently criticize it.

But, what does post* mean, anyway? Most people assume that the inclusion of "post" in the title is based on its chronological development "after" other theories. Instead, and more importantly, the post* refers to a theoretical position that calls for "a constant critique or deconstruction, an afterthought, or a revisiting of that which already 'exists' or will exist" (Berbary, 2017, p. 724). Therefore, to understand poststructural viewpoints, one must also understand the viewpoints or theories that already exist, or are becoming into existence, to be critiqued or troubled.

According to Lather and St. Pierre (2005), post* theories, such as postmodernism, poststructuralism, queer theory, post-colonialism, and posthumanism, are all connected by their general critique or troubling of Humanist theoretical positions such as positivism, interpretivisms, and Critical theories (critical, feminisms, critical race theory, etc). These theories are critiqued by post* theories for their reliance on Humanism[1] and its use of binary structures, belief in "progress," desire for mass movements, defined Truths, metanarratives, and epistemologies of objectivity or constructionism (Berbary, 2017; St. Pierre, 2000).

Poststructural feminism, formed as a combination of critical, feminist, poststructural, and anti-Humanist theories, departs from Humanism to engage in constant questioning of its tenets specifically in relation to the notions and functions of gender/gender identities. In particular, poststructural feminism employs post* critique to de-center the Humanist "man," de-essentialize the subject of "woman,"[2] and open up ways of doing gender differently in our material realities. The ability of poststructural feminist thought to do this work through redeploying language, challenging status quo, and reconceptualizing stable identities as fluid ones, all move towards creating spaces for alternative meanings, reverse discourses, and disruptive counterhegemonic narratives of gender in leisure studies research. Such material-discursive reconceptualizations encourage small ruptures in dominant gendered expectations, allowing for different ways of doing gender in the world. In a moment when theoretical pluralism gives us the best hope to illuminate our complicated realities, thinking with poststructural feminist thought offers yet another way to advance feminist social justice within our leisure research. With the goal of promoting the inclusion of post* thought in our field's feminist scholarship, this chapter will outline the historical roots and major contributions of poststructural feminist thought, discuss tensions and critiques of post* thinking, consider the ways in which such thought can be applied to leisure research to engage acts of social justice, illuminate relevance for thinking through fourth wave feminism, and suggest shifts towards anti-Humanist, posthumanist thought in the uncharted feminist territories of the future of leisure research.

Historical and (anti-)disciplinary rhizomatic roots: palimpsests of anti-Humanist, poststructural feminism

Poststructural feminism, also sometimes referred to as feminist anti-Humanism (Braidotti, 2013), is a *palimpsest* – the writing of one theory onto another partially visible theory – of Critical Humanist theories that have been redeployed, expanded, and reorganized to depart from Humanism, show its limits, and reinvest thought differently to increase possibilities for useful political change (Berbary, 2017). Although Humanism has at times served us well, and feminisms grounded in Humanism have made undeniable and meaningful change, the legacy of Humanism is also fraught with complexities that have had negative consequences for intersectional identities at the margins, including the various combinations of identities that fall under such signs as women, people of color, and people of various socio-economic statuses, abilities, and sexualities/gender identities. Such negative consequences occur because the same structures, cultural grids of intelligibility, and accepted social regularities that uphold Humanism simultaneously uphold the structures, organizing grids, and regularities required for sexism, racism, homophobia, ageism, and other oppressive forces (St. Pierre, 2000). Showing the limits of Humanist theories and redeploying them for social justice is therefore an ethical imperative of poststructuralist theories, including poststructural feminism.

To be sure, thinking through feminism with poststructural frames does not call for a full dismissal of Humanism or an escape from all of its organizing conditions; for Humanism is not an error (Foucault, 1984), and pluralism across philosophies of sciences is necessary to create change across multiple points of resistance. However, drawing feminism and poststructuralism together in an anti-Humanist frame provides us with the tools to constantly interrogate Humanism, make useful departures from it, and engage in the constant critique of our feminist, political engagements. Such departure towards more rhizomatic roots *is* the historical shift of poststructural feminist thought – a shift that can only occur through engagements with the history of ideas that have come before and continue to evolve. These historic shifts move through Humanist ontology toward anti-Humanist onto-epistemology; tree-like foundations of knowledge toward rhizomatic roots of anti-foundational knowledges; Critical theories toward post* frames; desires of stability toward constant contingencies; ideology toward discourse; power structures toward power relations; binaries toward multiplicities; foundational hierarchies toward anti-foundational flattened logic; man as the center toward de-centering man; humans above and apart from passive matter toward humans being a part of agentic matter; and ... and ... and ... borrowing and departing from Humanism's legacies.

And, in particular, poststructural feminism shifts us away from the Humanist underpinnings of most critical feminist work towards feminist philosophies of sexual difference (Braidotti, 1991; Irigaray, 1993; Kristeva, 1991) that are theorized through new[3] materialist, Deleuzian onto-epistemologies.[4] These anti-Humanist feminisms, which can include postmodern, poststructural, queer, post-colonial, and post-Humanist rearticulations of critical feminisms, work to expand upon and relocate the onto-epistemological allegiances, critiques of dominant masculinity, and ethnocentric universalisms permitted through Humanism's particular privileging of the stable, essentialized, coherent Man as central to analyses of power. Such expansions most importantly outline three major contributions of poststructuralism to feminist theory: rejecting the Humanist Man, redefining Humanist notions of gendered subjectivity, and transforming Humanist conceptualizations of gendered power and resistance through performativity.

The Humanist Man

This stable, coherent, centered Man is always already the abstract ideal of masculinity and is specifically a "white, European, handsome and able-bodied" representation that is "objectionable not only on epistemological, but also on ethical and political grounds" (Braidotti, 2013, p. 24) even when used for feminist critique. In particular, due to the Humanist Man's reliance on Eurocentric, colonizing whiteness (hooks, 1981) and its focus on only patriarchy (Man as patriarch) in lieu of other global oppressive sex/gender systems (i.e., gender-stratified systems of New Guinea) (Rubin, 1975),[5] poststructural feminism refuses this Humanist Man and the essentialized Woman – his second sex. Poststructural feminism rejects the starting point for political action as one that can begin with this man/woman binary, these notions of abstract masculinity embodied in whiteness, and this priority of stable gender identities that follow from privileging the Humanist Man as the center of analysis apart from other matterings. In particular, as Braidotti (2013) explains, anti-Humanist, poststructural feminism must reject the Vitruvian Man, and Woman, as the centered subjects of political change because:

> The human of Humanism is neither an ideal nor an objective statistical average or middle ground. It rather spells out a systematized standard of recognisability – of Sameness – by which all others can be assessed, regulated and allotted to a designated social location. The human is a normative convention, which does not make it inherently negative, just highly regulatory and hence instrumental to practices of exclusion and discrimination. The human norm stands for normality, normalcy, and normativity. It functions by transposing a specific mode of being human into a generalized standard, which acquires transcendent values as the human: from male to masculine and onto human as the universal format of humanity. This standard is posited as categorically and qualitatively distinct from the sexualized, racialized, naturalized others and also in opposition to the technological artefact. The human is a historical construct that became a social convention about "human nature."
>
> (p. 26)

The continuous re-theorization of this Humanist subject of the Vitruvian Man, and other gendered subjectivity that it enables, has been of great importance in poststructural feminist efforts toward deconstructing – taking an essentializing term and opening it up for new more useful redeployments – our social positions as essentialized subordinates to men. For if the Humanist subject who relies on such a man/woman sex/gender system remains intact, feminist understanding of self in Western feminism would continue to be grounded in this essentializing patriarchal structure of Humanist binaries in which women and all we are claimed to represent are continuously categorized into the less privileged half of a binary – the Not-A of the master binary, A/Not-A. Alcoff (1988) further explains the problems with being essentialized in general, and with being essentialized as lesser than the Humanist Man in particular:

> Man has said that woman can be defined, delineated, captured – understood, explained, and diagnosed – to a level of determination never accorded to man himself, who is conceived as a rational animal with free will. Where man's behavior is undetermined, free to construct its own future along the course of its rational choice, woman's nature has overdetermined her behavior, the limits of her intellectual endeavors, and the inevitabilities of her emotional journey through life. Whether she is construed as essentially immoral and irrational or essentially kind and benevolent, she is always construed as an essential something inevitably assessable to direct intuited apprehension by males.
>
> (p. 426)

These essentialist positions assigned to women have not only categorized women as having "natural" roles such as caretakers, nurturers, and, in modern/postmodern societies, nurses, housewives, and teachers, but have also set up inequitable sex/gender systems, including patriarchy, in which these positions are less privileged than men's roles.

Redefining gendered subjectivity

Feminist thinkers across feminist theories have worked to re-theorize this essentialist and "lesser than" Humanist female subjectivity in many ways. Cultural feminists, for example, have attempted to disrupt Humanist definitions of women by redefining "women" through a feminist-created description, shifting concepts like "housewife" to "supermom" to give devalued positions a more positive connotation. Although some may view such feminist re-theorizations as the most useful responses to Humanist notions of "women," poststructural feminism considers these reinscriptions of "women" as yet another attempt to tie women's identities to just another essentialist definition (Alcoff, 1988).

To combat these problematic theorizations and re-theorizations of women, a disruption of Humanist binaries and the "essentialist" social structures they reinforce must occur by stepping outside of Humanism itself. Therefore, rather than engage in critical Humanist moves to re-conceptualized new dualities where male/female have equal worth, poststructural feminism instead rejects hierarchical Humanist binary positions to begin with and opens them up into multiplicities offering "flattened" contingent positionalities with far more than two equitable options. Poststructural feminism therefore calls for a very different response to Humanist, essentialist definitions of "woman." Rather than redefining women in positive terms to bring equity to binaries, poststructural feminism instead rejects the possibility of a stable definition of "woman," since any definition of women should always remain contingent and up for grabs to avoid the reinforcement of phallocentric, essentialist notions of gender. As Alcoff (1988) further explained:

> Feminists who take this tactic go about the business of deconstructing all concepts of woman and argue that both feminist and misogynist attempts to define woman are politically reactionary and ontologically mistaken. Replacing woman-as-housewife with woman-as-supermom (or earth mother or super professional) is no advance. Using French post-structuralist theory these feminists argue that such errors occur because we are in fundamental ways duplicating misogynist strategies when we try to define woman, characterize woman, or speak for women, even though allowing for a range of difference within the gender. The politics of gender or sexual difference must be replaced with a plurality of difference where gender loses its position of significance.
>
> (p. 427)

Therefore, poststructural feminism rejects attempts to define "women" in any specific terms since the definition will always remain essentialized and caught within political structures. Instead, poststructural feminism deconstructs such a category and problematizes notions of what it means to be a "woman," ultimately keeping notions of gendered subjectivity constantly up for grabs. By leaving subjectivity open to such possibility, poststructural feminist gendered subjectivity purposely fails to provide a description of a Truth of the sign of woman and instead leaves it contingent, local, partial, and fluid, highlighting the interaction of power, Truths/truths, knowledge, and discursive practices on the processes of subjectivity as they interact again and again within culturally and historically specific discourses.

Reconceptualizing gendered power and resistance through performativity

One move used to make a departure from some of the oppressive structural legacies of Humanism and these potentially essentializing projects, is to shift feminist thought from the tree-like foundations of structuralism and its hierarchical organizing conditions, towards instead the rhizomatic, flattened root-like entanglements of poststructural thought. Such a move can enable feminists to bring together and simultaneously depart from the focus on performed gender and *power structures* of critical feminism with/towards notions of perform*ative* gender and *power relations*, contingencies, and constant critique of poststructural, anti-Humanist theories. This move significantly shifts the starting point of how to begin dismantling inequitable gendered power.

Rather than see power as a structure where some have power and others have not, theorizing power instead as relations moves feminists away from only supporting acts of larger revolutionary movements meant to empower others whom "have not" – an act which in itself can sometimes be read as maternalistic due its assumption that some women have no voice of their own. Instead, poststructural feminists leave such overthrows of power structures to critical feminists and shift to focus on relations in which all gendered subjects can resist, even within strongly disciplined discourses through subversive acts of misrepeats (Berbary, 2014a).

Because gender is constructed and must be repeated to be legible, it can also be mis-repeated, both intentionally and unintentionally, as an act of resisting dominant gender discourses. These resistances are not large overthrows of power, but rather are small points of resistance across multiple points of oppression that eventually can add up to create larger scale transformations. This process of resistance through mis-repeats is particularly apparent in Butler's theorization of gender as a performative act – one of the most notable contributions of poststructuralist thinking to feminist and queer theory.

To theorize performativity, Butler built on the Foucauldian notions of subjectivity, specifically the notion that the soul was always-already constituted by the power/knowledge relations of specific discourses (Butler, 1990). Since there is no internal "Truth" to the subject, the subject instead is always only the construction of the laws, beliefs, and behaviors appropriate to a specific discourse. How a subject behaved, and even what was thinkable or speakable in relation to that behavior, was always-already constituted by the power and discipline of the dominant discourse within which the subject existed.

This was also how Butler perceived gender: *as a construction within specific discourse*. For Butler, there is no "innate" masculinity or femininity, but rather only that which is deemed a normative masculine or feminine act by discursive power. A subject is gendered not by its own innate or natural "disposition," but rather is gendered as it is first "hailed" as male or female and then as it "performatively acts out" the specific discursive expectations or norms of gendered behaviors. However, rather than an agentic actor who has multiple choices in costumes and masks of gender that can be taken on and off at any moment, performativity denies this agentic doing behind the deed. Instead, performative gender is not a performance chosen or created anew within the moment by a pre-existing actor, but rather is a repetitive act of historically gendered expectations carried out by a body constituted within a particular gendered discourse. The repetition of the culturally appropriate norms legitimizes the body as a gendered subject, yet "there is no 'being' behind the doing, acting, becoming; 'the doer' is merely a fiction imposed on the doing – the doing itself is everything" (Nietzsche, as cited in Butler, 1990, p. 33). Therefore, for Butler, gendered performativity is not the process of an actor choosing to put on a performance of gender; rather, it is the repetition of the performance of discursively sanctioned normative acts of gender that constitute *the appearance* of a gendered subject – *the appearance* of a legible doer behind a deed. As Butler (1995) further explained:

> A performative act is one which brings into being or enacts that which it names, and so marks the constitutive or productive power of discourse. To the extent that a performative appears to "express" a prior intention, a doer behind the deed, that prior agency is only legible as the effect of that utterance ... In other words, when words engage actions or constitute themselves a kind of action, they do this not because they reflect the power of an individual's will or intention, but because they draw upon and reengage conventions which have gained their power precisely through a sedimented iterability. The category of "intention," indeed, the notion of "the doer" will have its place, but this place will no longer be "behind" the deed as its enabling source.
>
> (p. 134)

A critique of Butler's gendered subject is that it lacks agency because it seems always already constituted by discursive power. However, like Foucault, Butler theorize space for the subversion of gendered norms. If, as Butler contended, gender is produced through a system of performances and it is the repetition of such acts that constitute the gendered subject, there is the possibility for one to inevitably, even if by accident, repeat an act "incorrectly" (Mansfield, 2000). Therefore, although both Foucault and Butler contended that subjects are constituted by discursive power, they also both remain optimistic about the subject's ability to use that same power to subvert, produce, open up, and redeploy new subject positions. As Butler (1991) wrote:

> If sexuality is compelled to *repeat itself* in order to establish the illusion of its own uniformity and identity, then this is an identity permanently as risk, for what if it fails to repeat, or if the very exercise of repetition is redeployed for a very different performative purpose? If there is, as it were, always a compulsion to repeat, repetition never fully accomplishes identity. That there is a need for a repetition at all is a sign that identity is not self-identical. It requires to be instituted again and again, which is to say that it runs the risk of becoming *de*-instituted at every interval.
>
> (p. 24)

Butler, therefore, recognized that, while the repetition of normative discursive practice constitutes the gendered subject, the potential of a mis-repeat or a failure to repeat provides the space for a subversion or redeployment of power and discursive norm. This subversive mis-repeat aligns well with poststructural notions of power relations and small ruptures and resistances in status quo. With each mis-repeat, the constructedness of gender is revealed – and once revealed as a construction, sex/gender systems themselves can be understood as constructed rather than innate, and thus deconstructed and reconstructed more equitably.

By rejecting the Humanist Man, recognizing the complexity of gendered subjectivity, and transforming concepts of gendered power and resistance through performativity, poststructural feminism works to challenge dominant Humanist expectations of gender; complicate the idea of gender as an act put on or chosen by an actor; highlight the interactions of discursive practices, power relations, and gendered interpellation; and open a space for gendered subjects to de-institute discursive norms and do gender differently. Using such alternative meanings, reverse discourses, and disruptive counterhegemonic narratives of gender as starting points for feminist leisure research also shifts the purpose of our inquiries, the types of research questions we ask, and the ways in which we interpret our data on gendered leisure experiences. Before providing examples of how poststructural feminism can work to redefine our leisure inquiries, it is useful to consider the critiques of positioning our work within this anti-Humanist frame.

Tensions and critiques from the exterior

Although poststructural feminism is one of many useful theories with which to think about gender within leisure studies, the theory itself is still often met with much critique from the exterior. The three most common critiques of post* theories, poststructural feminism or otherwise, are that they are inaccessible, relativistic, and not useful for political action. Unpacking these critiques will help to show some of the ways in which post* theories are instead purposefully inaccessible, not relativistic, and differently useful for political action than Critical theories, yet still useful. Challenging these critiques requires a departure from Humanism, a rearticulation of taken-for-granted realities – a move critics are often unaware of or unwilling to make.

Purposeful inaccessibility

Yes, poststructural feminism can be very inaccessible and strong critique has been made that such inaccessibility can lead to exclusionary practices among feminists – both by those outside of feminism and within. However, poststructuralism asserts that there is potential, if not ethical, imperative to take up commonsense language *differently* to subvert the linguistic structures of Humanism that uphold the oppressive structures of society. For if we "word our worlds" (St. Pierre, 2000) – changing *thought* and *language* into *practice* and *behavior*, then the language we choose to use is of utmost importance to changing material conditions. Since day-to-day language, language that is deemed accessible, is always already grounded in status quo, any call for transparent, accessible, clarity in speaking is really just a call to reinforce the taken-for-granted structures of Humanism and does not allow for departure. As Lather (1996) suggested:

> To speak so as to be understood immediately is to speak through the production of the transparent signifier, that which maps easily onto taken-for-granted regimes of meaning. This runs a risk that endorses, legitimates, and reinforces the very structure of symbolic value that must be overthrown.
> (p. 528)

Hence, the inaccessibility of poststructuralism is an attempt to *do language differently* as a move against commonsense, status quo *dominant linguistic structures* that perpetuate *dominant material structures* and in turn uphold *oppressive power structures* of Humanism. This move to reinscribe language differently is itself therefore a political aspect of poststructural feminism (Berbary, 2017) that warrants critique, but also support because, at times, using language differently can transform the world.

Relativistic

Poststructural feminism is focused on the local, partial, contingent knowledges about situated gendered experiences. However, for some grounded in Humanism, a claim of not knowing stable, deep, full, universal, and constant Truths can be unnerving and lead to critiques of relativism concerning post* theories. *Relativism* is

> commonly considered the view that all beliefs, or belief systems, are equally valid and true in relation to their specific contexts, rather than in relation to a foundational structure of universal Truth(s) that would assign hierarchical value to beliefs across humanity.
>
> (Berbary, 2017, p. 726)

Critics argue that the contingent nature of post* truths means that our work has no evaluation system to judge that which is more or less useful to humanity, and therefore cannot contribute to positive transformation in the socio-political realm. However, it is important to understanding the nature of poststructural feminism's constant critique of taken-for-granted, universal Truths of Humanism. Such critique need not rely on a foundational structure or deep Truth to make evaluations. Rather, as Berbary (2017) explained:

> The distinction of "more useful or just" within post* thought is not made *based on* inherited, uncontestable, universal structures – particularly because, according to post* thought, those structures, while they *can* be mobilized to serve "the oppressed," also simultaneously construct the binary structure that enabled and maintains "the privileged" in the first place (Foucault 1970). Hence, in order to resist this dangerous double bind of the universal, post* evaluations of "useful and just" reject making judgments in relation to notions of foundational structures. Instead, evaluations are *based in constant political critique* of the usefulness of ongoing *evolutions of material-discursive practices* in the local, partial, contingent, and momentary realities of the current now. This lack of belief in a foundational structure against which to objectively determine good/bad, forces us to do the difficult work of *evaluating* and *re-evaluating human practices* over and over again across time, space, and history to reaffirm that they remain the most useful, most just, and most inclusive, contextualized practices *again and again and again*.
>
> (p. 727)

Therefore, while relativism *within* Humanism can lead to the inability to evaluate the usefulness of cultural practices, claims that poststructural feminism is relativistic are unwarranted. Rather, the denial of a foundational, unified Truth from which to judge universal practices instead requires a much more complex and consistently aware process of constant critique of all material-discursive practices in their local contexts in order to continuously evaluate their usefulness and equity. This again is the political action of poststructural feminism – the *constant continued critique* of gendered equity over and over again in each historical and cultural moment.

Seeing things differently: putting poststructural feminist tenets to work in leisure research

There are many ways that my own scholarship has put to work this continued constant critique enabled by poststructural feminism and its tenets. Specifically, my work has used it to think through the theorizations of my data, as well as engaging with it in my methodological choices to represent my data through creative analytic practices – a move that is grounded in poststructural notions of language and representation (Berbary, 2011, 2012, 2013a, 2014a, 2014b, 2015, 2017; Berbary & Johnson, 2012; Kumm & Berbary, 2018). For this chapter, I will draw examples from my dissertation research on sorority women in the Southern US. Sororities are women-only academic, social, philanthropic groups aligned with American universities that are often juxtaposed against their male-only counterparts – fraternities. Sorority women are often portrayed as caricatures of dumb, hypersexual, blonde, straight, white females who have little care in the world other than looks, boys, fashion, and female competition (Berbary, 2012). However, during my first interactions with sorority women, I became intrigued with this popular perception of them and wondered what would happen to this assigned subjectivity if I were to spend time with sorority women themselves – would it hold up, would it be completely wrong, could I see them differently? Therefore, in 2007 I began a year-plus-long ethnographic study to illuminate the ways that gender played out within a popular Southern sorority. My choice to use poststructural feminism to think through this project resulted in my use of two major concepts that shifted my work outside of Humanism to "do feminist leisure research differently" – *deconstruction* and *performativity*.

Transforming purpose and research questions: deconstruction

Knowing that my work would be grounded in poststructural feminism, the first adjustment I made to depart from Humanism was to reconsider the purpose of my inquiry. Rather than focus on explaining (post-positivist), understanding (interpretivist), or critiquing (critical) sorority culture, my use of poststructural feminism secured my purpose strongly in a post-Humanist paradigm in which the purpose of this inquiry became to deconstruct taken-for-granted notions of gendered subjectivity within sororities as they were constituted within particular gendered discourses of the South. This line of inquiry led me away from interpretivist concerns of understanding shared experiences or essences and away from critical concerns such as critiquing ideology, adding silenced stories to meta-narratives, or empowering individual woman perceived not to have their own voice. Although interpretivist and critical inquiries are necessary, this particular poststructural feminist project instead focused on deconstructing discourses of gendered power relations, illuminating the ways that such discourses functioned to constitute "appropriate" sorority subjects, and highlighting the potential ways that women might mis-repeat the disciplinary discourses enabling/enforcing such subjectivity. Hence, while making the shift towards a poststructural feminist guided project, my research questions shifted away from being about who all women are, what they share, what their essences are, or how we could empower them by showing them their own complicity. Instead, my questions became about discourse, function, and negotiation. Specifically, based on my theoretical allegiances, my research questions were: (i) What discourses of femininity are enabled within Zeta Chi sorority? (ii) How are such discourses disseminated and disciplined? And (iii) How do women in Zeta Chi negotiate the gendered expectations disciplined by this discourse? Hence, shifts in purpose and questions are the ways in which my inquiry was transformed by my onto-epistemological and theoretical allegiances to poststructural feminism.

Transforming the analytic frame: performativity

Using poststructural feminism also transformed how I thought about the data I generated with sorority women. Rather than analyze it for notions of identity and gender performance, as one might from a critical perspective, my inquiry shifted towards speaking of gendered subjectivity – the ways one becomes a subject, a self, a position, an identity, or an "I" as constituted through performativity within a specific discourse. As discussed above, focusing on performativity shifts thinking about how we come to see gender – not as a stable, chosen performance by an actor – but rather as a prescribed behavior that legitimizes the legibility of a body within a culturally constituted frame of intelligibility. It works to question the stability of gender, illuminates both sex and gender's construction vs. natural innateness, and shows the limitations and boundaries set around the possibilities for becoming woman within the specific context of study. Such a shift also illuminates notions of discipline and resistance, where gendered expressions of sorority women are understood as being enabled by a particular discourse that disciplines bodies into appropriate gendered subjects within specific power relations (Berbary, 2012). Notions of hierarchical observation, normalizing judgement, and examination can also be brought to light as Foucauldian notions of discipline and self-surveillance are added to the theorizations of gendered performativity within sorority space (Foucault, 1977). Because where there is power/discipline there is also resistance, this analysis, thinking through poststructural feminism, also enabled me to speak about sorority women's resistance of dominant gendered discourses through mis-repeats of "appropriate gendered expectations" even within this highly disciplined space

(Berbary, 2012; Berbary & Johnson, 2012). Shifting away from the critical to the poststructural feminist frame, therefore, enabled a different starting point and path for analysis that relied upon reading the data through a productive anti-Humanist frame that shifted the taken-for-granted traditions of critical feminist, Humanist inquiry in leisure studies.

No longer can we rely on only the accepted traditional notions of the purpose of our research to explain, understand, or critique the expectations of our research questions to primarily illuminate what exists. No longer can we depend on Humanist notions of concepts like gender, identity, power, or even leisure within our analysis or conclusions. Rather, poststructural work focused on gender in leisure studies gives us the purpose to deconstruct; enables research questions to illuminate, not just how things are, but how they came to be and continue to function; and necessitates that we constantly question, transform, and think differently about our longest and strongest held attachments to Humanist concepts that we often take for granted as we think through our analyses.

Advancing feminist social justice: engaging oppositional politics of resistance

How do we, then, put poststructural feminism to practice in deconstructing some of the more problematic sexist, patriarchal, sex/gender inequalities perpetuated by the structures of Humanism in our own field? Such work begins with an oppositional politics of resistance where each of us in our constituted reality must challenge the taken-for-granted grids of intelligibility across multiple lines of flight, points of resistance, and regimes of possibility. We are called to think where these oppressive powers began to repeat themselves, how they function and are perpetuated, and how we might construct things differently to transform the material-discursive conditions of our lives and our communities. Poststructural feminism assumes that all human practices take place on the surface where both language and reality exist together, rather than as in Humanist constructionism where surface language names that which resides in the metaphysics of depth (St. Pierre, 2013). Because of this belief, those aligned with poststructural feminism "are reminded that we are each complicit in the maintenance of unjust structures and relations" of gendered power and that we each also have the duty to revolt every day (Berbary, 2017, p. 730).

We can answer the call for revolt in our leisure research and practices by deconstructing notions of gender in our lives, our teaching, our practices, and our research. Deconstruction "is not to negate or to dismiss, but to call into question and, perhaps most important, to open up a term … to a reusage or redeployment that previously has not been authorized" (Butler, 1992, p. 802) so that we can interrogate the types of gender and gender relations that we perpetuate with the intention of deliberately creating positive transformation.

Poststructuralist feminist research therefore uses deconstruction to push us toward dismantling patriarchal meta-narratives; deconstructing gendered/raced/classed binaries to allow for multiple, intersecting subject positions; illuminating complex power relations as they play out within gendered discourses; and challenging dominance through small disobediences in our constituted realities to create change through the opening of ideas, presentation of multiplicity, and failure to repeat status quo (St. Pierre, 2000). This break from Humanist thought troubles the questions that are typically asked within traditional feminist leisure studies and instead challenge us to ask *different* questions, with the intention of exposing *different* "modes of unbecoming" (Halberstam 2011, p. 23) in order "to repeat terms subversively, and to displace them from the contexts in which they have been deployed as instruments of oppressive power" (Berbary, 2017; Butler, 1992, p. 168).

What are the kinds of questions we can ask about gendered intersections in our field to "do feminist leisure research differently" in ways that work to increase gender equity in our teachings, practices, and research? We must ask questions that will engage with ideas of *function*, *processes*, *silences*, *production*, *meaning*, and *materiality* such as (revised from Berbary, 2017, p. 733):

> How have gender and dominant gendered discourses been constructed? What holds such dominant discourses together? What do these dominant gendered discourses produce?
>
> (St. Pierre, 2000)

> In what specific contexts, among which specific communities of people, and by what textual and social processes has meaning about gender been made? How do these gendered meanings change? How have some gendered meanings emerged as normative and others have been eclipsed or disappeared? What do these processes reveal about how gendered power is constituted and operates?
>
> (Scott, 1988, p. 35)

> How do dominant gendered discourses function? Where are they to be found? How do dominant notions of gender get produced and regulated? What are the linguistic and material social effects of dominant gendered discourses?
>
> (Bove, 1990, p. 54)

> How do we keep dominant disciplinary discourses of gender at bay? How do we avoid forms of knowledge about gender that relegate other modes of doing gender differently to the redundant or irrelevant? How do we engage in and teach anti-disciplinary knowledges about gender and its intersections?
>
> (Halberstam, 2011, p. 11)

> How do we re-conceptualize "how different differences get made, what gets excluded, and how those exclusions matter" in relation to gender and gendered expectations?
>
> (Barad 2007, p. 30)

By engaging poststructural feminism to ask a different set of questions differently in feminist leisure research allows scholars to open up alternative ways of thinking about gender that are not permitted within Humanism. It is through these deconstructions of Humanist legacies, the asking of different questions differently, and the political moves associated with inaccessibility and constant critique, that all move towards creating spaces in leisure studies for alternative meanings, reverse discourses, and disruptive counterhegemonic narratives of gender. Such material-discursive reconceptualizations encourage small ruptures in dominant gendered expectations, allowing for different ways of doing gender in our worlds.

Engaging fourth wave feminisms: diffractive disturbances from within

How might all of these discussions of poststructural feminism engage with the fourth wave of feminism? As mentioned by Parry, Johnson, and Wagner in Chapter 1, fourth wave feminism is concerned with four major moves: (1) blurred boundaries across waves; (2) technological mobilization; (3) interconnectedness through globalization; and (4) a rapid, multivocal response to sexual violence. Engaging these notions through anti-Humanist feminisms, including poststructural feminism, highlights intersections between these feminisms and these tenets of the fourth wave.

In particular, anti-Humanist feminisms such as poststructural feminism, with their focus on resistances, biopower, globalized politics, technologically mediated realities, postcolonial critiques, cyborg, and material-discursive entanglements, arguably have much to offer all four of these tenets (Barad, 2007; Braidotti, 2013; Clough, 2009; Coole & Frost, 2010; Haraway, 1991). However, the following discussion will focus most specifically on anti-Humanist, poststructural feminist abilities to contribute to the first major move of fourth wave feminism; to blur the boundaries of feminist waves. I have chosen to focus on this tenet because of the clear contribution that such commentary can lend to reconceptualizing the boundaries of the waves of feminism.

Although speaking about feminism in waves has become common vernacular, many would argue that the metaphor has become problematic because, as discussed by Parry, Johnson, and Wagler in Chapter 1, when feminist issues and actions are viewed in sequential order, there can be a tendency to view the earlier stance as 'less than' those that come after. Also, categorizing research within one wave or another can be difficult when work is neither one or the other and when it may take inspiration from different 'waves'.

However, this critique is most strongly mounted when the notion of waves is understood as one wave washing clean past waves to move forward with a fresh slate, or when waves are understood as creating strong generational boundaries around feminist thought. Typical notions of feminist waves also often begin with perceptions of feminism beginning in the West and being spread to those in need of saving in the East (Ahmed, 2017). Such a perceived trajectory of feminism is colonizing, Eurocentric, and another major issue perceived as a danger of Western, white, middle-class feminist use of the waves metaphor.

By thinking with Barad's (2007) notions of waves as "not things per se; rather, they are disturbances" (p. 72), we begin to challenge waves that wash clean, create boundaries, or have unidirectional trajectories of West to East. Using Barad to reconceptualize waves works to even move beyond fourth wave feminist desire to simply blur boundaries between waves. Instead, reading waves through such anti-Humanist, poststructural feminism rejects them as separate moments with singular trajectories, and instead views waves as continuous cycles that shift directions from within, never manifesting only in the West to be dispersed through the world, but rather bringing together constant disturbances from across cultures, moments in time, generations, and histories. As Dejmanee (2016) noted, "the pervasive metaphor of the wave must be redeployed to encompass these qualities of plurality and continuity ... as multigenerational, transmediated entanglements" (p. 742).

Specifically, in line with fourth wave feminist calls, poststructural feminist and anti-Humanist reconfigurations call for waves of diffraction, always partial, entwined, palimpsests of histories of actions, rather than waves of erasure. Diffractive waves reject waves of erasure that result in altogether new waves of superiority – those that often contribute to rifts in feminist movements themselves (Dejmanee, 2016). Rather than erase and re-create, such diffractive waves multiply within as they encounter obstacles, bending, and overlapping; they respond to the limitations and erasures of those movements that have come before while making room within the flow of that which already is. They expand to submerge shifts for doing representation differently, increasing reflexivity in theorizing difference, and giving special attention to the ways in which the material-discursive effects of waves disrupt, create, reveal, and trouble the material realities of the world (Barad, 2007; Dejmanee, 2016). They do not have boundaries, generational allegiances, or disjointed histories – they instead are always already one body, one force.

Waves are then re-theorized through the metaphor of diffraction to be generative, partial, continuous reiterations of the same wave – no longer are waves moments in time with dated boundaries, theoretical allegiances, or correlated content. No longer are waves stable and reliable delimitations of feminist identity even when blurred (i.e., second waver). Rather, such waves are "generously and joyfully revelling in entanglements" (Dejmanee, 2016, p. 743) spanning continents, generations, social identities, historical moments, cultural contexts, and globalized material existences. Conceptualizing feminist waves through

Barad's notions of diffractive disturbances illuminate the agency of material–cultural relations and the mutual co-constitutions of being/knowing as ontologies and epistemologies have been, and continue to become, intra-active entanglements within social movements toward feminist action.

Therefore, when contributing to the fourth wave feminism desired to blur boundaries of the wave metaphor, anti-Humanist and poststructural feminist reconfigurations require that we think of waves as disturbances to status quo and challenge us to continuously ask ourselves: How might we create, direct, instigate such disturbances to manifest useful political and social effects. How do we celebrate disturbances, patterns of superposition (Barad, 2007) that combine to form "multi-generational, transmediated consumer and political entanglements" (Dejmanee, 2016, p. 744) within globalized political economies and technologically mediated communities? These are the questions that anti-Humanist, poststructural feminism enables us to ask as we move through feminist waves of continuity and pluralism across histories that are not over.

Unfinished business: towards unbecomings

Where do we go from here? Towards even more theoretical pluralism with deliberate intentions of igniting modes of unbecoming throughout these unending histories. Towards challenging the authority of any one theory, one methodology, or dominant discourses of gender in leisure studies. In particular, to add to the interdisciplinary, transdisciplinary, and anti-disciplinary nature of our field, many leisure scholars are beginning to move farther into the new materialist ontologies of posthumanism (Berbary, 2017; Kumm & Berbary, 2018; Kumm & Johnson, 2017; Lashua, 2017). Posthumanism offers many exciting avenues of hope, emerging to disrupt presumptive Humanist dichotomies of human–nonhuman, social–scientific, nature–culture to instead theorize humans as parts of the universe, a part of matter, and in mutual intra-active material constitution *with* nonhumans – not simply as beings *in* or *above* the universe of matterings (Barad, 2007). Humans no longer discover or construct their place in the world or interact as *a priori* beings within the preexisting material world. Rather, we are matter constituted *a praesenti* through mutually constituted intra-actions with other *a praesenti* subjects and objects to collectively configure and reconfigure the matters of the world. We are no longer the Humanist subject. We are no longer just human. And we are now forced to ask the question, Have we *ever* been *simply* human? (Braidotti, 2013; Buscher & Urry, 2009, p. 100). Thinking about ourselves and our universe in these ways significantly alters our commonsense assumptions, forcing different fields of possibility and impossibility within gendered material-discursive practices and phenomena in leisure studies research.

As we continue to move into these exciting pluralist modes of unbecoming, it is important not only to question our theories, but also our practices of putting these theories to use. This chapter will close by offering a list of questions to consider as we continue to engage in different theoretically rigorous terrains of feminist leisure research:

1 How might we at times be paralyzing/isolating ourselves with privileging ontological, epistemological, and/or theoretical thought?
2 What are the advantages of using out time on earth to read, reread, and keep reading in order to grasp fast-moving philosophical innovations?
3 How can we apply these philosophical concepts to our work in ways that make our life-work meaningful?
4 How can we use these ways of thinking to build connections rather than barriers?
5 What can we now see/do differently than before we started to read?
6 How can we turn ways of thinking of things into ways of acting that are more useful for humanity?
7 What does such a shift mean for the ways in which we embark on research? How would research "look" and how would it "function" as we move away from Humanism?
8 How does it redeploy our "taken-for-granted" notions of Humanist research?
9 How might a shift into anti-Humanist research be useful and/or detrimental to social justice-oriented leisure endeavors?
10 And, finally, what questions are left to ask and/or critiques are left to make as we encourage new ontological and epistemological possibilities for our leisure research?

Notes

1 "For broader discussion of Humanist social science, please see St. Pierre (2000), Braidotti (2013), and Bennett (2010). Specific to leisure studies, consider Berbary (2017), Kumm and Berbary (2018), and Kumm and Johnson (2017). Although not necessarily 'bad,' humanism is necessarily problematic. The most noble Humanist projects tend to erect hierarchical, binary divisions, structures with unintended, adverse consequences. Humanism sustains man/woman, adult/child, human/nonhuman power disparities via vertically structured chains of being (ontology), positioning standardized man as apex. These authors go to considerable lengths to demonstrate these problematics, offering insights for developing posthumanist alternatives" (Kumm & Berbary, 2018, p. 2).
2 For this chapter, the term *woman* refers to "all those who travel under the sign of woman" regardless of assignment or otherwise (Ahmed, 2017, p. 14).
3 "We agree that the 'new' in new materialisms and new empiricisms does not continue or accept a classificatory historiography of (academic) thinking that necessarily comes with a hierarchy or any kind of a priori logic" (St. Pierre, Jackson, & Mazzei, 2016, p. 100).
4 New materialist onto-epistemology is a complex, rhizomatic, multiple, and constantly fluid terrain of thought. Because of this complexity, it is difficult to thoroughly capture nuances in a book chapter, particularly details around issues of ontology and shifts towards post-Humanism (Fullagar's work further addresses this; see Chapter 3 in this volume). Due to this limitation, I have included multiple references at the end of this

chapter to provide a starting point for subversive scholars who wish to "read more" into the thinking(s) of such theorists as Braidotti, Bennett, Barad, Massumi, Haraway, and Spinoza.

5 Rubin (1975) defines a sex/gender system as any social system, not just those labeled by the term *patriarchy*, "which by a society transforms biological sexuality into products of human activity, and in which these transformed sexual needs are satisfied" (p. 159). According to Rubin, "it is important – even in the face of a depressing history – to maintain a distinction between the human capacity and necessity to create a sexual world, and the empirically oppressive ways in which sexual worlds have been organized. Patriarchy subsumes both meanings into the same term. Sex/gender system, on the other hand, is a neutral term which refers to the domain and indicates that oppression is not inevitable in that domain, but is the product of the specific social relations which organize it" (p. 168). Patriarchy is "a specific form of male dominance" grounded in the Old Testament-type Patriarch – other types of male dominance exist across cultures such as the gender-stratified system of New Guinea, which is similarly oppressive to women, yet is not founded on male roles as patriarch or father, but rather, for example, on collective adult maleness and exchange networks (p. 168).

References

Ahmed, S. (2017). *Living a feminist life*. London: Duke University Press.

Alcoff, L. (1988). Cultural feminism versus post-structuralism: The identity crisis in feminist theory. In W. K. Kolmar & F. Bartowski (Eds.), *Feminist theory: A reader* (2nd ed., pp. 426–436). Boston, MA: McGraw Hill.

Barad, K. (2007). *Meeting the universe halfway: Quantum physics and the entanglement of meaning*, Durham, NC: Duke University Press.

Bennett, J. (2010). *Vibrant matter: A political ecology of things*. Durham, NC: Duke University Press.

Berbary, L. A. (2011). Post-structural *writerly* representation: Screenplay as creative analytic practice. *Qualitative Inquiry*, *17*(2), 186–196.

Berbary, L. A. (2012). Don't be a whore, that's not ladylike: Discursive discipline and sorority women's gendered subjectivity. *Qualitative Inquiry*, *18*(7), 535–554.

Berbary, L. A. (2013a). Reflections of culture: A diary of a sorority girl. *Creative Approaches to Research*, *6*(1), 6–43.

Berbary, L. A. (2014a). "Even the good girls have their moments": Sorority women's misrepeats of ladylike discourse. *Qualitative Inquiry*, *4*(3), 2–21.

Berbary, L. A. (2014b). "Too good at fitting in": Methodological consequences and ethical adjustments. *International Journal of Qualitative Studies in Education*, 2–21.

Berbary, L. A. (2015). Creative analytic practices: Onto-epistemological and theoretical attachments, uses, and constructions within humanist qualitative leisure research. *International Leisure Review*, *2*(4), 27–55.

Berbary, L. A. (2017). Thinking through poststructuralism in leisure studies: A detour around "proper" humanist knowledges. In K. Spracklen, L. Lashua, E. Sharpe, & S. Swain (Eds.), *The handbook of leisure theory* (pp. 719–742). London: Palgrave.

Berbary, L. A., & Johnson, C. W. (2012). The American sorority girl recast: An ethnographic screenplay of leisure in context. *Leisure/Loisir*, *36*(3–4), 243–268.

Bove, P. (1990). Discourse. In F. Lentricchia & T. McLaughlin (Eds.), *Critical terms for literary study* (pp. 50–63). Chicago: University of Chicago Press.

Braidotti, R. (1991). *Patterns of dissonance*. Cambridge, UK: Polity Press.

Braidotti, R. (2013). *The posthuman*. Malden, MA: Polity Press.

Buscher, M., & Urry, J. (2009). Mobile methods and the empirical. *European Journal of Social Theory*, *12*(1), 99–112.

Butler, J. (1990). *Gender trouble: Feminism and the subversion of identity*. New York, NY: Routledge.

Butler, J. (1991). Imitation and gender insubordination. In D. Fuss (Ed.), *Inside/out: Lesbian theory, gay theories* (pp. 13–31). London: Routledge.

Butler, J. (1992). Contingent foundations: Feminism and the question of "post-modernism," In J. Butler & J. W. Scott (Eds.), *Feminists theorize the political* (pp. 21–39). New York, NY: Routledge.

Butler, J. (1993). *Bodies that matter: On the discursive limits of "sex."* New York, NY: Routledge.

Butler, J. (1995). For a careful reading. In S. Benhabib, J. Butler, D. Cornell, & N. Fraser (Eds.), *Feminist contentions: A philosophical exchange* (pp. 127–143). London, UK: Routledge.

Clough, P. T. (2009). The new empiricism, affect, and sociological method. *European Journal of Social Theory*, *12*(1), 43–61.

Coole, D., & Frost, S. (2010). Introducing the new materialism. In D. Coole & S. Frost (Eds.), *New materialisms: Ontology, agency, and politics* (pp. 1–43). Durham, NC and London, UK: Duke University Press.

Dejmanee, T. (2016). Waves and popular feminist entanglements: Diffraction as a feminist media methodology, *Feminist Media Studies*, *16*(4), 741–745.

Foucault, M. (1970). *The order of things: an archaeology of the human sciences*. New York, NY: Vintage Books.

Foucault, M. (1977). *Discipline and punish: The birth of the prison* (A. Sheridan, Trans.). New York, NY: Random House.

Foucault, M. (1984). What is enlightenment? In P. Rabinow (Ed.), *The Foucault reader* (C. Porter, Trans.). New York, NY: Pantheon Books.

Halberstam, J. (2011). *The queer art of failure*. Durham, NC: Duke University Press.

Haraway, D. (1991). A cyborg manifesto: science, technology, and socialist-feminism in the late twentieth century. In *Simians, Cyborgs and Women: The Reinvention of Nature* (pp. 149–181). New York, NY: Routledge.

hooks, B. (1981). *Ain't I a woman*. Boston, MA: South End Press.

Irigaray, L. (1993). *An ethics of sexual difference*. Ithaca, NY: Cornell University Press.

Kristeva, J. (1991). *Strangers to ourselves*. New York, NY: Columbia University Press.

Kumm, B. E., & Berbary, L. A. (2018). Questions for postqualitative inquiry: Conversations to come. *Leisure Sciences*, 40: 1–2, 71–84. doi:10.1080/01490400.2017.1376014

Kumm, B. E., & Johnson, C. W. (2017). Subversive imagination: Smoothing space for leisure, identity, and politics. In K. Spracklen, L. Lashua, E. Sharpe, & S. Swain (Eds.), *The handbook of leisure theory* (pp. 891–910). London: Palgrave.

Lashua, B. (2017). "Let's murder the moonlight!" Futurism, anti-humanism, and leisure. In K. Spracklen, L. Lashua, E. Sharpe, & S. Swain (Eds.), *The handbook of leisure theory* (pp. 487–506). London: Palgrave.

Lather, P. (1996). Troubling clarity: The politics of accessible language. *Harvard Educational Review*, 66(3), 525–545.

Lather, P., & St. Pierre, E. (2005). Post-positivist new paradigm inquiry. Class handout, ELAN 8560. *Theoretical Frameworks for Doctoral Students in the Human Science*.

Mansfield, N. (2000). *Subjectivity: Theories of the self from Freud to Haraway*. New York, NY: New York University Press.

Rubin, G. (1975). The traffic in women: Notes on the "political economy" of sex. In

Rayna R. Reiter (Ed.), *Toward an anthropology of women*. New York, NY: Monthly Review Press.

Scott, J. (1988). Deconstructing equality-versus-difference: Or, the uses of poststructuralist theory for feminism. *Feminist Studies, 14*(1), 33–50.

St. Pierre, E. A. (2000). Post-structural feminism in education: An overview. *International Journal of Qualitative Studies in Education, 13*(5), 477–515.

St. Pierre, E. (2013). The posts continue: becoming. *International Journal of Qualitative Studies in Education, 26*(6), 646–657.

St. Pierre, E. A., Jackson, A. Y., & Mazzei, L. A. (2016). New empiricism and new materialism: Conditions for new inquiry. *Cultural studies ←→ Critical Methodologies, 16*(2), 99–110.

Further reading: subversive readings for fugitive-type scholars

Barad, K. (2007). *Meeting the universe halfway: Quantum physics and the entanglement of meaning*, Durham, NC: Duke University Press.

Bennett, J. (2010). *Vibrant matter: A political ecology of things*. Durham, NC: Duke University Press.

Braidotti, R. (2013). *The posthuman*. Malden, MA: Polity Press.

Coole, D., & Frost, S. (2010). Introducing the new materialism. In D. Coole & S. Frost (Eds.), *New materialisms: Ontology, agency, and politics* (pp. 1–43). Durham, NC and London, UK: Duke University Press.

Deleuze, G., & Guattari, F. (2011). *A thousand plateaus: Capitalism and schizophrenia* (B. Massumi, Trans.). Minneapolis: University of Minnesota Press. (Original work published 1980 by Les Editions de Minuit, Paris.)

Chapter 3

Feminist theories after the poststructuralist turn

Simone Fullagar, Adele Pavlidis, and Jessica Francombe-Webb

In this chapter, we explore some of the key insights arising from feminist post-humanist and new materialist approaches, along with critical discussions of popular notions of post-feminism in the context of digital leisure and fourth wave feminism. Over several decades, rich and complex theoretical debates have emerged across social science and humanities disciplines about the ontological and epistemological assumptions that underpin notions of human subjectivity, human/non-human and digital relations, embodiment and the significance of affect in the circulation of power (Barad, 2007; Braidotti, 2013; Coole & Frost, 2010; Grosz, 1994; Haraway, 2013). A number of these post-structural and post-humanist approaches grouped under the rubric "new materialism" have begun to shape emergent fields of study that offer novel connections with feminist leisure scholarship: science and technology studies, animal studies, physical cultural studies, food studies, health and eco-humanities, digital sociology, material cultures, participatory design and arts as research practice, along with now more established queer, black, brown, Mad and crip feminisms – among others. Building upon Lisbeth Berbary's detailed account of post* ideas in Chapter 2, we have written this collaborative chapter through our particular interest in different ways of thinking through questions about power, women's[1] subjectivity or agency and the everyday politics of leisure.

Over the last two decades, there have been significant transformations in forms of feminist activism and broader debates in feminist scholarship that extend poststructural critique in new directions. With the rise of web 2.0[2] and the proliferation of digital media practices, the 1990s "girl power" popular cultural forms of post-feminism are being reinvented in the context of intensified political, economic, and cultural pressures that link women's local lives and global issues in new ways (Baer, 2016; Harris & Shields Dobson, 2015; McRobbie, 2015). Feminist leisure studies have begun to engage with these cultural shifts in what has been termed, not unproblematically, as fourth wave feminism (Parry & Fullagar, 2013). Knappe and Lang (2014) suggest that fourth wave feminists use "the web to re-link older and newer organizations, foster stronger networks, and encourage outreach to a new generation. Fourth-wave feminism has been defined by its focus on technology" (p. 364). Building on this analysis, we also offer some reflection on the utility and limitations of wave metaphors as we consider future avenues for feminist work.

In the desire to move-think-feel our way through advancing social justice (both within and beyond the academy), feminist leisure scholarship needs diverse theoretical, activist, and pedagogical approaches to open up different ways of materializing our feminist politics. New materialist thinking takes questions about the "personal as political" as serious embodied and conceptual matters, while also urging feminists to engage with ideas critically, creatively, and, hopefully, even playfully (Hinton & Liu, 2015). Perhaps at this point we should flash a warning sign for readers. Entering the terrain of new materialism may turn your thinking about gender, and knowledge itself, inside out and upside down, as we disrupt and diffract normative ways of knowing and being to imagine other possibilities for living.

One tactic that we have deployed in writing this chapter together is to entangle leisure studies with feminist work in related fields to forge broader alliances and networks around similar matters of concern. We view the boundaries of fields of knowledge as porous and open to the transformative movement of ideas back and forth. For example, there are overlaps with colleagues in education who have drawn upon new materialist theory-methods to challenge local and global stereotypes of British Muslim femininity through transformative dance and film projects. Hickey-Moody, Palmer, and Sayers (2016) work through a fleshy, embodied politics where

> building on a feminist investment in the agency of materiality, we think through the problem of the body as a site of learning, raising questions about how diverse bodies might fit in those environments that have traditionally suspended the body altogether, such as the university.
>
> (p. 214)

In this way, we understand writing as a material practice through which we draw different threads together to create feminist assemblages around particular problematics that we explore in the following sections: (i) historical and disciplinary context, (ii) tensions within feminist engagement with post* ideas, (iii) doing things differently through post theories and the feminist turn to affect, (iv) advancing feminist social justice, and (v) engaging with fourth wave feminisms and post-feminist debates. We conclude with a discussion of the limitations and possibilities for future feminist scholarship.

Historical and disciplinary context

In the recent history of leisure studies, Australian, British, and Canadian feminists, such as Betsy Wearing (1990, 1998), Sheila Scraton (1994), Cara Aitchison (2000), Susan Shaw (2001), and Simone Fullagar (2002), began to engage with poststructuralist theories as they "re-turned"[3] to earlier feminist critiques of masculine models of work and leisure, autonomous choice, and agency–structure debates (e.g., Deem, 1986; Green, Hebron, & Woodward, 1990; Henderson, Bialeschki, Shaw, & Freysinger, 1989). While we do not wish to reduce the complexity of these debates, there are some key shifts that significantly reshaped the field – such as the move away from defining leisure in terms of elements (space, time, activity and experience) and towards more relational, embodied and discursive accounts of leisure as a gendered practice.

As many other contributors to this book will discuss, feminist approaches to leisure importantly began to explore the "differences between women" and how gender intersected with race/ethnicity, religion, class, sexuality, (dis)ability, and age. Our own experiences as feminist scholars who cross different generations also troubles the notion that there are clearly identifiable waves of feminist thought. In the British context, Jessica's PhD completion in the early 2010s was written through an historical moment when leisure studies, feminism, and sport sociology were reconfigured as "physical cultural studies" to centralize embodiment as a problematic. As an undergraduate student in the late 1980s and early 1990s, Simone's honors thesis explored feminist philosophy under the supervision of Betsy Wearing, and, after having engaged with various post* theories in her PhD, several decades later she supervised Adele's PhD that explored feminist theories of affect in a new feminist sport.

Wearing (1998) also notes that ideas have complex trajectories, before the poststructuralist turn in symbolic interactionist theory brought an "awareness of the symbolic significance of the body and gestures to the interactional order" (p. 104). For example, explorations of emotion and affect in leisure before the poststructural turn primarily focused on how sport, particularly for men, enabled the expression of excitement and risk (e.g., Lyng, 1990; Norbert & Dunning, 1986). While, for women, much of the literature focused around friendship affiliations and making gender differences more visible (e.g., Green, 1998), Wearing's (1998) text sets out some of this historical terrain (see also Fullagar & Pavlidis, 2018; Pavlidis, 2017 for more recent outlines of the uses and trajectories of emotion and affect in leisure studies). The poststructuralist turn significantly influenced the more recent work of feminists in the "turn to affect," which has at its heart a desire to account for the *more than* symbolic aspects of the body and think about power beyond ideology in agency–structure debates (we attend to this more fully in the next section). Within feminist leisure scholarship questions of power and freedom have been central and the contribution of post* theories is very evident in the body of work that explores women's leisure as resistance to normative discourses and performative expectations. In this formulation, empowerment through leisure practices was not freedom or liberation from power; instead, there was a concern with identifying the strategies women deployed to create other modes of living and becoming for living *within and against* patriarchal institutions and practices.

Tensions and challenges within the theoretical perspective

Even with the emergence of poststructuralist ideas there have been tensions related to how qualitative methodologies were still situated within interpretivist and critical traditions that privileged a humanist notion of agency (romanticized notions of individual resistance and empowerment through leisure did seem to proliferate). As Berbary and Boles (2014) clearly articulate, the more recent turn towards new materialist theories open up key onto-epistemological questions that transform how we "do" representation, theory-method, and understand more-than-human agency. For example, feminist theories of affect seek to trouble binaries between "good' and "bad" feminism, "constrained" or "free" leisure as a means of questioning how the power manifests in material-discursive practices through which gender inequities and opportunities are felt, talked or not talked about, symbolized in cultural life, organized through the visible and invisible circuits of global capitalism, and digitally mediated. It is an approach which radically reconfigures notions of "empowerment," moving discourse about empowerment from a quality of being (tied to an individualized notion of subjectivity that interacts with a world that is somehow separate), to one that explores the relationality of becoming that produces agency as dispersed and co-implicated in the intra-actions of the world (Barad, 2007; Braidotti, 2013).

Accounts of feminist histories and theoretical "turns" are never straightforward, as they "cut" ideas in particular ways and we want to acknowledge this up front (Caudwell, 2011; Coleman, 2016; Parry & Fullagar, 2013). The emergence of new materialist feminisms as an onto-epistemological shift has been articulated by Van der Tuin (2009) as "the move towards relationality and non-dichotomous thinking [that] entails an epistemological practice that goes beyond the classificatory approach" (p. 18). Coleman (2016) extends this point by suggesting how feminist "theory is not [only] an epistemology – a way of knowing the world – but is also ontological in its imbrication in the becoming of these worlds" (p. 235). From a feminist perspective, new materialism asks questions that invoke ethical, ontological, and epistemological accountability about foundation claims that produce knowledge about "women" and gender (theory–method are understood as an apparatus; Barad, 2007).

Feminists have wrestled with the emphasis placed upon "new" materialism, as it assumes clear-cut departures of thought. Ahmed (2008), for example, argues that emphasizing a new materialism as a novel break from previous thinking presents "a false and reductive history of feminist engagement with biology, science and materialism" (p. 24). Different feminisms have posed critical questions from their location within particular sociohistorical milieus and Ahmed reminds us of the "need to appreciate the feminist work that comes before us, in all its complexity" (2008, p. 36). The feminist poststructuralist turn, within and beyond leisure studies in the 1990s, significantly informed theoretical debates in the 2000s about how we conceptualize freedom, resistance, and subjectivity.

Berbary (2017) makes the point that humanism still strongly influences scholarship in the field and, "without also making room for the possibilities of theorizing outside of this paradigm, only limits the potential breadth and application of our interdisciplinary field's social justice commitments" (p. 720).

Seeing things differently through post* theories

In sketching out the contemporary terrain of new materialist thinking, we wish to avoid repeating the analysis offered by Berbary in Chapter 2. As such, we will explore how this distinct "orientation or style of thought" can help formulate particular lines of inquiry to explore feminist leisure problematics (as we have done in different ways in our own research). Some of the problematics that we explore in this chapter, especially around post-feminism and digitality, could be described as situated "within and against" the interpretive humanist tradition with respect to issues of representation and agency, while the theorization of affect has been more closely entangled with onto-epistemological concerns. A significant departure point for feminist poststructuralist and post-humanist thinkers has been the challenge to assumptions about the human subject as masculine by default and positioned at the center of meaning.

The posts* have informed feminist thinking through questions that seek to reveal the assumptions (biological essentialism, social constructionism, human exceptionalism) that have informed knowing (epistemology) and being (ontology) "women." Judith Butler's (2004) work reoriented questions about women's experience of being oppressed (or liberated) by asking: How has gender been made thinkable as a subject position through (hetero)normative discourses that are *performative*? Similarly, Grosz (1994) asked: What are the effects of how gender difference is constituted through *binary oppositions* that work through hierarchical power relations to inferiorize the "other" in relation to the privileged first term: masculine/feminine, mind/body, reason/emotion, culture/nature, etc.? The influence of difference between feminists has also importantly shaped more intersectional and entangled thinking about the experiences of *becoming woman* within cultural formations (racism, homo/transphobia, Islamophobia, colonization, ableism, ageism, etc.), political institutions, economic relations, and local–global ecologies that are embodied, affective, mobilizing structures, and practices (Ahmed, 2004; Braidotti, 2013).

The turn towards new materialism has opened up questions to be formulated about what counts as political and ethical in terms of the entangled, intra-active, and co-implicated ontologies of knowing and becoming (Barad, 2007). Questioning any division between *matter* (human and non-human bodies, inorganic nature) and *meaning*, Hinton (2013) asks: "how might we approach the question of matter's participation in the very inequalities and exclusions that feminist political work attends to?" (p. 171). The influential feminist and quantum physicist Karen Barad calls her approach "agential realism," as she troubles the ontological assumptions about the reality of matter and works to "diffract" knowledge by questioning "how different differences get made, what gets excluded, and how those exclusions matter" – most often in relation to gendered ways of doing-knowing (Barad, 2007, p. 30). In this sense, feminists are "re-turning" to concepts such as patriarchy to open up more complex understandings of gendered power through examining bodies as entangled with more-than-human worlds. In Hook and Wolfe's (2017) work on gender-based violence, as an example, they give "new life" to the concept of patriarchy through new materialism rather than assuming a static representation that exists apart from its use in feminist knowledge.

One of the central critiques offered by new materialism concerns the onto-epistemological claims of *representationalism* that have informed positivist, interpretivist, and critical scholarship (Lather, 2015). Barad (2003) makes the point that "the representationalist belief in the power of words to mirror pre-existing phenomena is the metaphysical substrate that supports social constructivist, as well as traditional realist, beliefs" (p. 802). Feminist concerns have long been focused on the tensions around "representing" women (without essentializing categories of identity), which has also led to creative-critical ways of "doing" (theorizing–writing–re-creating) research that scholars interested in questioning the theory–method divide have named as "post-qualitative inquiry" (Berbary & Boles, 2014; Fullagar, 2017; St. Pierre, 2014). For example, van Ingen (2016) has written about her involvement in a Canadian boxing project for cis and trans women who have experienced gender-based violence. Rather than "represent" her findings about women's leisure lives, van Ingen (2016) draws upon creative practices as part of the research process to open up "space for voices and experiences that cannot be easily classified and that do not make easy sense" (p. 474). van Ingen's (2016) theory–method began with "getting lost" as an orientation to explore the complexities of women's leisure lives (Lather, 2015). While we do not have space to further discuss post-qualitative inquiry, we point towards the material-discursive possibilities produced through this theory–method approach (e.g., Berbary & Boles, 2014; Fullagar, 2017, 2018; Markula, 2006). In the rest of this chapter, we take up this concern with "representation" (beyond some assumptions about discourse reflecting a real world as matter) through feminist engagement with theories of affect, and then through issues of digitality and post-feminism.

The feminist turn to affect and emotion

> [I]n order to know differently, we have to feel differently... (feminist) politics can be characterized as that which moves us, rather than that which confirms us in what we already know.
>
> (Hemmings, 2012, pp. 150–151)

The emergence of theories of affect in cultural and feminist studies over the past few decades has been characterized by fierce proponents (e.g., Massumi, 1995;

Thrift, 2004) and a number of equally strong critical alternatives (e.g., Hemmings, 2005; Wetherell, 2013). Leisure practices provide us with a compelling site for feminist analyses into how affects are implicated in the micropolitics of embodied action, belonging, exclusion, and normalization. This is a complex terrain that follows scholarship across disciplines of cultural studies, queer studies, geography, pedagogy, and sociology – among others. Theories of affect are often attributed to masculine canon that includes the work of Deleuze (1994), both alone and with Guattari (1987); and authors such as Massumi (1995), Thrift (2004), and Anderson (2009), who have articulated the ways bodies and surfaces (human and non-human) are enfolded into productive "machinic" assemblages (Fox & Alldred, 2016). These scholars attempt to push the limits of "reason" to explore an ontology of surfaces and ways of knowing beyond language and the immediately knowable. Affect in these conceptualizations is relational, productive, generative, and vital. It is a capacity to act and be acted upon, to move and be moved. As Deleuze and Guattari (1987) write, rather than seek to know a phenomenon (pin down a singular meaning), "instead we will seek to count its affects" as multiplicity (p. 257). From the early work of scholars, such as Deleuze and Massumi, a range of disciplinary and theoretical engagements have emerged, contributing to an ever-growing attention to, and interest in, affect. Recent debates are less concerned with definitions of affect, of what affect *is* and instead focus on what affects *do*, as well as how they are implicated in the ever-changing power/knowledge relations in everyday life.

Feminist scholars have contributed substantially to debates concerning how affect can be deployed to better understand the rhizomatic relations of power that work to *reterritorialize* through assemblages, as well as open up *lines of flight* that enable becoming; "the personal" is always part of a political assemblage at any given moment. In different ways, feminists, such as Braidotti (2013), Ringrose and Renold (2014), Hemmings (2012), Wetherell (2013), Probyn (2005), and Ahmed (2004), have traced the desires that reterritorialize gender practices and identities – rather than assuming a genderless autonomy of affect that "follow(s) different logics and pertain to different orders" (Massumi, 1995, p. 88). Affective relations connect gendered bodies and practices through particular assemblages, which act as *arrangements*, bound up with economic effects, histories, and cultural intensities. For example, we can think about how shared pleasures of masculine sport fandom connect with practices of shaming and harassment of women in digital sportscapes.

The feminist focus on how bodies are practised is also echoed in Wetherell's (2012) work, which conceptualizes affect specifically in terms of "affective-discursive practices" (p. 364). Her primary charge against scholars such as Deleuze and Massumi is their insistence on the "autonomy" of affect as somehow separate from emotion and she argues that for an approach where affect is always entangled with the "discursive, already invaded by texts, symbols and representations" (Wetherell, 2012, p. 356). She cites researchers in psychology and neuroscience who find the separation of affect and emotion as "implausible" (Wetherell, 2012, p. 355). In response, Wetherell (2012) finds support for the principle that a burst of affect involves the "synchronous recruitment of somatic and mental resources" (Scherer, 2005, in Wetherell, 2012, p. 355). Indeed, affect is far more than a personal feeling; rather it is bound up with "embodiment, entanglement, the middle ranges of agency, patterns that organize but cannot necessarily be articulated, and the importance of taking action complexes as the main units of analysis" (Wetherell, 2012, p. 359).

Ahmed (2004) is another key feminist scholar who draws upon black feminist and post-colonial thought in her turn to affect and the affective economies that work on and through particular gendered, racialized, classed and sexed bodies. She too is concerned not so much with what affects are, but with what they can "do" (Ahmed, 2004, p. 4). For Ahmed (2004), any distinction between affect and emotion "can only be analytic" (p. 6). She writes:

> so emotions are not simply something "I" or "we" have. Rather, it is through emotions, or how we respond to objects and others, that surfaces or boundaries are made: the "I" and the "we" are shaped by, and even take the shape of, contact with others.
>
> (Ahmed, 2004, p. 10)

Like Wetherell (2012), then, Ahmed (2004) positions textures (and text) as central to research incorporating affect and emotion. In her work she demonstrates how experience is not simply constructed 'by' discourse or felt 'in' the body, but rather affects are produced through entangled material and discursive processes, "not just the textuality of emotions, but also the emotionality of texts" (Ahmed, 2004, p. 27).

The entangled gender relations of desiring bodies provides a different starting point for understanding injustice within normative, patriarchal relations; affects are not only part of the infrastructure of late capitalist society, but they are also transversal and hence disruptive in their effects. In their research on how gender is assembled through "body work" (e.g., cosmetic surgery and body image talk in schools), Coffey and Ringrose (2017) argue that transversal relations regulate and transform bodies through "practices that disrupt, rework but also productively inhabit hierarchies" (p. 177). The focus on gendered embodiment as assembled through material, performative, and affective relations disrupts conventional oppositions between (paid/unpaid) work and leisure, subject and world; leisure is increasingly bound up with working on the self (and for others). In a different context, Waitt (2014) explores active embodiment through a visceral analysis of young women's affective accounts of "sweating" that also draws together norms about femininity (i.e., men "sweat" and women "glow" in hyper-consumerist cultures) and the spatial relations through which bodies are enacted. The materiality of sweating produced affective, sensory responses – stickiness, smelliness, feelings of disgust, and feelings of dirtiness – and bring into relation an assemblage of forces that mobilize women's bodies in negative ways, which are often unrecognized as gendered practices (such as avoiding physical activity through shame).

Advancing feminist social justice

New materialist theories reorient thinking about social justice from foundational assumptions that would fix identity categories about gendered humanness as the main form of political address. Instead, feminist scholarship explores how power is materialized through "matter," and how gender comes to matter through entanglements of human and non-human bodies, affects, objects and cultural practices. As we have previously explored in relation to embodied movement practices,

> Such a shift reorients thinking around *relational questions* about the material-discursive forces that are complicated in what bodies can "do" and how matter "acts." This focus differs from more conventional social justice approaches concerned with what "is" a woman's body or the agentic meaning of experience that have characterized humanist interpretivist traditions (St. Pierre 2014, 2015).
>
> (Fullagar, 2017, p. 249)

Rather than adopt a social justice approach to leisure that equates participation with empowerment, a focus on the affective-material and discursive practices opens up analysis of the multiple desires and power relations that shape feminine subjectivity (see Braidotti, 2011). The turn to affect in leisure studies acts as a politics of hope – against the lack of hope that typifies the post-political (Mouffe, 2005) – as a generative, productive account of leisure practices that can forge new pathways, embrace uncertainty and also work *with* power as productive force for change. It is a theoretical and methodological shift in focus from categorizing "meaning" (what is leisure, what is gender) to understanding how gendered power relations materialize through bodies, patriarchal institutions, objects, and non-human nature in multiple ways: regulating, normalizing, and opening up trajectories of becoming (see also Pringle & Landi, 2017).

There has been less engagement with theories of affect in leisure studies than in other fields. Nonetheless, the work that has been published provides feminist accounts of leisure that make visible the embodied intensities and flows of affect (e.g., Markula, 2006; Newman, Thorpe, & Andrews, 2018; Roy, 2014). One of the first examples published in *Leisure Studies* was one of our articles (Fullagar, 2002), which worked through the materiality of embodiment to explore desire in the movement of feminine subjectivity through travel (preceded by an ecofeminist exploration of the assemblage of desire for nature via human–non-human relations; Fullagar, 2000). Reading Massumi's work on affect through French feminist theory, Fullagar (2002) conceptualized the gendered desire to travel as an affective self–other relation of becoming and hence beyond more static structure–agency formulations.

The affective relations that shape feminine subjectivities is a common theme in work that follows this trajectory. For example, a more recent article that we (Pavlidis & Fullagar, 2013) published explores the complex affective relations that women negotiate in forming leisure identities in relation to the gender relations of their lives (sexuality, class, geography, and so forth). Telling the stories of two roller derby participants in Australia and their negotiations of pride, shame, joy, and disappointment, we examined how affects played out differently for women in roller derby through distinct intersectional relations that (dis) assembled sport identities (Pavlidis & Fullagar, 2013). By engaging with the turn to affect, we were able to explore the gender relations (between women and involving masculine expectations) that shaped how different women (sexuality, motherhood, class, ethnicity) acted and felt in the flux of leisure spaces that involved more than "struggle and resistance to domination of the self and inferiorized subjectivities" (Wearing, 1998, p. 146).

In related fields, feminist scholars are engaging with methodological, conceptual, and theoretical dimensions of affect that have relevance to leisure. In education studies, for example, Ringrose and Renold (2014) explore the affective intensities involved in feminist activism in public leisure spaces with high-school-aged girls. These girls expressed a desire to participate in a local SlutWalk, which, as discussed in Chapter 1, is a global movement started in response to police instructions to women to "avoid dressing like sluts in order not to be victimized" (Ringrose & Renold, 2014, p. 4). Yet, the girls' teachers discouraged their participation. By focusing specifically on the interrogation of "slut" as a discursive and material category with affective intensity, Ringrose and Renold (2014) demonstrate how the girls were both regulated and how they reworked "slut" through a feminist assemblage.

In a very different context, Hickey-Moody (2013) considers the practices of affective pedagogy as a way of deploying art as an embodied space for young people (and educators) to reassemble subjectivity and move beyond normative categories. Her ethnographic work in a range of youth arts spaces (schools, community groups, and so on) is useful for thinking about how arts practice (dance, theatre, music) can be used by young women to enact gender by engaging with publics in new ways. As she writes, the opportunities afforded by arts "offer young people ways to understand themselves differently, to reassemble or augment their subjectivity, and to connect to unique communities … community youth art projects work through affective pedagogy" (Hickey-Moody, 2013, p. 146).

Next, we turn our attention to some interrelated questions concerning the rise of "post-feminism" as a cultural sensibility (dispelling some confusion surrounding this term) and the significance of digital leisure for feminist scholarship. Much of the feminist work on digital media has been informed by poststructural critiques of the discursive operations of power that seek to trouble how women's lives are "represented" or mediated through text and image. We draw primarily upon this work while also including examples of more materially oriented feminist explorations that understand "mediation" as an onto-epistemological relation that co-implicates self and world – Barad's (2007) notion of intra-action rather than inter-action. In this sense, digital leisure practices have particular material affects, and effects, as mediation is a material-discursive phenomenon, not just a "construction;" there is no assumed pre-existing separation of entities such as self and world, because all meaning is entangled. The extensive work of Donna Haraway (2013) (the figure of the cyborg and notion of diffraction) calls attention to how new materialist feminism has helped open up key questions about our relationship with technology – including in media studies where data is understood as having a "lively" materiality and affective relationality (Sumartojo, Pink, Lupton, & LaBond, 2016).

Engaging with fourth wave feminisms: postfeminism debates and digital leisure

Within this section, we map the gender relations that shape digital leisure practices and forms of online activism that offer mechanisms for political organization and the creation of feminist communities (Wajcman, 2000), and yet also participate in the oppressive relations of neo-liberal capitalism (Baer, 2016). This mapping offers an important contribution to feminist analyses as it ensures a critical exploration of the impact of fourth wave feminism articulated in terms of technology, online activism, and the "new" media-ecology (Darmon, 2013, p. 1). By interrogating these complexities and points of rupture, feminist analysis can contribute to new ideas and leisure practices that mobilize social change at the intersection of physical–digital culture. Critical engagement with digital leisure practices is imperative from a feminist perspective, as the digital offers a new form of "doing" feminist politics. Feminist scholars of digital leisure practices face a number of challenges when looking to better understand feminism, media practices, and moments of resistance and/or activism.

Most notably, there has not been extensive engagement with feminist activism online and postfeminist media culture. We require more complex understandings of how women's leisure choices are shaped beyond formulations of "constraints or barriers" that assume the self exists apart from the context that shapes gendered agency and desires. The circulation of material objects, discourses, and media within the markets of advanced liberal, global capitalism intensify the affective forces that produce a heady mix of "successful" individualism, consumerism, and heteronormative leisure (i.e., shopping, beauty and body image, social media, etc.) (Gerodetti & McNaught-Davis, 2017). It is in this contemporary moment that Baer (2016) claims the rise of digital feminist activism represents a "new moment or a turning point in feminism" in a number of ways (p. 18). First, feminist-inspired memes increase the consciousness of feminist issues in the public domain and promote new forms of feminist engagement. Second, through a democratization and sharing of knowledge and experiences, digital feminism is seen as a self-reflexive project whereby feminists from across the globe can learn from each other and begin intersectional conversations. Finally, "digital activism constitutes a paradigm shift within feminist protest culture" as feminist politics moves away from "conventional legal and legislative channels" (Baer, 2016, p. 18).

Nonetheless, questions remain about how we disentangle fourth wave feminism and post-feminism within online spaces as digital feminisms have emerged alongside the global dominance of neoliberal rationalities, markets, and modes of governing selfhood. Our engagement with fourth wave feminism necessitates that we pay attention to the complex ways in which women across the lifespan negotiate post-feminist physical and digital spaces or, in Renold and Ringrose's (2016) terms, *digital corporeal culture*. *Post-feminism* is a term fraught with conflicting meanings in academic and public circles. For some it is considered a theoretical position, for some it is thought synonymous with the third wave, for others it is a sentiment or critical object of inquiry. Our engagement with post-feminism follows the work of Gill (2007) and McRobbie (2004a, 2004b) in that we understand post-feminism as a *sentiment* across political, popular, and consumer culture. We engage with post-feminism as a critical object of inquiry that has come to indicate an undoing of feminism in the mainstreaming of empowered femininities that are self-governed and embodied. These self-styled feminine identities are produced in neo-liberal societies where women are offered normalized forms of equality through participation in consumer culture "in place of what a reinvented feminist politics might have to offer" (McRobbie, 2009, p. 2). As Latina and Docherty (2014) suggest, the "[k]ey questions that need to be addressed are thus: have social media really advanced the feminist cause? Do they really offer feminist activists previously unavailable privileges, and if so, in what ways?" (p. 703).

Working with different knowledges in a post-disciplinary context, and bringing them together to have different conversations about women's leisure, enables us to critically consider the performativity of gendered leisure and the ways that digital practices mediate affect, bodies, and affordances for feminist action. Our analyses shed light on the embodied experiences, shared social practices, material and discursive, human and more-than-human ways that individuals make sense of the world in the face of global policy challenges such as gender-based violence, sexualization, sexual discrimination, and entrenched gender inequalities in health, physical activity, and leisure. Understanding digital leisure practices as gendered and interrogating digital platforms and the feminist ideas disseminated requires an analysis of the wider socio-cultural context and how gender is negotiated in localized ways.

One such approach that we can adopt is thinking through theory as a practice of articulation (King, 2005). This involves constructing and reconstructing, speaking to/with, and listening back/from to generate research that is focused on exploring and theorizing embodied knowledge(s) in ways that contribute to a generative feminism (Braidotti, 2013). Borrowing from Kofoed and Ringrose's (2012) work on cyberbullying, we can see how critical post-humanism can offer "complexity-sensitive knowledge" of digital leisure, which articulates the performativity of gender in online spaces by taking into "consideration the number of forces that interact" (p. 7). Such an approach can move beyond critique to explore how the digital is reconfiguring women's leisure practices and how feminist analyses can work to materialize complexity as a contribution to matters of social justice. We begin to engage with this complexity by highlighting the contextual and emergent forms of feminist activism that take place online – with critical regard for their populist energy in leisure cultures (Phipps, Ringrose, Renold, & Jackson, 2017).

Feminist digital cultures

Fourth wave feminism is increasingly linked to the digital and technological innovations that shape contemporary culture. To begin, we want to spend time thinking about the ways that digital media technologies are being used by women and girls to "speak out" against patriarchy, hegemonic power relations, misogyny, rape culture, and everyday sexism (Keller, Mendes & Ringrose, 2016). Although a number of different social justice issues are taken up online, a dominant current in the feminist blogosphere involves challenging female visibility on the basis of bodily property and autonomy (Gill, 2007). For Keller, Mendes, and Ringrose (2016), the feminist blogosphere includes digital platforms such as Twitter, Tumblr, and Facebook, where feminist-inspired content functions as pedagogic devices that enable readers to learn about and be exposed to critiques that they may not have previously encountered (Baer, 2016). Across feminist research, the focus falls on some notable examples of recent feminist activism that have manifested differently in localized contexts but share a utilization of online platforms, particularly Twitter, to mobilize women globally and heighten visibility. Three notable examples are that of the SlutWalks organized around the world (predominantly in the global North), #everydaysexism, and #MeToo.

Since 2013, an increasingly global engagement with the feminist movement can be seen in the list of trending feminist hashtags, including: #FreeTheNip ple, #OscarSoWhite #ShoutYourAbortion, #ILookLikeAnEngineer, #AskHer More, #TamponTax, #GenderPayGap, #SolidarityIsForWhiteWomen, and #NotYourAsianSidekick. For Latina and Docherty (2014), these hashtags act as a form of socio-political campaigning that heighten the visibility of a particular cause or issue, but do not necessarily translate into other forms of activism on their own, given the narrow age ranges and gender diversity amongst most Twitter users, as well as the social positioning, digital literacy, and feminist vocabulary of the user. Nonetheless, #TraditionallySubmissive began trending in the UK in early 2016 when the (then)Prime Minister David Cameron's private suggestion that one of the reasons for radical extremism was the traditional submissiveness of Muslim women became public news.

This flippant suggestion prompted an immediate and global backlash on Twitter and inspired women from across the world to begin tweeting images of themselves holding pieces of handwritten paper emphasizing their competencies. One such example is an image of a woman holding a piece of handwritten paper that simply states: "Mother of 3, optometrist, Diehard LFC fan #Tradi tionallySubmissive." Unsurprisingly, the tweet that accompanies the image reads: "@david_cameron #TraditionallySubmissive Why don't you get to know us before you feel you have the right to comment on us." Another response incorporates an image of a Muslim woman holding a piece of handwritten paper that reads: "Working in the NHS 22 years, Mother of 3, Grandmother of 10, Know 5 languages AND English, Community Activist, Volunteer." The corresponding tweet succinctly notes: "Muslim women are not a problem that needs solving #TraditionallySubmissive @David_Cameron." Highlighting the interconnectedness of leisure, work, gender, this backlash from women on Twitter reminds us of Barad's (2007) new materialist notion of "intra-actions" that offers a critique of "representation" and urges researchers to move beyond "the view that the world is composed of individual entities with separately determinate properties" (p. 55). Extending this approach in her analysis of the materiality of digital practices, such as taking "selfies," Warfield (2016) calls attention to how the gendered apparatus of bodily production occurs through the entanglement of gendered postures, gazes, and camera angles. Indeed, intermingled senses of touch and vision are always a material-discursive "intra-action." In this context, digital intra-actions shape the possibilities of agency (rather than agency existing within a unified self) through the forces that are bound up in human and non-human assemblages (see also Lupton, 2017).

Within the context of leisure, health, fitness, and physical activity, increasing attention has been directed to the limited and essentialized forms of address that are aimed at women who are, or are encouraged to become, physically active. Across social media platforms such as Instagram, Facebook, and Tumblr there has been a rise in images, memes, vlogs, likes, shares, and status updates that can be categorized as forms of Fitspiration or "fitspo." Following Lucas and Hodler (forthcoming), Fitspiration posts commonly feature:

> [A] cropped image of a woman's body focusing on her thin, toned, white, hairless, six-packed torso … These images are generally paired with a pithy slogan or caption presumably aimed at inspiring the woman reader to exercise in order to achieve that fit-looking torso, hence the portmanteau "fitspiration."

Although presented as spaces of empowerment and self-expression, digital practices are performative sites that articulate normative ways of doing gender, sexuality, class, race, religion, age, and disability (Banet-Weiser, 2011; Dobson, 2015). The original aim of Fitspiration was to shift attention from overly slender bodies to a focus on health and fitness as key drivers for bodily appreciation.

Health and fitness practices such as eating "healthily" and exercising are therefore praised, and the gendered discourse of "strong is the new skinny" pervades much of the Fitspiration content across various digital media platforms. Whilst this shift in focus from the undernourished and over-exercised "size zero" body can be seen as inspiring, and perhaps even empowering for some in highly normalized ways, feminist criticism and activism online has begun to unpack the images, body types, activities, objectification, and textual elements of this online trend (Tiggemann & Zaccardo, 2016).

The hashtags #takebackfitspo and #stopfitspiration are now growing in number and significance. The images and mantras being shared function to challenge what have become the problematic features of fitspiration that jeopardize the potential for this online/offline movement to initiate significant change for women in active leisure contexts. For instance, people using the hashtag #takebackfitspo are "calling out" #fitspo on the basis of the individualized forms of address that assume: that physical activity is solely a matter of choice; the moralizing of women's active pursuits; the heteronormative and appearance-based notions of health and active leisure; and the surveillance of limited body-types that are on display (Hodler & Lucas-Carr, 2016; Tiggemann & Zaccardo, 2016). Instead, the online materialization of women's active leisure that is part of the #takebackfitspo trend mobilizes different affects – the pleasure and joys of exercise, the importance of listening to your body, and recognizing the competing priorities women face, as well as the place of exercise in their everyday lives (Lucas & Hodler, forthcoming).

Similarly, feminists have used online spaces to link their offline active leisure pursuits and their feminist activism. The blog "'Fit is a Feminist Issue" picks up on the two founders' experiences and deliberations about feminism and fitness. As feminist philosophers they hope to co-generate dialogue, debate, and engage with a feminist community who reflect upon and challenge common assumptions about women's fitness. Their guiding questions are: "What does it mean to be fit? What are appropriate measures for the goal? ... In what way(s) does women's quest for fitness and health contribute to empowerment and/or oppression?" The contributions on the blog speak to the notion of redoing feminism in a digital age as they reflect on the "*battle for sports inclusion*,"[4] challenge normalized healthism and functional approaches to fitness by not using "*training and racing to answer the questions*, '*Am I enough?*' *Instead ... trail run joyfully*," critiquing that "*Strong isn't a look*"[5] and promoting that "*All bodies are yoga bodies*."[6] By working through and providing space for discussion about some of the central tensions for feminists in fitness contexts, this blog is emblematic of a broader e-establishment of a "collective feminist politics beyond the realm of the self-styled individual" (Baer, 2016, p. 19). This is crucial, as "[r]eflecting on, and sharing personal experiences is a necessary first step to understanding how our personal circumstances relate to wider social structures" (Coleman, 2009, p. 11).

Doing feminism in the digital age: the complexities of post-feminism and neo-liberalism

Despite examples that highlight the potential offered by digital platforms "for broadly disseminating feminist ideas, shaping new modes of discourse about gender and sexism, connecting to different constituencies, and allowing creative modes of protest to emerge" (Baer, 2016, p. 18), we cannot take for granted that visibility will change patterns of gender inequity. This is because digital practices and digital feminism are constituted through assemblages bound up with global neo-liberalism. For Baer (2016), the relationship between digital feminism and neo-liberalism comes with many questions about the efficacy of digital activism by feminists when they become, as they inevitably will be, co-opted and work in tandem with individualized, "Do-It-Yourself" neo-liberal subjectivities and entrepreneurial forms of self-governance. Questions are raised about the political change that is likely to arise from these online backlashes and rebellions, especially in relation to the politics of the female body and the extent to which these body politics – which emphasize self-optimization, choice, and responsibility – make room for intersectional moments and non-binary identities that open up the category of "woman" as more than a homogenous group.

Due to its relationship with digital technology, the fourth wave treads a careful line, as feminism is seemingly being "redone" and yet "undone" in a post-feminist age of individualism, heteronormativity, whiteness, and consumerism. Noting that post-feminism has transpired as one of the most influential and disputed terms for feminist cultural studies, Gill (2007) highlights that there exists little consensus about how it is best understood. Rather than seeing post-feminism as a theory, historical shift, epistemological, and/or analytic perspective or as a form of "new," reworked or even dismantled feminism, Gill (2007) articulates post-feminism as a cultural sentiment (marked by ideas about femininity as a bodily property, intensified self-surveillance and discipline, and individualized empowerment linked to makeover paradigms).

As a populist discourse, the post-feminist sentiment proposes a discourse of autonomy and self-realization. Amy-Chinn (2006) emphasizes, however, these arguments often fail to contend with the extent to which discourses of femininity are founded upon a restrictive and already arrived at "normality." The post-feminist framing of women's experiences in terms of individualized autonomy positions them as having benefited "from the women's movement through expanded access to employment and education and new family arrangements" (Aronson, 2003, p. 904). Feminism and feminist concerns are thus seemingly redundant in this formulation; rendered as closure with key gains assumed as an historical given. For us, this points to the need to think critically and creatively about the ways in which we contend (theoretically and methodologically) with the notions of subjectivity, agency, empowerment, subversion, choice, and voice as they co-exist with, and are structured through, material-discursive practices that produce inequity in multiple and contradictory ways.

The challenge for feminism in a post-feminist age is about mobilizing a micropolitics to enact feminist desires related to gender equity and social justice (Coleman, 2009). We suggest that this can only come with developing an understanding of post-feminism as a critical object of inquiry, rather than an assumed reality, or an analytic perspective (Toffoletti, 2016). This critical post-feminist approach is not removed from the feminist wave metaphor but advances a politicized form of engagement that is not content with providing definitional accounts of post-feminism. Indeed, our approach aims to explore the way that post-feminist assemblages and rationalities are reterritorialized across women's digital leisure practices (see Depper, Fullagar, & Francombe-Webb, forthcoming; Francombe-Webb & Toffoletti, 2018). These assemblages need to be prioritized as objects of feminist inquiry to open up space for politicized intervention and activism that, among other things, engages with the work of new materialist scholarship to develop more nuanced understandings of digital-visceral bodies. Whilst this section has leant more heavily on a discursive reading of the Twitterscape and the micropolitics of women's digital leisure practices, we are mindful of the need to avoid the "teleological reduction in some poststructural accounts that subjects are simply captured and/or fixed within the structural/discursive order" (Kofoed & Ringrose, 2012, p. 8).

Unfinished business

At this historical moment, feminisms of various kinds are more visible in diverse public realms of global culture where gender issues play out within hostile digital and political contexts. In closing this chapter, then, we see the utility of new materialist theory to pursue questions of social justice through a focus on the micropolitics of gender and leisure assemblages as they are bound up with broader political, economic, ecological, technological and sociocultural relations, and affects. As a case in point, the election of American President Donald Trump has generated intense feminist affects (anger, outrage, despair, fear, and the desire for collective responses such as #makefeminismgreatagain and #womensmarch) in response to overt sexism and the erosion of institutional support for equality in advanced liberalism. Hard-fought gains for women's individual and collective rights, such as the inclusion of gender in the United Nations Sustainable Development goals,[7] can be all too easily undermined with shifting power relations that privilege a masculine notion of the subject as the norm (US restrictions placed on aid-funding around abortion access places women's lives at risk, the effects of climate change and poverty have greatest impact on women and children, etc.). Along with health, housing, work, and education, women's embodied leisure practices, virtual and physical spaces, and opportunities to act are thoroughly entangled with local and global flows of power. In terms of fourth wave feminism as a cultural formation, the engagement with feminist scholarship that explores the liveliness of digital landscapes, practices, and gendered infrastructures opens up new ways of conceptualizing agency beyond simply "woman" as an individualized, interpretive subject (or object) of knowledge or empowerment.

We have outlined how feminist engagement with the new materialist turn opens up onto-ethico-epistemological[8] questions that focus on the assumptions that inform all feminist thinking (the "cuts" of theory–method apparatus) about women's lives, (non-)normative gender (non-binary, cis and trans, intersex) practices, and intersectional relations. Building on earlier feminist theory that questioned what is meant by the normative category of "woman," new materialism continues to value different feminist ontologies that question "human exceptionalism" to explore how gender relations are co-implicated in human–non-human relations as material-discursive formations. While we have not had the space to explore diverse trajectories of thought that are opening up across multiple fields, we have aimed to introduce the possibilities of post-disciplinary dialogue for feminist leisure scholarship. As researchers, Hinton and Treusch (2015) remind us that new materialisms pose "questions of how we understand our relationship with what it is that we investigate, and therefore how we perceive our knowledge to be produced" (p. 3).

A materialist orientation to thought opens up questions about how difference comes to matter in ways that diffract normative ways of knowing-doing to create feminist alternatives. These include a diverse range of possibilities that also always recognize the fundamental limitations of generalized claims – for example, articulating Indigenous ontologies of nature–culture to inform policies on climate change, to queering family practices in performative ways, or mobilizing pedagogies of affect through creative arts and digital media with women and girls as feminist practices (Hickey-Moody, 2013; Renold & Ringrose, 2016). There is also a need for ongoing conversations about thinking through difference, as Hinton and Liu (2015, p. 130) ask in relation to questions of whiteness and race: "what has potentially been abandoned in new materialist discourse?" A number of scholars have articulated new materialist alternatives to representationalist conceptualizations of key ideas, such as intersectionality, to grapple with the limitations of identity politics and other political possibilities. They have deployed relational ways of thinking about how difference comes to matter, through queering assemblage theory (Puar, 2012) and evoking "interference" as a diffractive theoretical movement (Geerts & Van der Tuin, 2013). Reading-writing with these new ideas requires an orientation to living with uncertainty and not knowing, multiplicity rather than linearity and affective relations that unsettle and inspire at once. Engaging with how these ideas come to "matter" in feminist leisure scholarship is a transformative project, as Kumm and Johnson (2017) state: "The stakes are new modes of living, not reproductions of the same" (p. 905).

Notes

1 We use the term *women* to refer to a gender category that is a matter of self-identification and subject positioning (cis and transgender). We also note the limitations of either/or categories of gender for non-binary identifications.
2 Web 2.0 refers to the development of internet-based interactions from the early static interface to more interactive modes of engagement (social media, wearable technologies, etc.).
3 Barad (2014) articulates this process as far more than simply critique: "re-turning – not by returning as in reflecting on or going back to a past that was, but re-turning as in turning it over and over again ... We might imagine re-turning as a multiplicity of processes, such as the kinds earthworms revel in while helping to make compost or otherwise being busy at work and at play" (p. 168).
4 http://fb.me/1vvTcWcs
5 http://fb.me/8YjG1r38E
6 http://fb.me/70nFgxMQa; italics in original.
7 www.un.org/sustainabledevelopment/gender-equality/
8 Barad (2007) proposes that we ask questions that acknowledge the entanglement of ontological, ethical, and epistemological dimensions of all knowledge claims, methodologies, and ways of re-presenting matter.

References

Ahmed, S. (2004). *The cultural politics of emotion*. Edinburgh: Edinburgh University Press.

Ahmed, S. (2008). Open forum imaginary prohibitions: Some preliminary remarks on the founding gestures of the "New Materialism." *European Journal of Women's Studies*, *15*(1), 23–39.

Aitchison, C. (2000). Poststructural feminist theories of representing others: A response to the "crisis" in leisure studies' discourse. *Leisure Studies*, *19*(3), 127–144.

Amy-Chinn, D. (2006). This is just for me(n): How the regulation of post-feminist lingerie advertising perpetuates woman as object. *Journal of Consumer Culture*, 6(2), 155–175.

Anderson, B. (2009). Affective atmospheres. *Emotion, Space and Society*, *2*(2), 77–81.

Aronson, P. (2003). Feminists or "postfeminists"? Young women's attitudes toward feminism and gender relations. *Gender & Society*, *17*(6), 903–922.

Baer, H. (2016). Redoing feminism: Digital activism, body politics, and neoliberalism, *Feminist Media Studies*, *16*(1), 17–34.

Banet-Weiser, S. (2011). Branding the post-feminist self: Girls' video production and YouTube. In M. C. Kearney (Ed.), *Mediated girlhoods: New explorations of girls' media culture* (pp. 277–294). New York, NY: Peter Lang.

Barad, K. (2003). Posthumanist performativity: Toward an understanding of how matter comes to matter. *Signs: Journal of Women in Culture and Society*, *28*(3), 801–831.

Barad, K. (2007). *Meeting the universe halfway: Quantum physics and the entanglement of matter and meaning*. Durham, NC: Duke University Press.

Barad, K. (2014). Diffracting diffraction: Cutting together-apart. *Parallax*, *20*(3), 168–187.

Berbary, L. A. (2017). Thinking through post-structuralism in Leisure Studies: A detour around "proper" humanist knowledges. In K. Spracklen, B. Lashua, E. Sharpe, & S.

Swain (Eds.), *The Palgrave handbook of leisure theory* (pp. 719–741). London: Palgrave Macmillan.

Berbary, L., & Boles, J. C. (2014). Eight points for reflection: Revisiting scaffolding for improvisational humanist qualitative inquiry. *Leisure Sciences*, *36*(5), 401–419.

Braidotti, R. (2011). *Nomadic theory: The portable Rosi Braidotti*. Ithaca, NY: Columbia University Press.

Braidotti, R. (2013). *The posthuman*. Cambridge, UK: Polity Press.

Butler, J. (2004). *Undoing gender*. New York, NY: Routledge.

Caudwell, J. (2011). Sport feminism(s): Narratives of linearity? *Journal of Sport and Social Issues*, *35*(2), 111–125.

Coffey, J., & Ringrose, J. (2017). Boobs and Barbie: Feminist posthuman perspectives on gender, bodies and practice. In J. Lynch, J. Rowlands, T. Gale, & A. Skourdoumbis (Eds.), *Practice theory and education: Diffractive readings in professional practice* (pp. 175–192). London: Routledge.

Coleman, J. (2009). An introduction to feminisms in a postfeminist age. *Women's Studies Journal*, *23*(2), 3–13.

Coleman, R. (2016). Notes towards a surfacing of feminist theoretical turns. *Australian Feminist Studies*, *31*(89), 228–245.

Coole, D., & Frost, S. (2010). *New materialisms: Ontology, agency, and politics*. Durham, NC: Duke University Press.

Darmon, K. (2013). Introduction: Protest in the new media ecology. *Networking Knowledge*, *6*(3), 1–2.

Deem, R. (1986). *All work and no play? A study of women and leisure*. London: Open University Press.

Deleuze, G. (1994). *Difference and repetition*. Ithaca, NY: Columbia University Press.

Deleuze, G., & Guattari, F. (1987). *A thousand plateaus: Capitalism and schizophrenia*. London: Bloomsbury Publishing.

Depper, A., Fullagar, S., & Francombe-Webb, J. (forthcoming). This girl can? The limitations of digital do-it-yourself empowerment in women's active embodiment campaigns. In D. Parry, C. Johnson, & S. Fullagar (Eds.), *Digital dilemmas: Transforming gender identities and power relations in everyday life*. London: Palgrave.

Dobson, A. S. (2015). *Postfeminist digital cultures: Femininity, social media, and self-representation*. New York, NY: Palgrave Macmillan.

Fox, N. J., & Alldred, P. (2016). *Sociology and the new materialism: Theory, research, action*. London: Sage.

Francombe-Webb, J., & Toffoletti, K. (2018). Sporting females: Power, diversity & the body. In L. Mansfield, J. Caudwell, B. Wheaton, & R. Watson (Eds.), *The Palgrave handbook of feminisms in sport, leisure and physical education* (pp. 43–55). London: Palgrave.

Fullagar, S. (2000). Desiring nature: Identity and becoming in narratives of travel. *Journal for Cultural Research*, *4*(1), 58–76.

Fullagar, S. (2002). Narratives of travel: Desire and the movement of feminine subjectivity. *Leisure Studies*, *21*(1), 57–74.

Fullagar, S. (2017). Post-qualitative inquiry and the new materialist turn: Implications for sport, health and physical culture research. *Qualitative Research in Sport, Exercise and Health*, *9*(2), 247–257.

Fullagar, S. (forthcoming, 2018). Diffracting mind-body relations: Feminist materialism and the entanglement of physical culture in women's recovery from depression. In

J. Newman, H. Thorpe, & D. Andrews (Eds.), *Moving bodies: Sporting ecologies, assemblages, and new materialisms* (pp. 1–37). New Brunswick, NJ: Rutgers University Press.

Fullagar, S., & Pavlidis, A. (forthcoming, 2017). Feminist theories of emotion and affect in sport. In L. Mansfield, B. Wheaton, J. Cauldwell, & B. Watson (Eds.), *Handbook of feminism in sport, leisure and physical education* (pp. 1–22). Houndsmills, UK: Palgrave Macmillan. Retrieved from http://theconversation.com/this-girl-can-campaign-is-all-about-sexiness-not-sport-3623

Geerts, E., & Van der Tuin, I. (2013). From intersectionality to interference: Feminist onto-epistemological reflections on the politics of representation. *Women's Studies International Forum, 41*, 171–178.

Gerodetti, N., & McNaught-Davis, M. (2017). Feminisation of success or successful femininities? Disentangling "new femininities" under neoliberal conditions. *European Journal of Women's Studies, 24*(4). doi:10.1177/1350506817715045

Gill, R. (2007). Postfeminist media culture. *European Journal of Cultural Studies, 10*(2), 147–166.

Green, E. (1998). "Women doing friendship": An analysis of women's leisure as a site of identity construction, empowerment and resistance. *Leisure Studies, 17*(3), 171–185.

Green, E., Hebron, S., & Woodward, D. (1990). *Women's leisure, what leisure?* London: Macmillan Press.

Grosz, E. (1994). *Volatile bodies: Towards a corporeal feminism*. Sydney: Allen and Unwin.

Haraway, D. (2013). *Simians, cyborgs, and women: The reinvention of nature*. New York: Routledge.

Harris, A. & Shields Dobson. A. (2015). Theorizing agency in post-girlpower times. *Continuum, 29*(2), 145–156.

Hemmings, C. (2005). Invoking affect: Cultural theory and the ontological turn. *Cultural Studies, 19*(5), 548–567.

Hemmings, C. (2012). Affective solidarity: Feminist reflexivity and political transformation. *Feminist Theory, 13*(2), 147–161.

Henderson, K. A., Bialeschki, M. D., Shaw, S. M., & Freysinger, V. J. (1989). *A leisure of one's own: A feminist perspective on women's leisure*. State College, PA : Venture Publishing Inc.

Hickey-Moody, A. (2013). *Youth, arts, and education: Reassembling subjectivity through affect*. London: Routledge.

Hickey-Moody, A., Palmer, H., & Sayers, E. (2016). Diffractive pedagogies: dancing across new materialist imaginaries. *Gender and Education, 28*(2), 213–229.

Hinton, P. (2013). The quantum dance and the world's "extraordinary liveliness": Refiguring corporeal ethics in Karen Barad's agential realism. *Somatechnics, 3*(1), 169–189.

Hinton, P., & Liu, X. (2015) The im/possibility of abandonment in new materialist ontologies. *Australian Feminist Studies, 30*(84), 128–145.

Hinton, P., & Treusch, P. (2015). *Teaching with feminist materialisms* (P. Hinton & P. Treusch, Eds.). Nieuwegein: ATGENDER. Retrieved from atgender.eu/vol-12-teaching-with-feminist-materialisms/

Hodler, M. R., & Lucas-Carr, C. (2016). "Mother of all comebacks": A critical analysis of the fitspirational comeback narrative of Dara Torres. *Communication & Sport, 4*(4), 442–459.

Hook, G., & Wolfe, M (2017). Affective violence: Re/negotiating gendered-feminism within new materialism. *Journal of Gender Studies*, 1–10. doi: 10.1080/09589236.2017.1340151

Keller, J., Mendes, K., & Ringrose, J. (2016). Speaking "unspeakable things": Documenting digital feminist responses to rape culture. *Journal of Gender Studies*, doi:10.1080/09589236.2016.12115

King, S. (2005). Methodological contingencies in sports studies. In D. L. Andrews, D. S. Mason, & M. L. Silk (Eds.), *Qualitative methods in sports studies* (pp. 21–38), Oxford, UK: Berg.

Knappe, H., & Lang, S. (2014). Between whisper and voice: Online women's movement outreach in the UK and Germany. *European Journal of Women's Studies, 21*(4): 361–381.

Kofoed, J., & Ringrose, J. (2012). Travelling and sticky affects: Exploring teens and sexualised cyberbullying through a Butlerian-Deleuzian-Guattarian lens. *Discourse: Studies in the Cultural Politics of Education, 31*(1), 5–20.

Kumm, B., & Johnson, C. (2017). Subversive imagination: Smoothing space for leisure, identity, and politics. In K. Spracklen, B. Lashua, E. Sharpe, & S. Swain (Eds.), *The Palgrave handbook of leisure theory* (pp. 891–910). London: Palgrave.

Lather, P. (2015). The work of thought and the politics of research. In N. K. Denzin & M. D. Giardina (Eds.), *Qualitative inquiry and the politics of research* (pp. 97–107). Walnut Creek, CA: Left Coast Press.

Latina, D., & Docherty, S. (2014). Trending participation, trending exclusion? *Feminist Media Studies, 14*(6), 1103–1105.

Lucas, C. B., & Hodler, M. R. (forthcoming). #TakeBackFitspo: Building queer Futures in/through social media. In K. Toffoletti, J, Francombe-Webb, & H. Thorpe (Eds.), *New Sporting femininities: Embodied politics in postfeminist times*. London: Palgrave.

Lupton, D. (2017). Feeling data: Touch and data sense. *New Media & Society*, 1–19. Retrieved from implysociology.files.wordpress.com/2017/03/lupton-2017-feeling-data-touch-and-data-sense.pdf

Lyng, S. (1990). Edgework: A social psychological analysis of voluntary risk taking. *American Journal of Sociology*, 95(4), 851–886.

Markula, P. (2006). The dancing body without organs: Deleuze, femininity, and performing research. *Qualitative Inquiry, 12*(1), 3–27.

Massumi, B. (1995). The autonomy of affect. *Cultural* Critique, 31, 83–109.

McRobbie, A. (2004a). Notes on postfeminism and popular culture: Bridget Jones and the new gender regime. In A. Harris (Ed.), *All about the girl: Culture, power and identity*. (pp. 3–14). London: Routledge.

McRobbie, A. (2004b). Notes on "what not to wear" and post-feminist symbolic violence. *Sociological Review, 52*(2), 97–109.

McRobbie, A. (2009). The aftermath of feminism: Gender, culture and social change. Sage.

McRobbie, A. (2015). Notes on the perfect: Competitive femininity in neoliberal times. *Australian Feminist Studies, 30*(83), 3–20.

Mouffe, C. (2005). *On the political*. London: Routledge.

Newman, J., Thorpe, H., & Andrews, D. (Eds.) (forthcoming). *Sport, Physical Culture, and the Moving Body: Materialisms, Technologies, Ecologies*. New Brunswick, NJ: Rutgers University Press.

Norbert, E., & Dunning, E. (1986). *Quest for excitement: Sport and leisure in the civilizing process*. London: Wiley-Blackwell.

Parry, D., & Fullagar, S. (2013). Feminist leisure research in the contemporary era. *Journal of Leisure Research, 45*(5), 571–582.

Pavlidis, A. (2017). Affective and pleasurable bodies. In M. L. Silk, D. L. Andrews, & D. Holly Thorpe (Eds.), *Routledge handbook of physical cultural studies* (pp. 295–303). London: Taylor & Francis.

Pavlidis, A., & Fullagar, S. (2013). Narrating the multiplicity of "derby grrrl": Exploring intersectionality and the dynamics of affect in roller derby. *Leisure Sciences*, *35*(5), 422–437.

Pavlidis, A., & Fullagar, S. (2014). *Sport, gender and power: The rise of roller derby*. London: Ashgate.

Phipps, A., Ringrose, J., Renold, E., & Jackson, C. (2017). Rape culture, lad culture and everyday sexism: Researching, conceptualizing and politicizing new mediations of gender and sexual violence. *Journal of Gender Studies*, *27*(1), 1–8. doi:10.1080/09589236.2016.1266792

Pringle, R., & Landi, D. (2017). Re-reading Deleuze and Guattari's A *Thousand Plateaus*. *Annals of Leisure Research*, *20*(1), 117–122.

Probyn, E. (2005). *Blush: Faces of shame*. Sydney: University of New South Wales.

Puar, J. (2012). "I would rather be a cyborg than a goddess": Becoming-intersectional in assemblage theory. *philoSOPHIA*, *2*(1), 49–66.

Renold, E., & Ringrose, J. (2016). Selfies, relfies and phallic tagging: Posthuman participations in teen digital sexuality assemblages. *Educational Philosophy and Theory*, *49*(11). doi:10.1080/00131857.2016.1185686

Ringrose, J., & Renold, E. (2014). "F** k rape!" Exploring affective intensities in a feminist research assemblage. *Qualitative Inquiry*, *20*(6), 772–780.

Roy, G. (2014). "Taking emotions seriously": Feeling female and becoming-surfer through UK Surf Space. *Emotion, Space and Society*, *12*, 41–48.

Scraton, S. (1994). The changing world of women and leisure: Feminism, "postfeminism" and leisure. *Leisure Studies*, *13*(4), 249–261.

Shaw, S. M. (2001). Conceptualizing resistance: Women's leisure as political practice. *Journal of Leisure Research*, *33*(2), 186.

St. Pierre, E. A. (2014). A brief and personal history of post qualitative research: Toward "post inquiry." *Journal of Curriculum Theorizing*, *30*(2), 2–19.

Sumartojo, S., Pink, S., Lupton, D., & LaBond, C. H. (2016). The affective intensities of datafied space. *Emotion, Space and Society*, *21*, 33–40.

Thrift, N. (2004). Intensities of feeling: towards a spatial politics of affect. *Geografiska Annaler: Series B, Human Geography*, *86*(1), 57–78.

Tiggemann, M. and Zaccardo, M. (2016). "Strong is the new skinny": A content analysis of #fitspiration images on Instagram. *Journal of Health Psychology*, doi:10.1177/1359105316639436

Toffoletti, K. (2016). Analysing media representations of sportswomen – Expanding the conceptual boundaries using a postfeminist sensibility. *Sociology of Sport Journal*, *33*(3), 199–207.

Van der Tuin, I. (2009). "Jumping generations": On second and third wave feminist epistemology. *Australian Feminist Studies*, *24*(5), 17–31.

van Ingen, C. (2016). Getting lost as a way of knowing: The art of boxing within Shape Your Life. *Qualitative Research in Sport, Exercise and Health*, *8*(5), 472–486.

Waitt, G. (2014). Bodies that sweat: The affective responses of young women in Wollongong, New South Wales, Australia. *Gender, Place & Culture*, *21*(6), 666–682.

Wajcman, J. (2000). Reflections on gender and technology studies: In what state is the art? *Social Studies of Science*, *30*(3), 447–464.

Warfield, K. (2016). Making the cut: An agential realist examination of selfies and touch. *Social Media + Society*, *2*(2). doi:10.1177/2056305116641706

Wearing, B. (1990). Beyond the ideology of motherhood: Leisure as resistance. *Australian and New Zealand Journal of Sociology*, *26*(1), 36–58.

Wearing, B. (1998). *Leisure and feminist theory*. Sage: London.

Wetherell, M. (2013). Affect and discourse – What's the problem? From affect as excess to affective/discursive practice. *Subjectivity*, 6(4), 349–368.

Further reading

Coole, D., & Frost, S. (2010). *New materialisms: Ontology, agency, and politics*. Durham, NC: Duke University Press.

Fullagar, S. (2017). Post-qualitative inquiry and the new materialist turn: Implications for sport, health and physical culture research. *Qualitative Research in Sport, Exercise and Health*, 9(2), 247–257.

Hinton, P., & Treusch, P. (2015). *Teaching with feminist materialisms* (P. Hinton & P. Treusch, Eds.). Nieuwegein: ATGENDER. Retrieved from atgender.eu/vol-12-teaching-with-feminist-materialisms/

Newman, J., Thorpe, H., & Andrews, D. (Eds.) (forthcoming). *Sport, Physical Culture, and the Moving Body: Materialisms, Technologies, Ecologies*. New Brunswick, NJ: Rutgers University Press.

Taylor, C. A., & Hughes, C. (2016). *Posthuman research practices in education*. London: Palgrave Macmillan.

Chapter 4

Thinking intersectionally

Fourth wave feminism and feminist leisure scholarship

Beccy Watson

In June 2017, a tragic event occurred involving extensive loss of life at Grenfell Tower, a block of social housing flats (apartments) in the centre of London, United Kingdom, where (at the time of writing) the death toll is still unconfirmed as the investigation into the fire continues. The consequences facing victims and the context of how the fire occurred can be seen as an intersectional failure in the global North in the twenty-first century. That is, the tragedy acts as a stark reminder of social, economic and cultural inequalities that are inescapable indicators of differences and differential consequences of the materiality of everyday lives. The demographic profile of Grenfell residents is predominantly black and minority ethnic, including a number of refugees and asylum seekers, all are poor/low income, and it includes othered and excluded white 'working class' residents. Racialised, classed, gendered identities, intersecting with age, sexuality, disability, are made visible in this instance only through tragedy. Many of the individuals, families, communities, including the broader Grenfell Tower community, are acknowledged in the dominant discourse only because they are news items. In examining the details surrounding the fire at Grenfell Tower, critical commentators highlight deregulation, privatisation, austerity and inequality as culminating factors of such a devastating outcome (Freedland, 2017). Arguably there is no other obvious way to make sense of what happened than through an intersectional analytic framework.

My argument in this chapter is that "thinking intersectionally" is a crucially important endeavour for feminist leisure scholarship. An ongoing project with both possibilities and also potential pitfalls for feminist leisure scholars (Watson & Scraton, 2013), the "work" of intersectionality and definitions for intersectional thinking are by no means complete. Drawing on a view of intersectionality in process, it is important to note that feminisms are multiple and varied; to identify distinctive feminist theories and/or to group these theories into waves, in a linear/chronological sense at least, as a means of informing our feminist leisure work, can be limiting rather than liberating (Caudwell, 2011; Mansfield, Caudwell, Wheaton, & Watson, 2017; Parry & Fullagar, 2013; Watson & Scraton, 2017a). This is a key principle of ideas presented here. This chapter offers some commentary on if and how thinking intersectionally speaks to some of the central tenets of the fourth wave feminism and functions to advance feminist social justice. Sheila Scraton and I, along with many other leisure (and sport) feminists, have long since argued that leisure, as a complex and commonly divided set of cultural practices (that can incorporate and include sport and recreation, physical activity and so on) is an illuminating context for analysing gendering and gendered social relations more broadly.

In recent years I have been involved in work focused on feminisms across sport, leisure and Physical Education ('PE' in UK – compulsory part of education in school), (Mansfield et al., 2017) and my ongoing research and theorising on leisure, sport and social justice more broadly (Long, Fletcher, & Watson, 2017). This involvement resonates with Johnson and Parry's (2015) collection on leisure research for social justice outcomes. These edited collections build on previous work that applies critical theoretical perspectives to various political contexts of sport and leisure (e.g., Sugden & Tomlinson, 2002), and that examines questions of diversity, equity and inclusion across sport and leisure (Fletcher & Dashper, 2014). Remaining critically reflexive, using what Sheila Scraton and I term "reflexivity with responsibility" (Scraton & Watson 2001; Watson, 2017; Watson & Scraton, 2017b), is central to my engagement with social and gender justice-based research and is a fundamental aspect of my feminist leisure lens. Intersectionality, feminism and social justice are bound together in complex and dynamic interplay and this has numerous implications for leisure scholarship. This chapter is an attempt to outline some key characteristics of that interplay. To achieve this, I draw from my empirical research on masculinity, gender and recreational dance as an illustrative example of how thinking intersectionally is about "seeing things differently" in feminist leisure research. The chapter also outlines the historical and disciplinary roots of intersectionality, considers tensions and challenges within intersectionality, and, although the dynamics of intersectionality, feminism and social justice are implicit across the whole piece, I consider how we might advance feminist social justice and assess thinking intersectionally alongside fourth wave feminism in discrete sections. I return to my example of gender and dance in the final section to emphasise how thinking intersectionally is an ongoing process that is yet to be more meaningfully engaged with by feminist leisure scholars and leisure scholarship more broadly. Thus, this "unfinished business" section also acts as a reminder of how privilege and different manifestations of power remain embedded in our field of study.

Historical and disciplinary roots

Intersectionality is commonly believed to originate from the work of US-based legal scholar Kimberlé Crenshaw in the late 1980s and early 1990s (Crenshaw, 1989, 1991). Put simply, intersectionality is a conceptual framework that emerged as a way to recognise and account for what happens when different aspects of identity "collide". When Crenshaw outlined it as a theoretical framework, the specific categories of identity she was referring to at the time were race, gender and class. Thinking intersectionally, therefore, involves acknowledging the consequences of these collisions, which often remain invisible. Thus, intersectional feminism means "giving voice" and recognition to women who are discriminated against as a consequence of racism and sexism and for whom the feminist movement (and other social and political movements and protest groups) does not adequately account for or acknowledge.

In contemporary contexts, drawing on some of Crenshaw's recent and ongoing campaign work such as '#SayHerName' (Khaleeli, 2016), it is evident that concerns regarding sexual violence and harassment repeatedly stereotype white women as victims of sexual assault and black men as victims of racist violence on the street; as if (white) women are not racialised and (black) men are not gendered. Intersectionality is therefore concerned with highlighting absence as well as challenging stereotypical generalisation; it is problematic to talk in terms of black men, white women, and men and women per se. Absence of recognition that women are subject to private and public violence, and discrimination (as are some men), is referred to by Crenshaw as a form of intersectional failure. That is, some issues are persistently ignored and some voices are repeatedly kept silent.

Prior to Crenshaw, As Hill-Collins and Bilge (2016) explain, the underlying premise of intersectionality can be found in many ideas proposed by earlier Black feminists:

> Intersectionality's core ideas of social inequality, power, relationality, social context, complexity, and social justice formed within the context of social movements that faced the crises of their times, primarily, the challenges of colonialism, racism, sexism, militarism, and capitalist exploitation. In this context, because women of color were affected not just by one of these systems of power but by their convergence, they formed autonomous movements that put forth the core ideas on intersectionality, albeit using different vocabularies.
>
> (p. 64)

The reference to context is important and underpins my thesis throughout the chapter. Contextualisation acknowledges the significance of power relations and the process and processes in and through which these relations are both constituted and manifest. Intersectionality offers a useful lens into multiple axes of complex social relations and provides a workable analytic framework for understanding and addressing multiple social inequalities.

With reference to the Grenfell Tower incident, intersectional analysis highlights crucial questions be asked regarding the everyday lives of those affected (directly and indirectly), to more fully recognise and account for individual and collective subject positions vis-à-vis institutional, authority-based frameworks. This approach, accounting for individual difference in the context of social relations, is not without its challenges (Brah, 1996). I will expand on this as the chapter develops. For now, it is important to understand that intersectionality is referred to in myriad ways – as a theoretical perspective, as an analytical tool and as methodology.

As a theoretical approach, intersectionality is often associated with providing a more critically informed account of difference, something that directly informs my view of thinking intersectionally (Watson & Scraton, 2013). As Hill-Collins and Bilge's commentary above indicates, intersectionality did not suddenly appear in feminist rhetoric in the 1980s. Intersectionality is undoubtedly informed by established and ongoing critiques of white liberal feminism by black feminism that warn against a privileging of specific aspects of identity formation (Bilge, 2014; Brah, 1996; Hill-Collins, 1990; hooks, 1989; Yuval-Davis, 2011). Black and minority ethnic (a term referred to as BME and/or BAME and often used in the UK) feminism/s call for analysis of women's lives from a range of perspectives including standpoint and "strength in difference" (Amos & Parmar, 1984; Hill-Collins, 1990), postmodern blackness (hooks, 1991; Mirza, 1997), creolisation theory (Brah, 1996) and strategic essentialism (Spivak, 1987). These critiques demonstrated the need for a more critical analysis of difference (other than those valorising gender as the main explanatory framework). Following Crenshaw's initial conceptualisation, feminist writers and activists have continued to grapple with difference and identity (Cho, Crenshaw, & McCall; 2013; Hill-Collins & Bilge, 2016; Lutz, Vivar, & Supik, 2011; Lykke, 2010).

Davis (2008) suggests the core appeal of intersectionality as a theoretical approach is the way in which it brings together multiple identities in the context of postmodern difference without abandoning material relations of power. That is, intersectionality represents a rejection of additive approaches to gender, race, class, age, sexuality, (dis-)ability, yet seeks to account for the consequences of when these identity categories intersect and are routed through each other. In short, intersectionality offers a more nuanced approach to previously used identity categories (Cho et al., 2013; Davis, 2008; Hill-Collins & Bilge, 2016; Lewis, 2009; McCall, 2005; Nash, 2008; 2016; Yuval-Davis, 2011).

For all these writers, accounting for the historical context or conditions in which inequalities are manifest is vital. Yuval-Davies (2011) argues that "an intersectional mode of analysis which differentiates between the different analytical facets of social divisions and explores their connectivity in different historical contexts is a much more systematic and generally applicable mode of analysis" (p. 162).

Tensions and challenges

Intersectional approaches encourage and enable analyses of specific circumstances encountered by individuals, whilst maintaining an explanatory and analytical perspective that retains a focus on systems and processes of power relations (Brah, 1996; Cho et al., 2013; Valentine, 2007; Valentine & Harris, 2016). Intersectionality is often considered as a "middle ground" and herein lies both potential and peril; in terms of assessing more fully the consequences of difference, not all bases can be covered because there is no feasible way of assuming that context-specific complexity can be fully addressed. Intersectionality has at times been criticised for a somewhat overreliance on a fast-travelling concept of "raceclassgender" (Knapp, 2005) that veneers over difference rather than deconstructing it (Hill-Collins & Bilge, 2016). Gressgard (2008) warns centring multiplicity and complexity can place an overemphasis on diversity without adequate critical explanation; here, then, we can see how intersectionality is in danger of offering an *account of* difference, rather than *accounting for* difference.

This opens up another point of criticism, as, despite efforts to acknowledge and problematize identity categories, a potentially damaging result of employing intersectionality is the potential for race, gender and class to be defined deterministically (and in a somewhat reductionist manner). This raises pertinent questions regarding who defines various elements of feminist thinking and feminist activism; Bilge (2013, 2014), for instance, questions the limits of intersectionality in accounting for whiteness as power relations, and Nash (2016) challenges feminist commemorative claims of "originalism" when it comes to defining intersectionality (I return to this in discussion of fourth wave feminism later on). Hill-Collins and Bilge (2016) provide valuable commentary on how issues surrounding sexuality and sexualities were explicit in early black feminist writing and outline how various acts of black activism sought to engage with these challenges; yet there are concerns that intersectionality as a concept does not provide adequate coverage of sexuality and sexualities as a feature of identity (Puar, 2012). I touch upon the possibilities of queer and intersectional dialogue in the section on unfinished business.

Influential to the development of my feminist research and writing, Avtar Brah's (1996) analysis of the South Asian diaspora in the UK, provides a helpful articulation of "creolization theory" and "diaspora space" to explain that "difference and commonality are figured in non-reductive relationality" (p. 248). That is, individual identity and identities cannot be subsumed into collective notions of community any more than community be understood as uniform entities. For example, the Grenfell residents are constituted by multiple and complex identities of "minoritization" and marginalisation involving race and otherness in myriad ways. The ongoing tension of how social and individual identities are conceptualised continues to inform debates on intersectionality and its place within feminism (Cho et al., 2013; Hill-Collins & Bilge, 2016; Nash, 2016). Intersectionality remains particularly significant in a current political climate, across various areas of the global North, where suspicion and mistrust and hate fuel dominant discourses on migration, be they established diasporas, "new" and/or current, in transit, or yet to arrive.

In the introduction to her 1996 book *Cartographies of Diaspora*, Brah argued for "cartographies of intersectionality" grounded in political movements.

Looking back to the 1980s, she claims her work was based on distinctions between "experience," "culture" and "structure" – although they were seen, from the outset, to interact with one another (1996, p. 12). Brah's calls to engage with different levels of intersectionality, including organisational/institutional, intersubjective, experiential and representational, resonates with other feminists cited in this chapter who continue to inform my critical feminist leisure scholarship. A call for multi-level analysis would mean taking a multifaceted approach to making sense of the lives of those impacted by what happened at Grenfell. Accountability and tackling institutional failure runs much deeper than assessing the state of building and fire regulations in public sector/social housing. Defining intersectionality at an epistemological level has profound implications for how we seek to employ intersectional frameworks in practice in leisure (Watson, 2017; Watson & Scraton, 2017a, 2017b). In the next section, I expand on what I perceive my feminist leisure lens to be and, as indicated so far, it is premised upon power and centring difference as relational.

McCall (2005) suggested there are three key methodological approaches associated with intersectionality: anti-categorical, intra-categorical and inter-categorical. This analysis has had a significant impact on feminist engagement with intersectional-based research. In short, anti-categorical approaches reflect poststructuralist analyses, whereby deconstruction and refuting categorisation of identities as "knowable" is commonplace. In contrast, McCall's (2005) intra-categorical approach enables recognition of difference within identity categories such as gender. This approach tends to focus on marginalised identities with unmarked categories of privilege such as whiteness, heterosexuality and masculinity (Bilge, 2013, 2014; Lutz et al., 2011; Valentine, 2007). Thus, leisure contexts, as sites of privilege and power, require ongoing and further scrutiny.

Advocating for an engagement with categories whilst acknowledging and accounting their complexities (as opposed to anti-categorical perspectives) prompts questions about how intersectionality is put to work methodologically (Lykke, 2010; MacKinnon, 2013; McCall, 2005; Nash, 2008). Deconstructionist analysis refutes the existence of collective experience (at a conceptual level), but it does not eradicate oppression (hooks, 1989; Stanley & Wise, 1993; Walby, Armstrong, & Strid, 2012). There are understandable concerns about standpoint epistemologies (Haraway, 1988; Harding, 1987), which can potentially essentialize blackness, class or sexual identity (hooks, 1989), and yet there are ways in which being "essentialist" can be strategic (Spivak, 1987). However, debates about essentialism are not unique to intersectionality. What McCall (2005) and others argue is that intersectionality can (and must) inform research epistemologically and methodologically, that it be regarded as an entire process, not simply a research procedure (Cho et al., 2013; Winker & Degele, 2011).

McCall (2005) argues that an inter-categorical approach requires multi-level data that capture structural constraints and individual agency. This throws up methodological challenges in practical research terms, as it is likely that different aspects of categories – the anti, intra and inter – converge when we seek to understand leisure experience and its associated socio-cultural meanings (Watson, 2017). A persistent challenge for an inter-categorical approach is detailing and accounting for difference *and* inequality without reliance on assumptions about how different forms of inequality are accorded primacy (positioned hierarchically). One way to address this is to engage more fully and more critically with the contextualisation and the contexts of our research.

Seeing things differently and thinking intersectionally

Contextualisation of research requires epistemological sensitivity to *ongoing* issues surrounding dominant positions of knowledge production that are still commonly centred on a middle-class, Western, masculine, able-bodied, heteronormative self (Haraway, 1988; Harding, 1987, 1991). Context and contextualisation are therefore highly relevant to researchers engaging with intersectionality, because asking questions of the overall context – not least the overarching (or underlying) domain and/or parameters of our research – is a significant and necessary means of establishing our paradigmatic and epistemological starting points (Stanley & Wise, 1993). Alongside praxis and pragmatism, this is a fundamental premise of my feminist leisure lens.

I believe firmly that empirical studies make valuable contributions to understanding difference and that this usefully informs ways to achieve greater gender justice. Thinking intersectionally in feminist leisure scholarship includes questioning our research agendas throughout, from how we perceive leisure experience and its consequences, through to analysis and dissemination (Watson, 2017; Watson & Scraton, 2013). It is about linking our theoretical concerns to our methodological choices, though, as indicated above, I am not claiming that intersectionality is unique in that respect (as other chapters in this collection indicate). MacKinnon (2013) asserts that intersectionality is about people and experience and that intersectional research is thus seeking to account for multiple ways marginalisation impacts and is embodied (to account for the intersections, not just recognise and label them). Arguably MacKinnon's view builds on Brah's earlier assertions, and an emphasis on people, although seemingly obvious, reminds us how complex social relations are "lived" and are "felt" (to draw on the concept of affect). The impacts of Grenfell include fear, anxiety, depression and more. Where or how we contextualise leisure in this regard is beyond the scope of this chapter, though it is nonetheless pertinent.

It may seem obvious to state that studies seeking to expose and explain persistent gender (and other) inequalities require different methodological emphases (Nash, 2008). I draw on a couple of different research contexts here – one around space and one around embodiment – to illustrate where my ideas on thinking intersectionally have emerged and been put into practice. My entanglements with space and embodiment stem from my PhD research in the mid-1990s. I have stated elsewhere (Watson, 2017) that I came to intersectionality partway through this research, though I would suggest I was already engaged intersectionally in my thinking and in my research practice, if not by conceptual name at the time. My data collection and my analysis of young mothers' leisure, as time, as space and as identity, was only meaningful in the context of difference. I approached my participants as individuals whose identities were constructed through gender relations that only made sense in relation to race and class as well as gender. Looking back, I can see how I privileged gender as a category and, although I actively sought to refute additive models, I probably fell foul to ethnocentric and whitecentric feminisms, as I have gone on to consider elsewhere (Watson & Scraton 2001, 2017b). I share this experience to highlight how thinking intersectionally is a process rather than a procedure.

I remain committed to carrying out research that maps individual, micro experiences onto broader social, macro contexts and vice versa (Brah, 1996; Scraton & Watson, 1998; Watson & Scraton, 2001). It sounds simplistic in some ways yet it remains fundamental to my feminist scholarship. Researching difference represents a commitment to a (renewed) feminist politics for gender justice and hence the challenge of "thinking intersectionally" (Watson & Ratna, 2011; Watson & Scraton, 2013) about difference and multiple identities and inequalities and marginalisation and discrimination. It comes with a warning, too: intersectionality poses difficult questions for researchers and is not a shortcut to accounting for the heterogeneity of gendered experiences.

Space for leisure

Engaging intersectionality to analyse leisure spaces enables researchers to assess complex, interrelated social factors in dynamic, live situations. Space is socially constructed and a dynamic context in which identities and inequalities interact (Massey, 2005; Valentine & Harris, 2016). Scraton and Watson (1998) demonstrated, for example, how gender and leisure in urban space is simultaneously shaped by classed and racialised contexts. Watson and Ratna (2011) researched civic parks as racialised spaces and argue the term *space for leisure* captures how leisure and the appropriation of public space is an ever-changing and negotiated context. The research highlights the complex and contradictory nature of spaces of celebration within broader contexts of discrimination and alienation – in particular, events championing South Asian popular cultural activities. They assert how "thinking intersectionally" about leisure is meaningful in this respect. This involves seeing leisure spaces as contexts not just as sites; that is, the context is contested and not merely a leisure site or venue. The context of the park is, as a leisure space, one defined by outcomes and constituents of complex historical processes. In this analysis of space for leisure, the researchers incorporated an overview of the establishment and settlement of a South Asian diaspora in the city, identified populist and dominant discourses of racialised and gendered relations within and across the diaspora, considered dominant media narratives of the South Asian diaspora at the time and observed and documented myriad, embodied expressions of these identities at specific events. "Thinking intersectionally" enabled the researchers to critically engage with difference and explore expressions and negotiation of difference in situ whilst locating these findings in wider circuits informed by sociological, historical and geographical analysis.

Thinking intersectionally engages with multi-level data, multi-disciplinary approaches and prompts acknowledgement that the interactions occurring at a micro level need to be contextualised in the broader social and historical configurations (Yuval-Davis, 2011); that is, at the levels of experiential, intersubjective and institutional/organisational (Brah, 1996; Hill-Collins & Bilge, 2016; Lutz et al., 2011; Lykke, 2010). Some cultural analysts and sociologists regard 'public' leisure sites central to understanding complex identity formations, although the fact that these occur in leisure sites is often given limited analytical attention (Skeggs, 1999). Yet public spaces, be they formal, informal, spectacular and/or inconspicuous, are both core to the contexts of leisure research and have leisure at their core (Bairner, 2012; Scraton & Watson, 1998).

Examining space for leisure is just one facet of thinking intersectionally and by implication it is pertinent to consider embodiment and intersectionality. Though it may seem an obvious interdependency, there is little research that explicitly links these concepts in leisure and sport-related research, Flintoff, Fitzgerald, and Scraton's (2008) work on PE is an exception.

Leisure and embodiment

As bodies are the sites and situations where the complexity of identity is played out, leisure – as a context for negotiated expressions of identity and engagement in multiple forms of activity (and passivity) – has the potential to contribute to mainstream debates on intersectionality. The body, from a sociological perspective, represents the dynamic interaction of structure and agency. Thinking intersectionally about the body in varied leisure contexts contributes significantly to explaining how leisure is simultaneously liberating and constrained (Rojek, 2010). The social construction of the body and engagement with somatics (of the body) is an obvious way to examine difference as a living and breathing phenomenon, and to trace and examine power relations as embodied. "Embodiment is per se intersectional in its form" (Villa, 2011, p. 181), it is social process in action; people (bodies) are messy and do not fit neatly into discourse, yet categories retain relevance and resonance as individuals embody and represent various and varying combinations of social factors. For Villa (2011), the concept of intersectionality is useful for addressing "the complex entanglement of structure and action" (p. 177) and through her work on tango (dance) she draws out the context-specific inter-categorical expressions that are gendered, racialised and classed in this dance form. Bodies are also aged, sexed and sexualised, abled and disabled, and Villa is thus wary of the "hype of intersectionality" when attempts are made to reduce complexity at the expense of examining "how the exceedingly complex bodily practices are interpreted by actors themselves within these categories" (p. 183). Researching leisure and embodiment is a form of thinking intersectionally whereby contextualisation, in space as well as on and through the body, requires engagement with lived material circumstances to understand leisure experiences (Watson, 2017).

Advancing feminist social justice

I believe firmly that we can learn from different feminist epistemological perspectives and that we continue to be open to varying and various perspectives, particularly critiques offered by black and BME feminists, because feminism has not adequately or appropriately acknowledged and/or usefully engaged these perspectives (for an overview of the challenges of confronting whiteness in leisure research, see Watson & Scraton, 2001, 2017b). "We", feminist leisure scholars, can also benefit from and contribute to new and emerging analyses (that include rather than distinguish from black perspectives). Contextualising difference places emphasis on the consequences and constituents of difference as they are articulated and experienced in everyday life and specifically the roles that leisure plays within this. The range of questions and articulations of identity hitherto still marginalised is expansive – for example, applying queer and critical disability perspectives to explain gendered being and identity (Puar, 2012) – and I return to this in the following section.

The significance of social justice to intersectionality and thinking intersectionally remains central to my (and others') attempts to engage in meaningful and worthwhile empirical research that details leisure experiences in various contexts of difference and social inequalities; thus, it directly informs my feminist leisure lens. A commitment to research – to document and represent justly the materiality of people's lives, and in some cases make claims that such research can make a difference in challenging inequalities – is a raison d'être for much leisure (and sport) scholarship, through my ongoing research, teaching and activist work. Thinking intersectionally in research prompts feminist researchers to question experience as a discursive construction, to explore how experience features as one aspect of difference, and to locate it in the contexts of space and embodiment. The challenge, through the design, implementation and analysis of our research material, is not to *categorise* leisure experiences, rather it is to *contextualise* those experiences.

Watson and Scraton (2017a) argue that questions of social and gender justice require a sustained engagement with the dualism of materiality and culturalism rather than prioritising particular sets of theoretical accounts that favour structure or culture. In feminist leisure scholarship, this claim continues to attract some productive discussion (Aitchison, 2000; Parry & Fullagar, 2013; Watson & Scraton, 2013). Parry (2014) reminds us that social justice research in feminist leisure scholarship can be quiet and, in our attempts to confront whiteness, Sheila Scraton and I (Watson & Scraton, 2017b) indicate that small acts can be a significant aspect of embodying the personal as political activism. There is certainly a place for conceptual development in aspiring towards and attaining greater justice. Brah (1996) argues that understanding difference is a necessary means of achieving justice; that if we do not directly take on what difference is and examine critically how it manifests itself in everyday life, then we will not improve gender or social justice agendas. That call, made more than 20 years ago, is encapsulated in the quote from Nash above and points to how the work of intersectionality is incomplete.

Some feminists suggest that interdisciplinary work for justice, through employing an intersectional framework, can be effective in both challenging rhetoric and addressing a lack of resources; to raise and expose difficult questions rather than propelling a simplistic view of interdisciplinary work as a means to get answers (Lykke, 2010). A contextualisation of material that is "inter" rather than multi(-disciplinary) is appealing for gathering "evidence" and yet we need to be mindful of the power of positivist rhetoric regarding research (Lather, 1998, 1991, 2012). When I am engaged in feminist leisure scholarship I see myself as attempting to make sense of what is there, rather than attempting to provide definitive accounts. I am mindful of being reflexive with responsibility (Watson & Scraton, 2017a, 2017b), whilst recognising how that claim is possible only through my subject position of relative privilege. As Bilge (2013, 2014) warns, attempts at "un-doing" privilege can reproduce White epistemic certainty, consequently she argues for a critical intersectionality as "un-disciplinary". Puar's (2012) analysis of sexuality, racialisation and disability and the questions she poses regarding bodies and identities in neoliberal contexts is enlightening. In her calls for a rejection of normative and non-normative binaries and a recognition of the significance of affect, not just identity categories or markers, Puar (2012) states that "all bodies are being evaluated in relation to their success or failure in terms of health, wealth, progressive productivity, upward mobility, enhanced capacity" (p. 155). Different bodies in neoliberal contexts require ongoing recognition and analysis and Puar's thesis prompts new and ongoing challenges for feminist leisure scholarship in particular. This demands attention be paid to changing contexts that are simultaneously both constituents and outcomes of complex social relations.

Engaging with fourth wave feminisms

Intersectionality is a "live" critical framework and/or analytical tool, and the contexts to which it is relevant, arguably all aspects of social interaction, are not time- or epoch-bound. Consequently, I argue that to suggest intersectionality has had its day and/or is misplaced in its theoretical, methodological and political endeavours and should be usurped by another more contemporary theoretical analysis is misplaced. However, Nash's (2016) critique of commemorative approaches to intersectionality and wariness towards intersectional "originalism" is helpful here. That is, there is no definitive way of claiming authentic intersectionality. This resonates with Hill-Collins and Bilge's (2016) statement in the opening pages of this chapter that intersectionality should not be limited through reference to specific definitions and authors. It continues to evolve, as arguably all meaningful feminist analysis does. Although intersectionality is associated with middle ground (Watson & Scraton, 2013), I do not regard it as distinctly third wave. It is worthwhile reasserting that:

> Intersectionality, then, is a map of social structure that accounts for both "the bottom" and "the top", the privileged and the oppressed, the margins and the centre. Instead of describing multiple marginalisation, centring the experiences of the multiply-marginalised, or foregrounding the embodied knowledges of the multiply-marginalised, intersectionality is instead posited as an analytic that describes the systems of domination which ensnare us all, even as we are ensnared in different and socially contingent ways.
>
> (Nash, 2016, p. 16)

I have always grappled with how to usefully identify different aspects of feminism and various tenets of feminist theory. Rather than identify a best-fit explanation or analysis, we need contextually specific and conceptually relevant accounts for detailing the complexity and 'messiness' of everyday life. It is not helpful for feminists to get too drawn into discussions regarding who said what first and/or who came up with a particular term, unless that is done as a means to disrupt dominant subjective positions such as whiteness, heteronormativity and ableism.

Hill-Collins and Bilge's (2016) overview of the emergence of intersectionality suggests that, while Crenshaw may have labelled the term, she did not "invent" the concept. Rather, naming intersectionality helped to encapsulate shared frustrations and related, previously made articulations regarding the gendered nature of race and/or racialised gender and the particular contexts that ensued as a consequence. There are times when I privilege a feminist analysis even as I am continually aware of multiple, intersecting social relations. Perhaps adopting intersectional epistemological thinking is developmental, is on the way to contributing to more enlightened critical analyses that adequately accounts for difference and power, but I would not limit its location to third wave feminism. Indeed, it is not necessarily helpful to name a third wave as distinct, any more than a fourth wave. Further, referring to intersectionality as a third-way concept potentially negates the fact that black feminists have been demonstrating its significance for some considerable time (certainly alongside what might be considered as part of late second wave), as outlined in earlier sections.

An assessment of the value of different feminisms and their respective contributions quite often draws on a discourse or narrative of feminist theories occurring in linear and/or wave-like ways (Caudwell, 2011; Hemmings, 2005; McDonald, 2014; Parry & Fullagar, 2013). The use of a waves metaphor in feminism, and in sport feminisms in particular, has been refuted by Caudwell

(2011). In her appropriation of Hemmings (2005), Caudwell challenges the idea of linear development in feminist scholarship, arguing that an array of feminist perspectives, not just "new" or current modes of thinking, inform ongoing feminist analysis. This questions how some feminist voices come to be dominant. This is echoed in commentaries that warn against how discursive shifts – politically and theoretically – play to a neoliberalist tune of individual choice that can fragment feminism and heighten competitive femininity (McRobbie, 2015). Ethnocentric (and heterosexist) assumptions remain embedded in these discourses, and efforts need to be made and revisited to confront normative knowledge production, such as in relation to whiteness (Bilge, 2013, 2014; Watson & Scraton, 2001, 2017b). As we consider what fourth wave feminism is and has to offer, as well as my hesitancy about intersectionality being located or defined as third wave, what is interesting are the dynamics across and throughout different feminist perspectives and their contributions to accounting for continually changing contexts.

When I first read about the fourth wave, it was via Arai and Kivel's (2009) valuable collection on challenging the limits of definitions of leisure, particularly in relation to leisure experience and race (Kivel, Johnson, & Scraton, 2009). It was the context and implications of these arguments that stood out and not really what they were called or how they were labelled (perhaps there is a theme emerging here about my somewhat ambivalence towards waves of feminism). Sheila (Scraton) and I continue to reflect upon how feminist leisure studies has come to be known and what its priorities might be moving forward. In doing so, we have rehearsed, in relation to teaching leisure and sociology courses, some ideas about what a fourth wave might contribute (Scraton & Watson, 2015). As Chapter 1 suggests, there is a view that fourth wave feminism represents attempts to capture the complexity of global contexts, not least as constructed, communicated and constituted through new digital formats.

Online activism is associated with this wave of feminism and it is understandable that the presence and prevalence of reactions to sexism and misogyny in everyday life, including institutional and cultural representational contexts, particularly for young/new generations of feminisms, is attracting analysis (Schuster, 2013). There are some connections made to intersectionality and an implicit view that perhaps fourth wave is attending to gaps in intersectional thinking in ways that "older", more established feminisms miss. It will be interesting to see how this unfolds. There are links, it would seem, with claims regarding the significance of popular cultural forms and alternative ways in which marginalised populations voice their experiences and opinions (see, for example, Hill-Collins and Bilge's (2016) discussion of hip-hop). There are also concerns from black feminists interested in sport and popular culture (Ifekwunigwe, 2017) that some online expressions of contemporary feminism (such as "Care Free Black Girl" online) fall prey to neoliberal and postfeminist discourses and do not further intersectional emphasis on difference as power. It is undeniable how significant social media and feminism's relationship is becoming, and some commentators claim that fourth wave feminism and intersectionality are interdependent (Zimmerman, 2017). What is interesting is how leisure is the context for the expression and manifestation of these subject positions and articulations via online activity. It would be interesting to address, for example, online environments in the contexts of space for leisure and embodiment in relation to thinking intersectionally. The potential for detailing such leisure scholarship is beyond the scope of this present chapter and I am certain that others will and/or already are examining this.

Unfinished business

Over the past few years I have been privileged to work with community-based organisations that provide recreational dance to young people in my home city of Leeds, UK, with a particular focus on boys' engagement. I have highlighted this empirical work here because researching dance questions how participants express various articulations of masculinity through opportunities that dance allows (and denies), and I aim to identify how and where boys act, perform and produce gendered and intersectional identities when in male-only dance environments. This has led me to consider how a feminist leisure lens informs analysis of various ways in which boys and young men exhibit and embody diverse articulations of masculinity in recreational dance spaces. In short, how does engaging in dance in leisure time reflect, inform, reproduce, as well as disrupt, masculinity and masculinities? That of course necessitates entanglements with working definitions for masculinity and for gender, which in turn demands recognition that such 'gendering' is always relational to and with other social factors, notably class and race in researching dance thus far with community-based organisations (RJC Dance, rjc.org and Dance Action Zone Leeds, dazl.org). Rather than claim that it is intersectional research, I am more comfortable with describing it as research that is informed by thinking intersectionally. I approach the dance research with a conscious view of identities as gendered and locate those articulations and negotiated identities in ways informed by "space for leisure" and "leisure and embodiment", as outlined above (see Watson, 2017 for further discussion of methodological issues).

With my feminist leisure lens in mind, I am particularly interested in how boys reproduce and parody stereotypes of being male in the context of expressions, articulations, representations and practices of masculinity available to them through recreational dance (including street, hip-hop, cheer dance and carnival styles). Thus, the overarching context of my research on dance is to explore how it both reflects and constructs gender relations. I place firm emphasis on the way in which gender intersects with other social relations, including social class and racialised identities, though arguably marginalising some key issues, including disabled youth and dancing. Through conceptualising leisure spaces as contested and negotiated, my analysis calls attention to how dance is a space, a context and a leisure setting in which boys "belong" in different ways

(Watson & Ratna, 2011; Watson & Scraton, 2013). Hence, leisure is a significant context for the dynamic construction (and reproduction) of identities.

A key theme of my research is where and when boys appear to be in a minority in dominant, populist discourses of dance. Within localised dance settings and contexts, boys' engagement in dance is significantly influenced by their social class (Watson & Rodley, 2015) and varying intersections with gender and race (Watson, Tucker, & Drury, 2013). Thinking intersectionally involves recognition of complexity and contradiction as well as exploring, examining and mapping social relations at a micro level in relation to broader social, cultural and economic circumstances – that is, attending to where dance occurs, in what spaces, what types of provision, as well as assessing who the participants are, as individuals and as constituents, in local communities.

The different contexts of young people's everyday lives are crucial in any attempt to make sense of different and differing expressions of masculinity and dance. This might be considered as "good" ethnography and might be associated with attempts at being an active and imaginative sociologist of leisure. The dance research highlights ways in which boys' engagement in physically active recreation, displaying body competence and expressions of sporting capital, is normalised. Linking physicality and masculinity is a normative, common language for many boys, albeit if expressed differently in relation to class and race and discourses of sexuality. Some researchers call for a disruption of discourses of dance and masculinity to enable greater possibilities for participation and enjoyment (Gard, 2008). Yet we also need to unpack what we mean by seeking shifts or creating alternative masculinities for boys in dance; otherwise, we risk reproducing the stereotypes (as highlighted in opening sections of this chapter in reference to Crenshaw's recent work) that black boys do street dance and white boys do ballet. Thinking intersectionally prompts us to ask questions that explore and examine the backstory of who the boys involved in dance are, to challenge and question black and working-class masculinities as dangerous and non-normative (Archer & Yamshita, 2003; Bereswill & Neuber, 2011).

Dance research data (Watson & Rodley, 2015; Watson et al., 2013) highlights some interesting complexities and contradictions within configurations of masculinity – for example, the interplay between hyper-masculinity and hetero-normative masculinity. I have commented on this regarding the challenge of claiming that boys' participation in dance is/can be transformative (Watson et al., 2013). This research highlighted the significant influence of dance instructors on the expressions and possibilities of masculine identities available and articulated through dance (Risner, 2007).

Vulnerability is an interesting theme in researching masculinity, and this often appears in my dance research when boys are learning and/or trying out new movements. Boys will take risks amongst other participants when they cannot easily perform physical tasks, including those that require strength (such as full press-ups), those that require some grace and agility (such as cartwheels) or following dance rhythms. Observational data suggest boys disrupt some elements of dominant (sporting), masculine hegemony in that respect (Watson & Rodley, 2015); they offer support and encouragement rather than overt demonstrations of dismissal and ridicule. In this sense, when boys engage in a 'soft' activity like dance (Gard, 2008), they subvert an accepted "bad boy" image (Archer & Yamashita, 2003). Such expressions are, however, also distinctly about social class, and boys who have limited resources and capital demonstrate a 'raw' willingness to give things a go and 'use' their bodies that arguably stems from historical contexts of classed and racialised bodies. Here, further analysis about the power relations of bodies being owned and sold through a capitalist division of labour and enslavement of black and other bodies can inform commentary about contemporary articulations of masculinity (Watson & Rodley, 2015). Boys and young men's (dancing) bodies are simultaneously expressions of gendered identities whereby boys can capitalise (perhaps literally at times) on expectations of physicality and levels of body competence, even when dance moves are not easily acquired by those involved. My observations arguably require further consideration and analysis and Schippers' (2007) work on hegemonic femininities is potentially useful in this regard. Schippers draws on empirical-based studies to demonstrate how embodied gendered experience and expressions are at once intersectional and context-specific, assessing a variety of examples where discourses of gender are potentially disruptive.

To conclude my consideration of intersectionality as a framework for feminist leisure scholarship, intersectionality does have significant potential for ongoing assessment of the divide between structuralist or agentic accounts of women's leisure. When I discovered intersectionality in others' writing whilst studying for my PhD in the 1990s, it gave me great impetus to account for complex interrelationships I observed in women's leisure. This framework continues to inform my ongoing research activities and my engagement with ongoing methodological challenges (Watson, 2017). In relation to framing our research ideas, to responding to the call from external partners, through to analysis and representation of our data, thinking intersectionally means rearticulating some firm beliefs, grounded in empirical study, that structure and agency, micro and macro, are always relational. It sounds rather simplistic and somewhat dated, but those challenges have neither gone away in the context of understanding and appreciating the complexity of people's everyday lives, nor have feminist thinking and feminist activism sufficient reason to abandon the push and pull of individual and collective experiences, identities, subject positions and lived material relations.

Intersectionality is not just an attempt to name or know inequalities and injustices. In drawing attention to what happened (and continues to happen) at Grenfell Tower I am not proposing that intersectional perspectives provide ready-made formulae for accounting for social inequality. Rather, thinking intersectionally, usefully and crucially, reminds us that we have to be prepared to engage with the complex, complicated and often messy contexts of everyday life. I am unashamed about claiming a realist ontology and believe that, despite challenges in articulating it, a post-positivist realist ontology has credibility. Other contributions in this present collection (see Chapter 2) help to inform that debate. I am convinced by Patti Lather's (2012) arguments for post-qualitative or even post-post-qualitative research, but I do not believe that has inevitably to involve the expulsion of the grounded, political basis of intersectionality. Unless it is a misreading of intersectionality that posits intersectionality as a misguided form of identity politics (Hill-Collins & Bilge, 2016), but it could be that I am (Just) philosophically naïve. Watson and Scraton (2013) indicate a usefulness in complexity theory, and yet as I write that I can see the dangers of clinging to versions of wanting to know (for sure) or being able to demonstrate (definitely and at times defiantly) rather than letting go of such a venture and being more open to possibilities.

I opened this chapter with a reference to work with Sheila Scraton where we conclude that, to be effective, intersectionality needs to remain disruptive. I want to reassert that position here – thinking intersectionally is a dynamic and a disruptive process. Drawing on recent empirical work on boys and recreational dance, the chapter offers an example of how conceptualising masculinity engages thinking intersectionally as a meaningful lens through which to account for masculinity within and across leisure. This was contextualised alongside space for leisure and leisure and embodiment as means of addressing everyday lived practices and the significance of contextualising leisure within and across these domains. Drawing on Schippers' (2007) reference to symbolism and culturalism more broadly, the chapter argues that thinking intersectionally is an epistemological frame of mind that consistently and persistently raises questions about identity and structure. The chapter unashamedly highlights the central voice of Black and minority ethnic feminist perspectives at the heart of intersectionality. This is not done in an attempt to reaffirm feminist standpoint perspectives (Black and/or other standpoint epistemologies included); rather, it is about recognition and a plea to look at leisure (and social relations more broadly) from a relational, critically informed position.

References

Aitchison, C. C. (2000). Poststructural feminist theories of representing Others: A response to the "crisis" in leisure studies discourse. *Leisure Studies*, *19*(5), 127–144.

Amos, V., & Parmar, P. (1984). Challenging imperial feminism. *Feminist Review*, *17*, 3–19.

Arai, S., & Kivel, B. D. (2009). Critical race theory and social justice perspectives on whiteness, difference(s), and (anti)racism: A fourth wave of race research. *Journal of Leisure Research*, *41*(4), 459–470.

Archer, L., & Yamashita, H. (2003). Theorising inner-city masculinities: Race, class, gender and education. *Gender & Education*, *15*(2), 115–132.

Bairner, A. (2012). Between *flânerie* and fiction: Ways of seeing exclusion and inclusion in the contemporary city. *Leisure Studies*, *31*(1), 3–19.

Bereswill, M., & Neuber, A. (2011). Marginalised masculinity, precarisation and the gender order. In H. Lutz, M. T. H. Vivar, & L. Supik (Eds.), *Framing intersectionality: Debates on a multi-faceted concept in gender studies* (pp. 69–88). Farnham, England: Ashgate.

Bilge, S. (2013). Intersectionality undone. *Du Bois Review: Social Science Research on Race*, *10*(02), 405–424.

Bilge, S. (2014). Whitening intersectionality: Evanescence of race in intersectionality schorlarship. In W. D. Hund & A. Lentin (Eds.), *Racism and sociology* (pp. 175–205). Berlin: Lit Verlag/Routledge.

Brah, A. (1996). *Cartographies of diaspora*. London: Routledge.

Caudwell, J. (2011). Sport feminism(s): Narratives of linearity? *Journal of Sport and Social Issues*, *35*(2), 111–125.

Cho, S., Crenshaw, K., & McCall, L. (2013). Toward a field of intersectionality studies: theory, applications and praxis. *Signs*, *38*(4), 785–810.

Crenshaw, K. (1989). Demarginalizing the intersections of race and sex: A black feminist critique of antidiscrimination doctrine, feminist theory and antiracist politics. *University of Chicago Legal Forum*, *140*, 139–167.

Crenshaw, K. (1991). Mapping the margins: Intersectionality, identity politics and violence against women of color. *Stanford Law Review*, *43*, 1241–1299.

Davis, K. (2008). Intersectionality as buzzword: A sociology of science perspective on what makes a feminist theory successful. *Feminist Theory*, 9(1), 61–85.

Fletcher, T., & Dashper, K. (Eds.) (2014). *Diversity, equity and inclusion in sport and leisure*. London: Routledge.

Flintoff, A., Fitzgerald, H., & Scraton, S. (2008). The challenges of intersectionality: Researching difference in physical education. *International Studies in Sociology of Education*, *18*(2), 73–85.

Freedland, J. (2017, June 17). Grenfell will forever stand as a rebuke to the right. *Guardian*, p. 39.

Gard, M. (2008). When a boy's gotta dance: New masculinities, old pleasures. *Sport, Education and Society*, *13*(2), 181–193.

Gressgard, R. (2008). Mind the gap: Intersectionality, complexity and "the event." *Theory and Science*, *10*(1). Retrieved from http://theoryandscience.icaap.org/content/vol10.1/Gressgard.html

Haraway, D. (1988). Situated knowledges: The science question in feminism and the privilege of partial perspective. *Feminist Studies*, *14*(3), 575–600.

Harding, S. (Ed.) (1987). *Feminism and methodology*. Milton Keynes, UK: Open University Press.

Harding, S. (1991). *Whose science? Whose knowledge? Thinking from women's lives*. Ithaca, NY: Cornell University Press.

Hemmings, C. (2005). Telling feminist stories. *Feminist Theory*, 6(2), 115–139.

Hill-Collins, P. (1990). *Black feminist thought: Knowledge, consciousness and the politics of empowerment*. London: Routledge.

Hill-Collins, P., & Bilge, S. (2016). *Intersectionality*. Cambridge, UK: Polity.

hooks, b. (1989). *Talking back: Thinking feminist, thinking black*. London: Sheba.

hooks, b. (1991). *Yearning: Race, gender and cultural politics*. Boston: Southend Press.

Ifekwunigwe, J. (2018). "And still Serena rises": Celebrating the cross-generational continuities of black feminisms and black female excellence in sport. In L. Mansfield, J. Caudwell, B. Wheaton, & B. Watson (Eds.), *The handbook of feminisms in sport, leisure and physical education* (pp. 111–131). London: Palgrave Macmillan.

Johnson, C. W., & Parry, D. C. (Eds.) (2015). *Fostering social justice through qualitative inquiry: A methodological guide*. Walnut Creek, CA: Left Coast Press, Inc.

Khaleeli, H. (2016). #SayHerName: Why Kimberle Crenshaw is fighting for forgotten women. *Guardian*. Retrieved from www.theguardian.com/lifeandstyle/2016/may/30/sayhername-why-kimberle-crenshaw-is-fighting-for-forgotten-women

Kivel, B. D., Johnson, C., & Scraton, S. (2009). (Re)theorising leisure, experience and race. *Journal of Leisure Research, 41*(4), 473–493.

Knapp, G. A. (2005). Race, class, gender: Reclaiming baggage in fast travelling theories. *European Journal of Women's Studies, 16*(3), 203–210.

Lather, P. (1988). Feminist perspectives on empowering research methodologies. *Women's Studies International Forum, 11*(6), 569–581.

Lather, P. (1991). *Getting smart: Feminist research and pedagogy with/In the postmodern.* New York, NY: Routledge.

Lather, P. (2012). Becoming feminist: An untimely meditation on football. *Cultural Studies/Critical Methodology, 12*(4), 357–360.

Lewis, G. (2009). Celebrating intersectionality? Debates on a multi-faceted concept in gender studies: themes from a conference. *European Journal of Women's Studies, 16*(3), 203–210.

Long, J., Fletcher, T., & Watson, B. (Eds.) (2017) *Sport, leisure and social justice*. London: Routledge.

Lutz, H., Vivar, M. T. H., & Supik, L. (2011). *Framing intersectionality: Debates on a multi-faceted concept in gender studies*. Farnham: Ashgate.

Lykke, N. (2010). *Feminist studies: A guide to intersectional theory, methodology and writing.* London: Routledge.

MacKinnon, C. A. (2013). Intersectionality as method: A note. *Signs: Journal of Women in Culture and Society, 38*(4), 1019–1030.

Mansfield, L., Caudwell, J. Wheaton, B., & Watson, B. (Eds.), (2017). *The handbook of feminisms in sport, leisure and physical education.* London: Palgrave Macmillan.

Massey, D. (2005). *For space*. London: Sage.

McCall, L. (2005). The complexity of intersectionality. *Signs: Journal of Women in Culture and Society, 30*(3), 1772–1800.

McDonald, M. G. (2014). Mapping intersectionality and whiteness: Troubling gender and sexuality in sport studies. In J. Hargreaves & E. Anderson (Eds.), *Routledge handbook of sport, gender and sexuality* (pp. 51–159). London: Routledge.

McRobbie, A. (2015). Notes on the perfect: Competitive femininity in neoliberal times. *Australian Feminist Studies, 83*(3), 3–20.

Mirza, H. S. (Ed.) (1997). *Black British feminism: A reader*. London: Routledge.

Nash, J. C. (2008). Re-thinking intersectionality. *Feminist Review, 89*, 1–15.

Nash, J. C. (2016). Feminist originalism: Intersectionality and the politics of reading. *Feminist Theory, 17*(1), 3–20.

Parry, D. C. (2014). My transformative desires: Enacting feminist social justice leisure research. *Leisure Sciences, 36*, 349–364.

Parry, D. C., & Fullagar, S. (2013). Feminist research in the contemporary era. *Journal of Leisure Research, 45*(5), 571–582.

Puar, J. (2012). Coda: The cost of getting better: Suicide, sensation, switchpoints. *GLQ: A Journal of Lesbian and Gay Studies, 18*(1), 149–158.

Risner, D. (2007). Rehearsing masculinity: Challenging the "boy code" in dance education. *Research in Dance Education, 8*(2), 139–153.

Rojek, C. (2010). *The labour of leisure*. London: Sage.

Schippers, M. (2007). Recovering the feminine other: Masculinity, femininity, and gender hegemony. *Theory and Society*, *36*(1), 85–102.

Schuster, J. (2013). Invisible feminists? Social media and young women's political participation. *Political Science*, *65*(1), 8–24.

Scraton, S. (2001). Reconceptualising race, gender and sport: The contribution of black feminism. In I. McDonald & B. Carrington (Eds.), *Race and sport in British society* (pp. 170–187). London: Routledge.

Scraton, S., & Watson, B. (1998). Gendered cities: Women and public leisure space in the postmodern city. *Leisure Studies*, *17*(2), 123–137.

Scraton, S. & Watson, B. (2015). 'Leisure and consumption: A critical analysis of free time. In M. Holborn (Ed.) *Contemporary Sociology*. London, Polity Press.

Spivak, G. (1987). *In other worlds: Essays in cultural politics*. New York, NY and London: Methuen.

Stanley, L., & Wise, S. (1993). *Breaking out: Feminist ontology and epistemology*. London: Routledge.

Sugden, J., & Tomlinson, A. (Eds.) (2002). *Power games: A critical sociology of sport*. London: Routledge.

Valentine, G. (2007). Theorising and researching intersectionality: A challenge for feminist geography. *Professional Geographer*, *59*(1), 10–21.

Valentine, G., & Harris, C. (2016). Encounters and (in-)tolerance: Perceptions of legality and the regulation of space. *Social and Cultural Geography*, *17*(7), 913–932.

Villa, P. I. (2011). Embodiment is always more: Intersectionality, subjection and the body. In H. Lutz, M. T. H. Vivar, & L. Supik (Eds.), *Framing intersectionality: Debates on a multi-faceted concept in gender studies* (pp. 171–186). Farnham: Ashgate.

Walby, S., Armstrong, J., & Strid, S. (2012). Intersectionality: Multiple inequalities in social theory. *Sociology*, *46*(2), 224–240.

Watson, B. (2017). Thinking intersectionally and why difference (still) matters in feminist leisure and sport research. In L. Mansfield, J. Caudwell, B. Wheaton, & B. Watson (Eds.), *The handbook of feminisms in sport, leisure and physical education*. London: Palgrave Macmillan.

Watson, B., & Ratna, A. (2011). Bollywood in the park: Thinking intersectionally about public leisure space. *Leisure/Loisir*, *35*(1), 71–85.

Watson, B., & Rodley, I. (2015). Dazzling yet invisible: Boys in cheerdance. In C. Hallgren et al. (Eds.), *Invisible boy: The making of contemporary masculinities* (pp. 95–106). Umea, Sweden: Umea University Press.

Watson, B., & Scraton, S. (2001). Confronting whiteness? Researching the leisure lives of South Asian mothers. *Journal of Gender Studies*, *10*(3), 265–277.

Watson, B., & Scraton, S. (2013). Leisure studies and intersectionality. *Leisure Studies*, *32*(1), 35–47.

Watson, B., & Scraton, S. (2017a). Gender justice and leisure and sport feminisms. In J. Long, T. Fletcher, & B. Watson (Eds.), *Sport, leisure and social justice* (pp. 43–57). London: Routledge.

Watson, B., & Scraton, S. (2017b). Re-confronting whiteness: Ongoing challenges in sport and leisure research. In S. Farooq & A. Ratna (Eds.), *Race, gender and sport* (pp. 85–106). London: Routledge.

Watson, B., Tucker, L., & Drury, S. (2013). Can we make a difference? Examining the transformative potential of sport and active recreation. *Sport in Society*, *16*(10), 1233–1247.

Winker, G., & Degele, N. (2011). Intersectionality as multi-level analysis: Dealing with social inequality. *European Journal of Women's Studies*, *18*(1), 51–66.

Yuval-Davis, N. (2011). *The politics of belonging: Intersectional contestations*. London: Sage.

Zimmerman, T. (2017). #Intersectionality: The fourth wave feminist Twitter community. *Atlantis*, 38(1). Retrieved from journals.msvu.ca/index.php/atlantis/article/view/4304

Further reading

Brah, A. (1996). *Cartographies of diaspora*. London: Routledge.

Hill-Collins, P., & Bilge, S. (2016). *Intersectionality*. Cambridge, UK: Polity.

Lutz, H., Vivar, M. T. H., & Supik, L. (2011). *Framing intersectionality: Debates on a multi-faceted concept in gender studies*. Farnham: Ashgate.

Nash, J. C. (2016). Feminist originalism: Intersectionality and the politics of reading. *Feminist Theory*, *17*(1), 3–20.

Watson, B., & Scraton, S. (2013). Leisure studies and intersectionality. *Leisure Studies*, *32*(1), 35–47.

Chapter 5

Queering leisure

Teasing out queer theory's legacies

Judy Davidson

How are we to understand the term *queer* in the early 21st century, especially in the context of the field of leisure studies? What is at stake in the word that has so tenaciously connected shame and powerlessness to the idea of homosexuality and/or gender dissonance to be mobilized as the vile epithet to produce abjected and minoritized identities and pathologizations over the course of the 20th century (Sedgwick, 1993)? And what is feminism's history and role in the rich theoretical tradition that emerged 30 years ago and bears queer's name (Rubin with Butler, 1994)?

This chapter will consider a genealogy of how leisure studies has (and has not) been queered. The notion of *queer theory* emerged in the early 1990s with the promise to be a reflexive, ethical alternative to certain rigidities in both feminist theories and gay and lesbian studies. Its ability to address intersectionality has been under scrutiny ever since. Queer has now become a very capacious term, often mobilized in multiple and contradictory ways. Sometimes used as a descriptor of identity (most often standing in for the LGBT umbrella – lesbian, gay, bisexual, trans/trans*/trans+),[1] it can denote transgressive disruption of norms, or reference a post-foundational, anti-identity politics or theoretical frame. Paradoxically, queer can be deployed to mark the abjectable, disposable other, as well describe certain homonormative and liberal privileges (Abelove, Barale, & Halperin, 1993; Eng, Halberstam, & Munoz, 2005). I will historicize one story of queer theory's genesis and trace its sometimes-overlooked imbrication with feminism. I then selectively overview how queer has moved in leisure studies through notions such as gay and lesbian leisure, queer sports studies, and critical spatial and touristic analyses of leisure and sexuality. Finally, I consider some of the perhaps unintended consequences produced by particular LGBT leisure community projects. To do this, the chapter will conclude with a discussion of how a certain homonationalist leisure formation (a localized analysis of Pride hockey tape) reconsolidates White racial, classed, gender, and citizenship privilege, at the expense, particularly in setter colonial states, of Indigenous and people of colour justice movements.

Historical and disciplinary roots

The early years and the sexuality debates

It might be possible to mark something of a shared historical condition of possibility for leisure studies and queer theory. Arguably, both are effects of mid-20th-century modernity and emerge from that historical moment in the form that we recognize them each today. The ascendency of industrial capitalism in the Westernized world meant that waged work, almost full employment, and the increase in leisure time for certain populations who had not had it before (primarily an emerging White male, middle-class), made non-work pastimes more possible with increased free time and financial resources. Leisure studies emerged as scholars recognized this important cultural change. The subject field converged through three main threads in the late 1970s – critical social science research, leisure policy and management analysis, and practical debates among professionals about how to improve people's leisure time (Spracklen, 2014). Not long after that, feminist leisure scholars started to question the androcentric bias of the field and the lack of analysis involving women (Parry, 2016).

The emergence of queer theory was a result of the development of a gay and lesbian community and identity in North America that became solidified more publicly than ever after the Stonewall Riots in 1969 and into the 1970s. While Michel Foucault's (1978) first volume of *The History of Sexuality* traces the emergence of the "homosexual"[2] through the 18th and 19th centuries, John D'Emilio (1983) argues that capitalism makes possible gay identity in the 20th century. The shift in population demographics, from rural to urban, materialized as agrarian and self-sufficient forms of life and kinship gave way to large numbers of people moving to industrialized cities for waged work in factories, businesses and other professions. In *Capitalism and Gay Identity*, D'Emilio (1983) writes, "in divesting the household of its economic independence and fostering the separation of sexuality from procreation, capitalism has created conditions to allow some men and women to organize their personal lives according to an erotic/emotional attraction to their own sex" (p. 104). In addition to the underground minority sexual communities that persevered through this era, early homophile organizations in the United States (US), such as the Daughter of Bilitis (formed in 1955 as a lesbian social club to be an alternative to the bars) and the Mattachine Society (a very early gay rights organization founded by Harry Hay in 1950), were created in response to the very repressive, moralistic postwar McCarthy era (Faderman, 1992; Rubin with Butler, 1994). These were leisure-based identities that in the 1970s celebrated many of the gains made by gay liberation and the women's movement. Gay male culture became increasingly recognized as gay men developed their own enclave communities in major cities, such as the Castro District in San Francisco. Lesbian feminism worked to build "alternative institutions and an alternative culture that attempted to embody a liberatory vision of the future" (D'Emilio, 1983, p. 100).

Interestingly, in 1979, William Devall published an article in the *International Review of Modern Sociology* entitled "Leisure and Lifestyles Among Gay Men: An Exploratory Essay." It is a remarkable piece, not only because it is the earliest instance of academic work that explicitly puts leisure in conversation with gay sexuality, but because the article positions gay men, gay sexual practice, and gay identity and community as central. In it, Devall (who later went on to write extensively in the Deep Ecology movement) boldly asserts that the gay lifestyle is a leisure lifestyle. Based on interviews with gay men in the San Francisco Bay Area and the Castro District, Devall (1979) systematically lays out an important set of parameters for how gay men were the leading edge of a new "modern" leisure lifestyle, which is worth quoting at length from the conclusion:

> The elements of emergent lifestyles among gay men in metropolitan areas of North America include the following. Gay men tend to be individualistic. Creativity, subjectivity, individualism tend to be more salient than duty, obligation, the "work ethic" and conventionality. Gay men tend to be hedonistic in leisure lifestyles. Whether it be recreational sex and the erotic conversion of conventional settings or use of drugs, nude beaches and parties, gay men are at the frontiers of erotic hedonism. There is an avid and elaborate proliferation of recreational sex scenes.
>
> There is parody and exaggeration in leisure scenes whether it be the extremes of cross-dressing or the parodies on "macho man." The exaggeration is partly mocking and partly flaunting conventional society but in the process of playfully flaunting conventional society, gay culture allows conventional society to be transformed through mixing superficial and serious elements. Gay social identities and explicitly gay lifestyles are after-work, leisure lifestyles. Gay men in their leisure lifestyles are developing social networks, which are national and even international in scope and cosmopolitan in content. Finally, travel and playing at scenes are part of the process of developing gay self and social identities and as gay men play at this culture they are part of the trend of modernity in North America.
>
> (p. 193)

This description of a gay leisure lifestyle in some ways anticipates many aspects of how both leisure studies and queer theorizing take up studying sexuality. Importantly, Devall (1979) can be used to read parts of Gayle Rubin's (1984) crucial and oft-cited treatise, "Thinking Sex: Notes for a Radical Theory of a Politics of Sexuality." Her groundbreaking and influential article has been a very important contribution to the development of both feminist and queer theory (Duggan, 2011; Love, 2011). This text is one of the earliest pieces of North American sexuality studies work to be informed by Michel Foucault's genealogical analysis of the emergence of homosexuality. Indeed, Rubin provocatively argued that, while the analysis of sexuality and gender are related, they must be separately analyzed even while being linked.

Sex had its politics and this was on full display when Rubin first presented "Thinking Sex" at a Barnard College conference in 1982. On the one hand, anti-pornography feminists such as Catharine MacKinnon and Andrea Dworkin promoted the position that patriarchal gender hierarchies and sexuality were synonymous, and that particular sexual practices (especially pornography, sadomasochism, and role-playing) were essentially and always violent and exploitative (MacKinnon & Dworkin, 1985). On the other hand, in these feminist sex wars of the 1980s, pro-sex feminists argued that if any of those practices listed above resulted in women's pleasure, especially in the context of lesbianism, they were a feminist act, effectively subverting patriarchal sexual relations (Duggan, 2011; Love, 2011; Turner, 2000).

Rubin's (1984) intervention into that second wave feminist discourse was to ethnographically think through the oppressive dimensions of various practices of sexuality. She did this by conceptualizing the "charmed circle," which outlines "good, normal, natural, blessed" sexuality from the "outer limits," which included homosexual, unmarried, promiscuous, non-procreative, commercial, alone or in groups, casual, cross-generational, in public, pornography, with manufactured objects, and sadomasochism (Rubin, 1984, p. 281). It was a sexual values system where hierarchies were clearly delineated and legitimated in similar ways that other ideological systems function.

What is remarkable about Devall's (1979) gay leisure lifestyle article is that it is so articulate about sexual acts and pastimes, and claims them as the foundation for leisure, not as an injurious identity-seeking retribution to a heteronormative ideal. This centering of examples of some of the "outer limits" of queer sexual practice is unusual in the literature on leisure and sexuality that follows over the next four decades.[3] Later in this chapter, I will explore a few variations of this hierarchical ordering in the context of 21st-century LGBT leisure and its politics. Particularly, I will explore this through the idea of abjectable and queered populations, a phenomenon that has emerged as a different generational inflection of the "outer limits" of a continuously shifting sexual order.

The rise of gay and lesbian studies

Concurrent with Rubin's work through the 1980s, a new academic field called gay and lesbian studies started to gain institutional recognition. It focused (and focuses) on culturally marginalized sexual identities (primarily, but not exclusively, gays and lesbians), which emerged from 1970s grassroots organizing and community building out of the gay liberation movement. It has become a diverse field, marked by various tensions in various places throughout the world at various times. Generally, its object of study has been "the lives of gays and lesbians themselves – identities, experiences of oppression, [and] struggles for recognition" (Weeks, 2000, p. 2). Writing about gay and lesbian sexuality tentatively started to appear in the leisure studies literature starting in the 1980s and continued into the 1990s. Primarily this work took (and takes) up the applied professional focus of leisure studies to make suggestions for how practitioners can effectively program and strategize for this stigmatized group. Its presumptions are informed by the tenets of a minoritized gay or lesbian identity (Sedgwick, 1993). This ameliorative, liberal approach to sexuality and leisure continues today (see Theriault & Witt, 2014).

Notably, the work about leisure that emerged in the 1980s clearly identifies and acknowledges the importance of the gay liberation movement for the possibility to live openly as a person with a gay or lesbian identity, and the subsequent ability to create communities from which leisure opportunities become possible (Pitts, 1988; Shallenberger, 1988). The impact of the AIDS epidemic crisis is also noted in these pieces. Into the 1990s, the focus primarily shifts to one of the negotiation between lesbian and gay participation/experience in leisure and the mainstream, heteronormative context in which that occurs. This early body of work considers the special needs of lesbian and gay youth (Caldwell, Kivel, Smith, & Hayes, 1998; Grossman, 1992, 1993; Johnson, 1999; Kivel, 1994, 1997; Kivel & Kleiber, 2000), aging gay men and lesbians (Catalano, 1982; Jacobson & Samdahl, 1998), and depicting the experiences of lesbian mothers (Bialeschki & Pearce, 1997). In a book chapter on sport, gender, and queer theory, Johnson and Kivel (2007) point out how the main focus of analysis in the first wave of lesbian and gay leisure scholarship is very much based in an individualistic and social psychological framework which fails, on their argument, "to lodge any substantial critique against the homosexual/heterosexual binary" (p. 94) and "offer[s] little insight into the cultural forces and structural inequalities that create and reproduce that binary" (p. 95).

Tensions or challenges within the theoretical perspective

Queer theory – Judith Butler and the question of identity

At around the same time that leisure research about sexuality "comes out" (so to speak), queer theory bursts onto the scene in the early 1990s through debates within both gay and lesbian studies and feminist theory.[4] While Rubin's "Thinking Sex" (1984) had disrupted a particular feminist orthodoxy in the early 1980s, the publication of Judith Butler's book *Gender Trouble: Feminism and the Subversion of Identity* in 1990, and her 1993 follow-up, *Bodies that Matter: On the Discursive Limits of "Sex,"* fundamentally altered the contours of feminist theory and was a critical contribution to inaugurating queer theory. In both books, she draws extensively on the work of Foucault, as well as Derridean deconstruction and Lacanian psychoanalysis. Butler's work on performativity intervened into the debates about the question of the identity "woman" as the foundational object of analysis for feminist theory. Based on a poststructuralist understanding of subjectivity, Butler radically argued that it is "discourses of gender that produce sex as a causal category. Without these discourses, and the acts to which they give rise, there would be no gender and the gendered body has no ontological status outside of those acts" (Jagger, 2008, p. 8). Furthermore, Butler's (1990) critique extended to the categories of sexuality, bodies, and desire as well as gender and sex, suggesting that they are all "effects of a specific formation of power" (p. x).

Through her theorizing of gender performativity, Butler proposed that heterosexuality was nothing more than imitation and parody, unseating it from its position as natural and inevitable. This led to her argument for political agency and resistance, particularly in its "critically queer" form. Butler held that merely reversing an identity form only reconsolidated the original referent. It was not queered if it was merely a resistant mirroring. "There is no guarantee that exposing the naturalized status of heterosexuality will lead to its subversion. Heterosexuality can augment its hegemony *through* its denaturalization, as when we see denaturalizing parodies that reidealize heterosexual norms *without* calling them into question" (Butler, 1993, p. 231; emphasis in the original). This critical injunction has rarely been taken up in queer sport and leisure research on gay and lesbian subjects.

At the same time, there are two important exceptions I want to highlight. In "We Are All Royalty," Joshua Trey Barnett and Corey Johnson (2013) employ a narrative methodology to explore how a drag queen (Dominique) and drag king (Dickie) each contextualize their genderqueer lives and performances in their queer leisure contexts, their activist communities, and in their lived experiences as gender nonconforming. Barnett and Johnson (2013) use Butler's work on gender performativity to highlight the constructedness of gender, the fragility and queering of the work/leisure binary, and the importance of drag for queer community and world-making. Twenty-five years later, it hearkens back to Devall's (1979) work by being another rare piece of leisure scholarship that foregrounds and celebrates the subcultural contexts and practices of a 21st-century version of Rubin's "outer limit" of sexuality and gender.

A second, more theoretically dense example of Butler's queering is from my own work with Michelle Helstein (Davidson & Helstein, 2016) about an ice hockey team for which we have both played – the Booby Orrs. In 2007, this women's team played in a gay and lesbian hockey tournament where, in a consolation final game, there were multiple episodes of breast flashing – originally by fans, and in the subsequent iterations by fans and players back. In our analysis, we use psychoanalytic theory to help us think through the dynamics of desire and the production of subjectivity through the function of the hegemonic player gaze.

An identity-based reading of these breast flashings would suggest that the baring of lesbian breasts was a resistive act in a hockey arena. Against this, we argue that, regardless of the female gendered or lesbian sexual identities in play in the arena, it is not until the players lift their jerseys and chest protectors to reveal their own breasts on the ice that the hegemonic player gaze (what we suggest is structurally the heteropatriarchal gaze) is queerly subverted by forcing the fans (who were hegemonically positioned as flashers) to become consumers of a queered flashing.[5] I argue this is an example of Butler's queering. "The resignification of norms, is thus a function of their *inefficacy*, and so the question of subversion, of *working the weakness in the norm*, becomes a matter of inhabiting the practices of its rearticulation" (Butler, 1993, p. 237; emphasis in the original). Not presuming in advance what political effects a practice might have, and unseating what constitutes the fixed referent of queer politics, constitutes the radical potential that queerly denaturalizes social processes and identities in leisure contexts.

Lesbian and gay leisure studies

Butler's foundational work was written alongside a whole explosion of queer theorizing in the 1990s, which informed most gay and lesbian studies analysis into the 2000s. Changing political and social conditions also meant that lesbigay civil rights battles were slowly being recognized throughout the Anglo-Western world, neoliberal capital started aggressively courting the pink market, and gay and lesbian leisure activities and organizations became more plentiful. These are some of the hallmarks of an era of queer liberalism (Eng et al., 2005). As the new millennium proceeded, scholarship in the leisure field started to reflect these changes, primarily conducted through a sexual identity theory lens and/or a focus on the sexualized spatialization of leisure activities. Four general themes emerge: issues in and for gay and lesbian tourism (among others, see Jarvis & Weeden, 2017; Therkelsen, Blichfeldt, Chor, & Ballegaard, 2013; Vorobjovas-Pinta & Hardy, 2016), sexualized leisure spaces (among others, see Browne & Bakshi, 2011; Johnson & Samdahl, 2005; Pritchard, Morgan, & Sedgly, 2007), lesbian and gay leisure identity management (among others, see Oakleaf, 2013; Theriault & Witt, 2014; Trussell, 2017), and sport and sexuality studies. This literature also emerges as part of the larger epistemic shift in the North American academy, which occurred in the latter part of the 20th century.

The "cultural turn" impacted leisure studies in its critiques of individualism, post-positivist hegemony, and its reliance on social psychological renderings of identity (Aitchison, 2000, 2001, 2006; Kivel, 2000). And with this challenge to the research and knowledge hegemonies within leisure scholarship, calls were made for a more nuanced and critical approach to social and political differences. In some cases, leisure research about sexuality started to integrate more than one axis of difference in their analyses of power. Among these studies are Yvette Taylor's (2007) research on how working-class lesbians are subtly excluded from leisure "scene" space by middle-class lesbians, gay men, and straight women through forms of fashion and conspicuous consumption, bringing class, gender, and sexuality together in her analysis. Taylor (2007) builds on the foundational work of Beverley Skeggs' (1999), which analyzed how power relations are reproduced through space and sexuality by comparing the disidentifications performed by White working-class straight women with the territorialization and visibility strategies employed by lesbians in urban leisure contexts. Importantly combining gender and sexuality with a feminist approach, Johnson and Samdahl's (2005) work on gay masculinities in country and western bars considers how misogyny penetrates a minoritized sexualized community. Jasbir Puar (2002) offers a trenchant critique of queer tourism pointing out its neo-colonial impulses and effacement of women in its practice and analysis. These few examples illustrate some of the tentative steps leisure studies started to take towards a fuller and more complex analysis of social differences.

The provocations to attend to the complex entanglements of intersectionality extended to work within feminist theory and gay and lesbian studies as well. As early as 1993, Butler anticipated the intersectional challenge that queer theory would surely face. "The inquiry into both homosexuality and gender will need to cede the priority of *both* terms in the service of a more complex mapping of power that interrogates the formation of each in specified racial regimes and geopolitical spatializations" (Butler, 1993, p. 240). However, as queer theory developed throughout the late 1990s and early 2000s, critique emanated from within the field – identifying a certain unmarked White, masculinist privilege that often wielded inaccessible high theory to create a new insular canon that in effect systematically marginalized many other groups (both within and outside of the academy) including people of colour, crips, dykes, and poor queers (Perez, 2005). In this context, the criticisms levelled by both Perez (2005) and Eng et al. (2005) need to be heeded by those of us who work in leisure studies generally, but especially for those of us who do work on sexuality and leisure.

Much of the work on sexuality in leisure studies, by default and without note, centers and foregrounds middle-class, White, gays and lesbians, often with money and time to travel. As Burdsey (2015) reminds us about racialization in particular, "the discipline still has some way to travel in its understandings and analyses of the ways that leisure constructs, maintains, reproduces and challenges whiteness" (p. 385). Samantha King (2008) notes a similar impulse in queer sports studies, arguing that the field

> remains predicated on the resistive potential of visibility and identity and focused on the experiences of a narrow stratum of North American and European lesbian and gay athletes whose sexual subjectivities are rendered in isolation from the processes of racialization and capital accumulation through which they are constituted.
>
> (p. 420)

In response to these concerns, I will trace how one thread of critical queer theoretical analysis (homonationalism) moves through an interrogation of large sport spectacles (e.g., the Gay Games, the Olympic Games, and the National Hockey League) in the latter part of this chapter.

Seeing things differently: queering the field of leisure

Over the last decade, there has been a call for more intersectional work on sexuality and leisure studies. One of the first essays to do this was included in Jayne Caudwell's (2006) groundbreaking edited anthology, *Sport, Sexualities and Queer/Theory*. In her essay "Beyond the Pale: The Whiteness of Sports Studies and Queer Scholarship," Mary McDonald (2006) exhorts scholars who work in the area queer sport and leisure studies to incorporate work by queer of colour theorists such as José Esteban Muñoz, Roderick Ferguson, Jasbir Puar, and David Eng, but also integrate the crucial intersectional work by Chicana feminists, the traditions of Black feminist thought, and postcolonial feminist critics such as Chela Sandoval, Gloria Anzaldúa, Barbara Smith, and Emma Perez.

The increased mainstreaming of an "acceptable" queer subject is one index of the entrenchment of homonormativity in the 21st-century LGBT movement. The homonormative, coined by Lisa Duggan, is the "new neoliberal sexual politics that hinges upon the possibility of a demobilized gay constituency and a privatized, depoliticized gay culture anchored in domesticity and consumption" (Duggan in Puar, 2007, p. 38). Typical examples of homonormative political campaigns include gay marriage, advocating for gays in the military, and other initiatives that seek lesbigay acceptance in conventional social contexts (much gay tourism could be included here). Far from a Butlerian queering, this kind of visibility and recognition by capital and state-sanctioned systems is complicit with the very power structures against which a queer politics struggles. While one of the hallmark claims of a third wave feminism has pointed to increased sexual freedom, I think it is incumbent upon us to consider that assertion within the contexts of who has access to that freedom, and with what structural privileges. Interestingly, to bring Gayle Rubin back to the conversation, homonormative queers have simply manoeuvred themselves into the 21st-century version of the "charmed circle." Sexual hierarchies persist, only in new reconfigured forms. And in fact, the "outer limits" of Rubin's circle have perhaps expanded in the era of the war on terror. One of the new kids on queer theory's block, homonationalism, helps us to see how.

Homonationalism

In wake of the events of September 11, 2001, the world experienced an upswing of global warfare, political exceptionalism (particularly by the United States) where the rule of law was suspended with disturbing regularity, and increased Islamophobia. In 2007, Puar published the book, *Terrorist Assemblages: Homonationalism in Queer Times*, which responded to both the fallout of 9/11 and to an earlier tendency in transnational feminist and queer theory to position queer as always an outlaw in relation to the heteronormative nation state (Puar, 2013). Homonationalism importantly attends to Eng et al.'s (2005) and

McDonald's (2006) call for more attention to global forces, political economy and racialized, classed, and gendered hierarchies within the fields of both queer theory and leisure studies. Hence, this concept has helped us to sketch another "facet of modernity and a historical shift marked by the entrance of (some) homosexual bodies as worthy of protection by nation-states" (Puar, 2013, p. 337). In exchange for that nominal and contingent acceptance of homonormative queer citizens, there must be a queering abjection of a disposable Other. In Puar's (2007) *Terrorist Assemblages*, that Other is the constructed monster-terrorist-fag, the ubiquitous and always murderous Arab terrorist threat (Davidson, 2013; Puar, 2007). As Travers and Shearman (2017) elaborate, Puar (2007) developed "a radical critique of the rights-oriented campaigns by which some LGBT folks are granted respectability or "folded into life" at the expense of racialized/impoverished LGBT and non-LGBT people" (p. 44).

In recent years, homonationalism has started to be taken up by several scholars in the leisure field (Davidson, 2013, 2014; Davidson & McDonald, 2018; Sykes, 2016; Travers & Shearman, 2017). These analyses focus not just on participation in and management of large-scale leisure phenomena, such as the Olympic Games or the Gay Games, but on the political effects these mega-events have and the implications for queer interrogations of leisure sexualities. In this context, I will now use my own research career and its development as an example of how the debates within queer theory and feminist studies have shaped my thinking about leisure contexts. It involves a queer move to a more intersectional approach to studying sexualities, to which homonationalism (and settler homonationalism) have been crucial contributions.

My doctoral dissertation research was a cultural history and queer analysis of the Gay Games (Davidson, 2003). Relying on Judith Butler's reading of melancholic queer subjectivity and psychoanalysis of culture, it offered an analysis that rejected sexual identity-based claims for gay pride, and instead demonstrated how unresolved losses and homophobic refusals mobilized gay shame in service of the death drive (Davidson, 2004, 2006, 2007, 2017). After its completion, I was insistently haunted by the knowledge that, while it was a sophisticated "queer" theorization, it did not attend at all to the racialized dynamics of whiteness. This was a problem. It was Puar's (2007) book that shifted my analysis of the Gay Games to collude less in the production of unmarked, White queer work.

And so, ten years after the completion of my dissertation, I was able to revisit the project by overviewing how, since their inception, the Gay Games have been a technology of White supremacy and how they willingly contributed to regimes of normalization. In "Racism Against the Abnormal?" (Davidson, 2014), I use Ladelle McWhorter's (2009) very important re-reading of Foucault's idea to argue "the question that needs to be the starting point is 'What were the technologies of White racialized privilege and sexuality that produced a Gay Games population in the context of mid to late twentieth century racism and homophobia?'" (Davidson, 2014, p. 363). In doing so, I outline specific Gay

Games' participation policies, handling of the AIDS crisis in the 1980s, political lobbying for waivers with U.S. immigration, and a global storytelling event as examples of these technologies.

In "Sporting Homonationalisms," I continue the analysis post-9/11 to demonstrate both Orientalist and genocidal impulses at international gay and lesbian athletic events. Examples here include displays of militarism and the veneration of gay marriage at the Chicago Gay Games in 2006 and the juxtaposition of neoliberal human rights with Arab exoticization at the Montreal OutGames in 2006 (Davidson, 2013). The paper ends with a reading of the first Pride House for LGBT athletes and spectators at the 2010 Vancouver Winter Olympics. I argue this space worked to concomitantly produce the queered population that was Indigenous and activist opposition by allowing particular homonormative queers a place inside the securitized perimeter (see also Sykes, 2016 for a much-elaborated analysis of settler homonationalism at the 2010 Olympics).

Here, I turn to settler homonationalism, which has a particular relevance for my location in Canada. The idea, developed by Scott Morgensen (2010), draws from both Indigenous studies and queer studies and is characterized by the notions of settler colonialism and homonationalism. According to Patrick Wolfe (1999), settler colonialism is at "base a winner-take-all project whose dominant feature is replacement. The logic of this project, a sustained institutional tendency to eliminate the population, informs a range of historical practices that might otherwise appear distinct – invasion is a structure, not an event" (p. 163). In Canada, this structure has involved in part decimating sacred and life-giving buffalo herds, incarcerating Indigenous nations on reserves, stealing land and resources, instituting the genocidal practice of enforced residential schooling and thereby almost destroying Indigenous forms of family and kinship relations, rampant (sexual) violence against Indigenous women, and incarcerating high numbers of Indigenous people. Morgensen (2010) suggests that through these practices, Indigenous sexualities, and genders, were almost completely wiped out, while settler (hetero)sexuality was rewarded by the nation state, for both Indigenous and non-Indigenous people. Settler colonialism was the apparatus through which modern sexual identity categories emerged – whether straight or gay. The 20th-century struggle for gay and lesbian recognition is made possible by this violent settler sexuality. As I will suggest in my analysis of Pride Tape, attempts to eradicate Indigenous presence continue today, inadvertently perhaps, but through LGBT pride initiatives.

I want to close this chapter with a more extended analysis of a particular LGBT pride event that happened in the context of the city in which I live – Edmonton, Alberta. It is a critically queer reading of Pride hockey tape. It highlights how sport and leisure formations that purportedly work for the improvement of lesbian and gay youth in minor hockey can simultaneously work to reinjure and reconsolidate already pre-existing forms of disenfranchisement and marginalization, particularly differentially affecting women and female-identified people. I use it as an exemplar of how the best of critically queer theory can importantly enrich an emerging fourth wave feminist leisure studies – not because it only champions women or gays or lesbians, but because it demands an unrelenting commitment to intersectional political theorizing. It is queer because it unsettles the norm.

Advancing (queer) feminist social justice

Pride Tape

In 2016, players from my local NHL hockey team, the Edmonton Oilers, used rainbow-coloured "Pride Tape" on their hockey sticks during their annual skills competition. Remarkably, it was the first explicitly anti-homophobic campaign ever conducted on ice by NHL players (Tumilty, 2016). This very popular "community" fundraiser not only cultivates and resolidifies fan support, but it is also used as a social marketing cause for some of the Oilers' corporate backers. The vast majority of attendees are young boys with their fathers and other male hockey fans occupying commercialized arena space in a wide array of Oilers jerseys. The action on the ice comprises predictable displays of hard, aggressive athletic masculinity – vigorous displays of strength, speed, and power dominate the action. It is a quintessential instance of one of the most hegemonically celebrated faces of leisure in Edmonton – White prairie masculinity celebrating the national religion called professional men's hockey (Adams, 2006).

In a game where homophobic behaviour on and off the ice is entrenched, as evidenced by the slurs that still regularly pervade both locker room talk and invective flung at officials and opponents, this public embrace of LGBT acceptance seems to be an important start towards changing entrenched norms and attitudes within this iconic national sport culture and leisure formation. And it proved to be very popular. The Kickstarter campaign for Pride Tape reached its $54,000 financial goal within four months of launching. Prominent professional men's hockey organizations and local businesses readily supported the popular sport and its social marketing cause ("Oilers become," 2016; "Pride Tape," 2016).

The local Edmonton hockey fan community has not always been so open to lesbians and gay men. The last time the Edmonton Oilers won a Stanley Cup was in 1990. In that historical moment, there was absolutely *no* articulation of a hegemonic Oilers boosterism with anything related to gays or lesbians in coverage by the local media. Homophobia has a long, entrenched history in this province, the last in Canada to begrudgingly comply with Charter sexual orientation human rights legislation in 1998. In 2006, nearly 20 years later, the Oilers *almost* won a Stanley Cup, but missed it in the end. This time around, the local media did the subtle (but historically notable) job of articulating the situated interests of gay and lesbian fans *with* the hegemonic (albeit diverse) group known as "Oilers" fans. *Edmonton Journal* columnists wrote about watching a playoff game with a gay fan in a gay bar, or connected the playoff run with the local Pride parade. This ideological work was one of the new neoliberal twists of Oilers communitas produced in the 2006 campaign. Arguably, this now acceptable, prestige-based "queer" community – particularly the upwardly mobile, professional gays and lesbians who were coveted as the new index of the creative class – was being hailed not only for taking its rightful place at the tolerant, diverse, and multicultural table that is Canadian identity, but also as a new, potentially untapped market for the Oilers brand (Scherer & Davidson, 2011).

Ten years further on, the Edmonton Oilers logo sits prominently on the Pridetape.com website. It is in this historical moment that all mainstream print media (circulated widely on social media) locally, provincially, and nationally heralds the Pride Tape event as an example of an inclusive, human rights breakthrough. Boys are being encouraged not to use homophobic language in locker rooms, and professional men's hockey is being represented as a leader in human rights and acceptance. It has provided remarkable public exposure for some local lesbian and gay advocacy organizations, but it has also been a marketing dream for the local NHL franchise.

The Edmonton Oilers have relied on public funding and subsidies since their inauguration as a World Hockey League franchise in 1974. Since 2002 Daryl Katz, the billionaire owner of the Oilers and former pharmacy mogul, has mobilized both civic fears and pride to be the beneficiary of one of the most privately profitable, publicly funded arena deals ever written in North America. While Katz will "generously" contribute close to $140 million towards the total cost of the project, the taxpayers of the City of Edmonton will bear the brunt of the debt, a $614 million mortgage financed over the next 35 years, while also assuming all of the financial risk. Moreover, although the City will "own" the building, all of the revenue generated in the arena will go to the Oilers Entertainment Group (OEG) owned by Katz. Even in the "substandard" Rexall Place, the Oilers' previous arena, Katz had been the beneficiary of substantial annual revenues. Indeed, the Oilers are one of the most profitable NHL teams, small-market team status notwithstanding. Getting the arena deal signed has been one of the most divisive municipal debates the City has engaged in in recent memory (Scherer, 2016).

While there was some local opposition to the use of public funds for the new arena, there was little, if any, discourse about how such a development would affect the existing communities in the inner city, and/or any discussion of this as yet another instance of settler territoriality. And it is here that I want to turn to a discussion of the production of populations, and how the Pride Tape event contributed to a version of settler homonationalist discourse that stubbornly and effectively keeps itself quietly hidden. Apparently, riffing on Sara Ahmed (2010), I am intent on being a rainbow killjoy.

Indigenous studies scholar Mark Rifkin (2014), following Foucault, asks: "What defines a population as such? … It could be asking how groups of people are constituted as a population or populations – how the contours of a population are determined, by whom, and through what institutional and ideological mechanisms" (p. 149). I will put forth that there are two targets (those who will be supported in life, and those who will be left to die) for whom there are different strategies – some institutional and some ideological in this particular Pride Tape scenario. The Oilers' decision to move to the new state-of-the-art Rogers Place Arena in downtown Edmonton has more clearly delineated, and pushed further to the edges, an increasingly abjected and queered population in a central city space. The eastern edge of Edmonton's downtown is home to a large number of social service agencies who, in various ways with stagnant or shrinking resources in the face of greater and greater need, serve a diverse, primarily poor, community of people. Many of these individuals and agencies struggle to live with and through the often generational traumas that modernity and colonization have inflicted upon many of us. Not surprisingly, a disproportionately high number of Indigenous people live in this community.

What are some of the institutional and ideological mechanisms that are continuing to produce inner-city community members as "subject populations [that are] a potential threat to the welfare/life of the national people and thus [are] in need of extensive and intrusive management" (Rifkin, 2014, p. 154)? On the one hand, the connection to a particular version of men's hockey contributes to "the welfare/life of the national people" – and that welfare is about who is supported in life. As Mary Louise Adams (2006) reminds us, "the national community imagined through stories about hockey is a racialized community" (p. 75). The imagined recipients of the "good" produced by the Pride Tape initiative are hockey-playing, overwhelmingly White boys and men – now gay or straight – who have both the economic and cultural capital to participate in the national game.

If, as Rifkin (2014) also suggests, a "population is not given but produced in order to locate particular groups of people within a system of control that operates through distributions around a biologically imagined norm" (p. 150), a particular kind of gay man has been contingently invited to be in the discursive rainbow realm of that imagined, hockey norm, as long as they adhere to a narrow version of White settler masculinity – rugged, virile, aggressively athletic. However, as Puar (2007) reminds us, this is often a contingent form of recognition or acceptance. As a case in point – the Pride Tape has been used only once by an NHL team, and that was during a peripheral, local, fundraising activity. While players are free to tape their sticks as they see fit (one of the very few unregulated freedoms players actually have), no NHL hockey player has used the rainbow-coloured tape in a sanctioned game.

In another example, there is no representation online of the 2016 Skills competition – only the video from the previous year and properly normative white-taped sticks remains on the Oilers TV website ("Annual skills," 2016). And – while privileging "coming out" as a political tactic is fraught with complicated effects – the fact still remains that no active NHL player has come out as gay despite all sorts of inclusive and accepting rhetoric. All that said, the rainbow Pride

Tape campaign does paint the Edmonton Oilers hockey franchise as a progressive and inclusive corporate citizen who cares about minorities and the less fortunate, and supporting gay rights is now added to the list of good works.

But let us return to the second target of this biopolitical[6] moment. This is both where an intersectional feminist and queer analysis needs to be made. To reprise Rifkin (2014), "subject populations [are] a potential threat to the welfare/life of the national people and thus [are] in need of extensive and intrusive management" (p. 154). The building of the new arena downtown has inaugurated many changes and will continue to impact pre-existing inner-city communities. Faced with shrinking public funding and punitive neoliberal approaches to providing human services, supports for vulnerable inner-city people are changing or are being withered away. For example, the Women's Emergency Accommodation Centre (WEAC) ceased operation for almost a year after a small arson fire in April 2016, displacing 60 clients back into more dangerous survival situations (Wong, 2016). A $700,000-per-year funding request from the Boyle McCauley Health Clinic (an inner-city, non-profit, community-based health care centre) to provide 24/7 medical care for inner-city community members leaving hospital was denied (Stolte, 2016). Being left to die, literally and with disturbing regularity, is a management strategy in downtown Edmonton. While public funding for social services and support is diverted to debt financing a cultural sporting centre for middle- and ruling-class White men (Kidd, 1990), the City of Edmonton has now hired 33 new beat cops to patrol a 20-square-block area downtown. Rogers Place has a brand new 300-member private security detail to patrol inside and outside the new arena, and transit security is to be augmented during events. This well-documented phenomenon of the policing of inner-city communities is one example of "extensive and intrusive management," which produces many punitive effects for particular inner-city community members (Rifkin, 2014; Stuart, 2016).

While a Kickstarter campaign for rainbow-coloured hockey tape was able to quickly and easily attract tens of thousands of dollars, downtown social service agencies struggle to fundraise for basic operations. And these services are marked by gendered, sexualized, and racialized differences. There is substantially more capacity for emergency housing for men than women in the city core. Trans clients often face serious discrimination and/or are barred from particular agencies. And the massively profitable OEG is changing how it targets its charitable giving. One frontline agency that primarily serves inner-city women has for years received in-kind financial support from the team, which is substantial and crucial for the agency yet barely registers in Oilers' budget terms. This past year, for the first time, the OEG declined the agency's annual fundraising request. The message left was: "The Oilers Entertainment Group has decided to focus its non-profit giving on minor hockey." Presumably, White middle-class boys receiving anti-homophobia education in their dressing rooms while using rainbow hockey tape is far better marketing copy than supporting mostly Indigenous, female-identified individuals, many of whom are street-level, survival sex workers. Nonetheless, this approach further contributes to the precarity of those people and the few supported, safe places to which they have access. Perhaps there is no better leisure example of Foucault's famous maxim "to make live and to let die" (Foucault, 2003, p. 241). In the meantime, alongside many other ideological and institutional strategies, Pride Tape will have contributed to an attempt to normalize a sanitized and safe form of LGBT acceptance in men's hockey, a White, patriarchal form of acceptable difference that makes possible the racialized "abnormal" communities of the inner city who will continue to be represented as "dangerous" and unpredictable – a queered population against which settler hockey society must be defended (Foucault, 2003). This is another example of racism against the abnormal (McWhorter, 2009).

Engaging with fourth wave feminism

Almost 30 years ago, Bruce Kidd (1990) explicitly argued that the public and private financing of professional sports stadia was a feminist issue. It appears that in a new millennium the problem continues with even greater force and more complicated entanglements with racialized, classed, and sexualized inflections. These are important considerations to which fourth wave feminist leisure scholars must attend, as they comprise the larger apparatuses of 21st-century biopower in Edmonton. The continued provisional privileging of some specific sporting subjects and further territorial displacement and neglect of others – what Dean Spade (2011) calls the disproportionate distribution of "life chances" – reconsolidates the bifurcation of those supported to live, and those left to die in the ongoing production of queered, disposable populations on the Canadian prairies. In this story, the larger settler colonial apparatuses include the civic boosterism lobby to develop "world class" cities with scarce public resources, the LGBT visibility politics of diversity, human rights and inclusion, and the ongoing entrenchment of the interests of civic and business elites with professional men's sport nexuses. This form of White, settler patriarchal acceptance sought by homonormative gays and lesbians "produces the effect of 'queer as regulatory' whereby homonormative queer citizens strive to become 'subjects of life' rather than left for death" (Morgensen in Davidson, 2013).

What I have endeavoured to do with this overview of a recent piece of my leisure research is to take seriously the call by both McDonald (2006) and Eng et al. (2005) for a renewed queer theorizing, one that foregrounds racial, gender, and class hierarchies, and the nationalistic political economies that keep those disparities within leisure contexts in place. The best of fourth wave feminist tenets lines up with these commitments to justice, exposing the complex and selective structural underbellies of seemingly benign social marketing campaigns. While slick, persuasive social media strategies take advantage of the best technological advancements and appear to work in the service of social justice, understanding the textured micropolitics of layered and embedded contexts offers a very different kind of analysis. Fourth wave feminism aligns with critically queer theory when its commitment to deeply intersectional structural analysis is fulfilled. Careful attention must be paid to the focus on micropolitics and technology for how their multiple effects (both helpful and problematic) operate in complex socio-political situations.

Unfinished business

Tipi Confessions

As Foucault (1983) helpfully reminds us, "my point is not that everything is bad, but that everything is dangerous" (p. 231). While my analysis of Pride hockey tape points out the limits of homonormative/nationalist LGBT rainbow initiatives, there are dangers to how I represent the effects of this discourse. By framing Indigeneity in this chapter as impoverished and victimized queer abjection, I resediment a genocidal settler colonial stereotype and this is clearly a limitation to my analysis. It contributes yet again to a pathologizing form of settler knowledge production that robs vibrant, resilient Indigenous and other communities of their vitality and queer creativity. So I end this piece by briefly describing a community-based performance event called Tipi Confessions, which explicitly combines politics and sex to work in the service of decolonizing sexuality.

The storytelling show explores sex and sexuality through humour and vulnerability. In its Edmonton incarnation (the form has its roots in Austin, Texas, and other Canadian cities have hosted associated events), it has an all-Indigenous production team who foreground the ethos that

> decolonizing sexuality, and sex positivity and healing more broadly, is key to curbing violence in our society in both Indigenous and non-Indigenous communities. Tipi Confessions, informed by Indigenous experiences and perspectives on relationships, sexualities and gender, is and will continue to be an all-inclusive enterprise, welcoming all genders, races, and sexualities.
> (Tipi Confessions, 2017)

Each event has an auditioned program of storytellers as well as anonymous "confessions" generated from the audience that are read by the show's sexy emcees. This is not a whitewashed "it gets better" type of production. It clearly positions the post-apocalyptic conditions under which Indigenous communities have lived for more than the past century. The theme of a recent show was "Sex at the End of the World," where the team "indulge[d] in indigenized zombie metaphors and sex in an era of environmental apocalypse. Tipi Confessions is not only sexy. Our audiences are reminded that sex is always also political" (Tipi Confessions, 2017).

Perhaps this type of leisure event can be a kind of queer productive moment of decolonial love[7] in a fourth wave of feminism. Regardless, it is the kind of resilient initiative that is rigorously politicized, erotic, funny, heartbreaking, and pleasurable. It is a micropolitical intervention in a local context that exists precariously in, and in spite of, the massive juggernauts of professional men's hockey spectacles, the machinery of homonormative lesbigay politics, and the crushing power of neoliberal settler civic elites.

Notes

1 A note on trans, trans*, and trans+: All three of these terms are used as abbreviations of *transgender* and/or as ways to more explicitly communicate inclusion of the full breadth of people whose gender identities are something other than was expected of them at birth (Kapitan, 2017).

2 The "homosexual," as Foucault deployed the term, was a historically specific category that emerged as an effect of various social, political, moral, and medical discourses of the late 19th century in Northern Europe: "The sodomite had been a temporary aberration; the homosexual was now a species" (Foucault, 1978, p. 43). Foucault's insights are borne out in the term's colloquial usage in 20th-century North America, where it was wielded as a psychiatrized, medicalized form of pathologization for decades.

3 Important exceptions to this include D. J. Williams' fascinating work on consensual participation in BDSM (bondage/discipline, sadomasochism) as a leisure practice (among others, see Prior & Williams, 2015; Williams & Storm, 2012).

4 There are, of course, several other important authors and books that came out in the early 1990s and contributed to the rapid development of queer theory. Among others, see: Eve Kosofsky Sedgwick's (1990) *Epistemology of the Closet*, Michael Warner's *Fear of a Queer Planet* (1993), Michel Foucault's *The History of Sexuality* (1978), and *The Lesbian and Gay Studies Reader* (Abelove et al., 1993). I have chosen to privilege Butler's contribution here, given the direct connection to feminist theory.

5 See Davidson (2009) for an autoethnographic account of a different queering of the same event.

6 "Foucault suggests that biopolitics 'effects distributions around the norm,' and 'the judicial institution is increasingly incorporated into a continuum of apparatuses (medical, administrative, and so on) whose functions are for the most part regulatory,' 'a technology of power centered on life.' The positions various groups of people occupy within the political and economic configuration(s) that sustain the norm, then, are validated as merely expressive of their collective bodily dispositions, qualities that make them – as populations – less able to participate in the promise of augmented life represented by the norm" (in Rifkin, 2014, p. 150).

7 However, as Métis scholar Zoe Todd (2014) suggests,

> I hope people continue to write about decolonising sex, decolonising relationships, decolonising gender roles, decolonising how we are conditioned not to express emotional vulnerability (as a matter of survival in a traumatised, brutal world). But love itself never was, never can be colonised. It is inherently decolonising. So decolonial love, as two words strung together, is redundant. Love needs no decolonisation because it is itself a decolonial force.
>
> (n.p.)

References

Abelove, H., Barale, M. A., & Halperin, D. M. (Eds.) (1993). *The lesbian and gay studies reader*. New York, NY: Routledge.

Adams, M. L. (2006). The game of whose lives? Gender, race, and entitlement in Canada's "national game." In D. Whitson & R. Gruneau (Eds.), *Artificial ice: Hockey, culture, and commerce* (pp. 71–84). Peterborough, ON: Broadview Press.

Ahmed, S. (2010). Feminist killjoys (and other willful subjects). *S&F Online – The Scholar and Feminist Online*, 8(3). New York: Barnard Centre for Research on Women. Retrieved from sfonline.barnard.edu/polyphonic/ahmed_01.htm

Aitchison, C. (2000). Poststructural feminist theories of representing Others: A response to the "crisis" in leisure studies' discourse. *Leisure Studies*, *19*(3), 127–144.

Aitchison, C. (2001). Gender and leisure research: The codification of knowledge. *Leisure Sciences*, *23*(1), 1–19.

Aitchison, C. M. (2006). The critical and the cultural: Explaining the divergent paths of leisure studies and tourism studies. *Leisure Studies*, *25*(4), 417–422.

Annual skills competition – Oilers TV. (2016, September 16). Retrieved from video.oilers.nhl.com/videocenter/console?id=937985

Barnett, J. T., & Johnson, C. W. (2013). We are all royalty: Narrative comparison of a drag queen and king. *Journal of Leisure Research*, *45*(5), 677–694.

Bialeschki, M. D., & Pearce, K. D. (1997). "I don't want a lifestyle – I want a life": The effect of role negotiations on the leisure of lesbian mothers. *Journal of Leisure Research*, *29*(1), 113–131.

Browne, K., & Bakshi, L. (2011). We are here to party? Lesbian, gay, bisexual and trans leisurescapes beyond commercial gay scenes. *Leisure Studies*, *30*(2), 179–196.

Burdsey, D. (2015). Review of *Whiteness and leisure* by K. Spracklen. *Leisure Studies*, *34*(3), 385–388.

Butler, J. (1990). *Gender trouble: Feminism and the subversion of identity*. New York, NY: Routledge.

Butler, J. (1993). *Bodies that matter: On the discursive limits of "sex."* New York, NY: Routledge.

Caldwell, L. L., Kivel, B. D., Smith, E. A., & Hayes, D. (1998). The leisure context of adolescents who are lesbian, gay male, bisexual and questioning their sexual identities: An exploratory study. *Journal of Leisure Research*, *30*(3), 341–355.

Catalano, D. J. (1982). Reaching an invisible population: Leisure and recreation for aging lesbians and gay men. *Leisure Information Newsletter*, 9(2), 7–8.

Caudwell, J. (2006). *Sport, sexualities and queer/theory*. London: Routledge.

Davidson, J. (2003). The wannabe Olympics: The Gay Games, Olympism and processes of incorporation. Unpublished doctoral dissertation, University of Alberta, Edmonton.

Davidson, J. (2004). Remembering Tom: The Gay Games' ego ideal and ideal ego. *torquere: Journal of the Canadian Lesbian and Gay Studies Association*, 6, 116–142.

Davidson, J. (2006). The necessity of queer shame for gay pride: The Gay Games and Cultural Events. In J. Caudwell (Ed.), *Sport, sexualities and queer/theory* (pp. 90–105). London: Routledge.

Davidson, J. (2007). Homophobia, fundamentalism, and Canadian tolerance: Enabling Gay Games III in Vancouver. *International Journal of Canadian Studies*, *35*, 151–175.

Davidson, J. (2009). Lesbian erotics at women's hockey: Fans, flashing, and the Booby Orrs. *Journal of Lesbian Studies*, *13*, 337–348.

Davidson, J. (2013). Sporting homonationalisms: Sexual exceptionalism, queer privilege, and the 21st century international lesbian and gay sport movement. *Sociology of Sport Journal*, *30*, 57–82.

Davidson, J. (2014). Racism against the abnormal? The 20th century Gay Games, biopolitics, and the emergence of homonational sport. *Leisure Studies*, *33*, 357–378.

Davidson, J. (2017). The early Gay Games: The Bay Area years. In M. Smith & R. Liberti (Eds.), *San Francisco Bay Area sports: Golden Gate athletics, recreation and community* (pp. 235–251). Fayetteville: University of Arkansas Press.

Davidson, J., & Helstein, M. (2016). Queering the gaze: Calgary hockey breasts, dynamics of desire, and colonial hauntings. *Sociology of Sport Journal*, *33*(4), 282–293.

Davidson, J. & McDonald, M.G. (2018). Rethinking human rights: The 2014 Sochi Winter Olympics, LGBT protections and the limits of cosmopolitanism. *Leisure Studies*, *37*(1), 64–76.

D'Emilio, J. (1983). Capitalism and gay identity. In A. Snitow, C. Stansell, & S. Thompson (Eds.), *Powers of desire: The politics of sexuality* (pp. 100–113). New York, NY: Monthly Review Press.

Devall, W. (1979). Leisure and lifestyles among gay men: An exploratory essay. *International Review of Modern Sociology*, *9*(2), 179–195.

Duggan, L. (2011). Love and anger: Scenes from a passionate career. *GLQ: A Journal of Lesbian and Gay Studies*, *17*(1), 145–153.

Eng, D. L., Halberstam, J., & Munoz, J. E. (2005). Introduction: What's queer about queer studies now? *Social Text*, *23*(3–4), 1–18.

Faderman, L. (1992). *Odd girls and twilight lovers: A history of lesbian life in twentieth century America*. New York, NY: Penguin.

Foucault, M. (1978). *The history of sexuality*, *Vol. 1*, *An introduction* (R. Hurley, Trans.). New York, NY: Pantheon.

Foucault, M. (1983). On the genealogy of ethics: An overview of work in progress. In H. L. Dreyfus & P. Rabinow, *Beyond structuralism and hermeneutics* (2nd ed.) (pp. 229–252). Chicago, IL: University of Chicago Press.

Foucault, M. (2003). *Society must be defended: Lectures at the Collège de France 1975–1976* (M. Bertani & A. Fontana, Eds., D. Macey, Trans.). New York, NY: Picador.

Grossman, A. H. (1992). Inclusion, not exclusion: Recreation service delivery to lesbian, gay, and bisexual youth. *Journal of Physical Education, Recreation & Dance*, *63*(4), 45–47.

Grossman, A. (1993). Providing leisure services for gays and lesbians. *Parks & Recreation*, *28*(4), 26–29, 90–91.

Jacobson, S., & Samdahl, D. (1998). Leisure in the lives of older lesbians: Experiences with and responses to discrimination. *Journal of Leisure Research*, *30*(2), 233–255.

Jagger, G. (2008). *Judith Butler: Sexual politics, social change, and the power of the performative*. New York: Routledge.

Jarvis, N., & Weeden, C. (2017). Cruising with pride: The LGBT cruise market. In R. Dowling & C. Weeden (Eds.), *Cruise ship tourism* (pp. 332–347). Wallingford, UK: CAB International.

Johnson, C. W. (1999). Living the game of hide and seek: Leisure in the lives of gay and lesbian young adults. *Leisure/Loisir*, *24*(3–4), 255–278.

Johnson, C. W., & Kivel, B. (2007). Gender, sexuality and queer theory in sport. In C. C. Aitchison (Ed.), *Sport & gender identities: Masculinities, femininities and sexualities* (pp. 93–105). London: Routledge.

Johnson, C. W., & Samdahl, D. M. (2005). "The night *they* took over": Misogyny in a country-western gay bar. *Leisure Sciences*, *27*, 331–348.

Kapitan, A. (2017, August 31). The radical copyeditor's style guide for writing about transgender people. Retrieved from radicalcopyeditor.com/2017/08/31/transgender-style-guide/

Kidd, B. (1990). The men's cultural centre: Sports and the dynamic of women's oppression/ men's repression. In M. A. Messner & D. F. Sabo (Eds.), *Sport, men, and the gender order: Critical feminist perspectives* (pp. 31–43). Champaign, IL: Human Kinetics.

Kivel, B. D. (1994). Lesbian and gay youth and leisure: Implications for practitioners and researchers. *Journal of Park and Recreation Administration*, *12*(4), 15–28.

Kivel, B. D. (1997). Leisure, narratives and the construction of identity among lesbian, gay and bisexual youth. *Journal of Leisurability*, *24*(4), 31–38.

Kivel, B. D. (2000). Leisure experience and identity: What difference does difference make? *Journal of Leisure Research*, *32*(1), 79–81.

Kivel, B. D., & Kleiber, D. A. (2000). Leisure in the identity formation of lesbian/gay youth: Personal, but not social. *Leisure Sciences*, *22*(4), 215–232.

Love, H. (2011). Introduction: Rethinking sex. *GLQ: A Journal of Lesbian and Gay Studies*, *17*(1), 1–14.

MacKinnon, C., & Dworkin, A. (1985). *The reasons why: Essays on the new civil rights law recognizing pornography as sex discrimination*. New York, NY: Women Against Pornography.

McDonald, M. G. (2006). Beyond the pale: The whiteness of sports studies and queer scholarship. In J. Caudwell (Ed.), *Sport, sexualities and queer/theory* (pp. 33–45). London: Routledge.

McWhorter, L. (2009). *Racism and sexual oppression in Anglo-America*. Bloomington: Indiana University Press.

Morgensen, S. L. (2010). Settler homonationalism: Theorizing settler colonialism within queer modernities. *GLQ: A Journal of Lesbian and Gay Studies*, *16*(1–2), 105–131.

Oakleaf, L. (2013). "Having to think about it all the time": Factors affecting the identity management strategies of residential summer camp staff who self-identify as lesbian, gay, bisexual or transgender. *Leisure/Loisir*, *37*(3), 251–266.

Oilers become first NHL team to use pride tape. (2016, January 24). Retrieved from www.nhl.com/news/oilers-become-first-nhl-team-to-use-pride-tape/c-799371

Parry, D. C. (2016). The relational politics of gender and leisure. In G. Walker, D. Scott, & M. Stodolska (Eds.), *Leisure Matters: The State and Future of Leisure Studies* (pp. 206–216). State College, PA: Venture Publishing Inc.

Perez, H. (2005). You can have my brown body and eat it, too! *Social Text*, *23*(3–4), 171–191.

Pitts, B. G. (1988). Beyond the bars: The development of leisure-activity management in the lesbian and gay population in America. *Leisure Information Quarterly*, *15*(3), 4–7.

Pride Tape – Hockey tape to support young LGBTQ players (2016, September 19). Retrieved from www.kickstarter.com/projects/252024940/pride-tape-hockey-tape-to-support-young-lgbtq-play/posts/1483685

Prior, E. E., & Williams, D. J. (2015). Does BDSM power exchange among women reflect casual leisure? An exploratory qualitative study. *Journal of Positive Sexuality*, *1*(1). Retrieved from http://journalofpositivesexuality.org/archive/volume-1-feb-nov-2015/

Pritchard, A., Morgan, N., & Sedgly, D. (2007). In search of lesbian space? The experience of Manchester's gay village. In A. Pritchard, N. Morgan, I. Ateljevic, & C. Harris (Eds.), *Tourism and gender: Embodiment, sensuality and experience* (pp. 273–290). Wallingford, UK: CAB International.

Puar, J. (2002). A transnational feminist critique of queer tourism. *Antipode: A Radical Journal of Geography*, *34*(5), 935–946.

Puar, J. (2007). *Terrorist assemblages: Homonationalism in queer times*. Durham, NC: Duke University Press.

Puar, J. (2013). Rethinking homonationalism. *International Journal of Middle East Studies*, *45*, 336–339.

Rifkin, M. (2014). Making peoples into populations: The racial limits of tribal sovereignty. In A. Simpson & A. Smith (Eds.), *Theorizing native studies* (pp. 149–187). Durham, NC: Duke University Press.

Rubin, G. (1984). Thinking sex: Notes for a radical theory of a politics of sexuality. In C. S. Vance (Ed.), *Pleasure and danger: Exploring female sexuality* (pp. 267–319). Boston, MA: Routledge & Kegan Paul.

Rubin, G., with Butler, J. (1994). Sexual traffic. *differences: A Journal of Feminist Cultural Studies*, *6*(2–3), 62–99.

Scherer, J. (2016). Resisting the world-class city: Community opposition and the politics of a local arena development. *Sociology of Sport Journal*, *33*(1), 39–53.

Scherer, J., & Davidson, J. (2011). Promoting the "arriviste" city: Producing neo-liberal urban identity and communities of consumption during the Edmonton Oilers' 2006 playoff campaign. *International Review for the Sociology of Sport*, *46*, 157–180.

Sedgwick, E. K. (1990). *Epistemology of the closet*. Berkeley: University of California Press.

Sedgwick, E. K. (1993). Queer performativity: Henry James' "The art of the novel." *GLQ: A Journal of Lesbian and Gay Studies*, *1*(1), 1–16.

Shallenberger, D. (1988). Linking leisure and sexuality: The gay and lesbian experience. *Leisure Information Quarterly*, *14*(4), 4–6.

Skeggs, B. (1999). Matter out of place: Visibility and sexuality in leisure spaces. *Leisure Studies*, *18*(3), 213–232.

Spade, D. (2011). *Normal life: Administrative violence, critical trans politics, and the limits of the law*. Durham, NC: Duke University Press.

Spracklen, K. (2014). Leisure studies education: Historical trends and pedagogical futures in the United Kingdom and beyond. *Journal of Hospitality, Leisure, Sport and Tourism Education*, *15*, 20–23.

Stolte, E. (2016, June 9). Bed rest for the homeless: Edmonton inner-city health centre lobbies for 24 hour nursing care. Retrieved from edmontonjournal.com/news/local-news/bed-rest-for-the-homeless-edmonton-inner-city-health-centre-lobbies-for-24-hour-nursing-care

Stuart, F. (2016). *Down, out, and under arrest: Policing and everyday life in skid row*. Chicago, IL: University of Chicago Press.

Sykes, H. (2016). Gay pride on stolen land: Homonationalism and settler colonialism at the Vancouver Winter Olympics. *Sociology of Sport Journal*, *33*(1), 54–65.

Taylor, Y. (2007). "If your face doesn't fit ...": The misrecognition of working-class lesbians in scene space. *Leisure Studies*, *26*(2), 161–178.

Theriault, D., & Witt, P. (2014). Features of positive developmental leisure settings for LGBTQ youth. *Journal of Park and Recreation Administration*, *32*(2), 83–97.

Therkelesen, A., Blichfeldt, B. S., Chor, J., & Ballegaard, N. (2013). "I am very straight in my gay life": Approaching an understanding of lesbian tourists' identity construction. *Journal of Vacation Marketing*, *19*(4), 317–327.

Tipi Confessions. (2017). Tipi Confessions. Retrieved from www.facebook.com/pg/tipi-confessions/about/?ref=page_internal

Todd, Z. (2014, July 4). Love is inherently decolonising: Some thoughts on Junot Diaz' "decolonial love". Urbane Adventurer: Amiskwacî. Retrieved from https://zoestodd.com/2014/07/04/love-is-inherently-decolonising-some-thoughts-on-junit-diaz-decoloniak-love/

Travers, A., & Shearman, M. (2017). The Sochi Olympics, celebration capitalism, and homonationalist pride. *Journal of Sport and Social Issues*, *41*(1), 42–69.

Trussell, D. E. (2017). Parents' leisure, LGB young people and "When we were coming out". *Leisure Sciences*, *39*(1), 42–58.

Tumilty, R. (2016, January 26). Edmonton Oilers play with pride tape at skills contest. Retrieved from www.metronews.ca/news/edmonton/2016/01/24/edmonton-oilers-play-with-pride-tape-at-skills-contest.html

Turner, W .B. (2000). *A genealogy of queer theory*. Philadelphia, PA: Temple University Press.

Vorobjovas-Pinta, O., & Hardy, A. (2016). The evolution of gay travel research. *International Journal of Tourism Research*, *18*, 409–416.

Warner, M. (Ed.). (1993). *Fear of a queer planet: Queer politics and social theory*. Minneapolis: University of Minnesota Press.

Weeks, J. (2000). The challenge of lesbian and gay studies. In T. Sandfort (Ed.), *Lesbian and gay studies: An introductory, interdisciplinary approach* (pp. 1–13). London: Sage.

Williams, D. J., & Storm, L.,E. (2012). Unconventional leisure and career: Insights into the work of professional dominatrices. *Electronic Journal of Human Sexuality*, *15*. Retrieved from www.ejhs.org/volume15/BDSM.html

Wolfe, P. (1999). *Settler colonialism and the transformation of anthropology: The politics and poetics of an ethnographic event*. London: Cassell.

Wong, J. (2016, April 29). "It's a bit of a crisis": Arson forces closure of Edmonton women's shelter. Retrieved from globalnews.ca/news/2671194/its-a-bit-of-a-crisis-arson-forces-closure-of-edmonton-womens-shelter/

Further reading

Abelove, H., Barale, M.A., & Halperin, D. M. (Eds.) (1993). *The lesbian and gay studies reader*. New York: Routledge.

Butler, J. (1990). *Gender trouble: Feminism and the subversion of identity*. New York: Routledge.

Butler, J. (1993). *Bodies that matter: On the discursive limits of "sex."* New York: Routledge.

Morgensen, S. L. (2011). *Spaces between us: Queer settler colonialism and Indigenous decolonization*. Minneapolis: University of Minnesota Press.

Puar, J. (2007). *Terrorist assemblages: Homonationalism in queer times*. Durham, NC: Duke University Press.

Chapter 6

"We danced around the circle"

Feminist standpoint theories and turning old stories into something new

Felice Yuen

> We went to a pow wow in the spring,
> my mother and my grandmother.
> We danced around the circle.
> My grandmother turned to me and said,
> "You know I would have never been able to do this."
> (Sophia, *Journey Women*)

Sophia is an Indigenous[1] woman who was part of a Canadian arts-based project called *Journey Women*. This project was a collaboration between Minwaashin Lodge, an Indigenous women's support centre in Ottawa, Ontario, and Concordia University in Montreal, Quebec. The purpose of *Journey Women* was to explore Indigenous women's experiences and meanings of healing. Sophia, along with seven other Indigenous women from various Indigenous nations (i.e., Inuit, Métis, Cree, Algonquin, Innu), participated in a three-day body-mapping workshop and public art exhibit.

Body mapping was a process used in *Journey Women* for women[2] to explore and share their experiences of healing. An outcome of this process is a life-sized canvas, which represents the artists' healing journey (see www.journeywomen.ca). I share the stories of *Journey Women* because they were created to be shared, to raise awareness around the issue of violence against Indigenous women, and to celebrate Indigenous women's resilience and strength. Their stories are simultaneously painful reminders of Canada's colonization and its devastating impacts, and powerful reminders of a resiliency rarely heard or acknowledged (Smith, 1999; Spears, 2006).

In this chapter, I discuss how feminist standpoint theories (FST) can provide a methodological and theoretical platform for Indigenous women's stories to be seen and heard, as well as activate social justice. I present my experience with the *Journey Women* project and the women's stories as exemplars for this chapter's exploration of FST. To set the stage, I will begin with a brief discussion of colonization. This discussion is an important consideration for FST, because of the focus on situated and context-specific knowledges (Crasnow, 2009; Harding,

1991; Houle, 2009). Understanding the current experiences of Indigenous peoples begins with understanding past *and* present experiences of colonization (Razack, 1998).

As revealed by Sophia's powerful quote at the beginning of this chapter, *Journey Women*'s stories of resistance, strength, and healing are rooted in centuries of colonization and oppression. Colonization refers to discursive or political suppression of heterogeneity (Mohanty, 2003). For Indigenous peoples in Canada, colonization was enforced through cultural genocide – where practices and policies were used to destroy and eradicate a targeted group (Truth and Reconciliation Commission of Canada [TRC], 2015a). Tactics included land seizures, restriction of movement, banning languages, outlawing spiritual practices such as pow wows, and seizing children – often without consent or knowledge from their families and communities, and placing them in residential schools or with non-Indigenous families (Sinclair, 2007; TRC, 2015a). In Canada, residential schools played a major role in the cultural genocide of Indigenous peoples (TRC, 2015a). Approximately 150,000 First Nations, Inuit, and Métis children attended these schools, where they experienced severe punishment for speaking their Indigenous language, living their Indigenous spirituality and cultural traditions, and seeking out family. Sexual, physical, and emotional abuse was commonly inflicted upon children in residential schools by their teachers and others in positions of authority (TRC, 2015a).

While the last residential school closed in 1996, the impact lives on through *intergenerational trauma*. This trauma is manifested through symptoms of anxiety, depression, the over-representation of Indigenous peoples in prisons, and violence against oneself or other Indigenous peoples (Duran & Duran, 1995; Maracle, 1996). In this sense, it is important to note that Indigenous women's experiences of trauma are markedly different from non-Indigenous Canadian women. For example, although Indigenous peoples make up 2 percent of the Canadian population, one in four women murdered in Canada are Indigenous ("Wake up. The threat to our Indigenous women is Canada's problem," 2015). Further, the Native Women's Association of Canada (2015) reports that Indigenous women are at a greater risk than non-Indigenous women of experiencing various forms of family violence, such as having a gun or knife used against them, or being beaten, choked, or sexually assaulted by their partner. Indeed, Indigenous women report spousal abuse at three times the rate of non-Indigenous women (Statistics Canada, 2004, as cited by Native Women's Association of Canada, 2015). This violence can be traced back to the horrendous impact of colonization on Indigenous peoples (Duran & Duran, 1995; Maracle, 1996). As Wesley-Esquimaux (2006) argues, "'present' Indigenous communities are a direct legacy of their traumatic 'past'" (p. 6). In other words, Indigenous peoples' experiences of marginalization and oppression are directly linked to colonization and associated experiences of trauma.

By honouring the stories of Indigenous women, FST facilitate the acknowledgement of colonization and the continued impact of marginalization and oppression on Indigenous women's lives. I begin this chapter by considering the historical and disciplinary roots, and three basic tenets of FST. Following this discussion, I will review some of the tensions within FST and propose decolonizing methodologies as an approach to mediate some of these challenges. Towards the end of the chapter, I present the *Journey Women* project as an example of how FST enabled me to view and engage in research differently – specifically, how I came to privilege relational knowledge and emotional ways of knowing. The possibilities of engaging FST within the fourth wave of feminism are also explored as I reflect upon the potential for FST to create a strong methodological and theoretical foundation for Indigenous women to inspire social justice through social media, specifically as it relates to technology, intersectionality, and globalization. In this context, I argue that FST provide a methodological and theoretical foundation that can ignite social justice by evoking a political *and* emotional consciousness. I conclude this chapter with an acknowledgement that the epistemological direction of *Journey Women* is still unclear, despite my attempts to combine FST with decolonizing methodologies. I will consider this dilemma in relation to the potential for FST to advance social justice agendas within the fourth wave of feminism.

Historical and disciplinary roots: the history of FST

FST emerged in the 1970s and 1980s, and was largely influenced by standpoint theory, which began as a methodology in the social sciences to decentre Eurocentric knowledge and practice (Crasnow, 2009). Influenced by Marxism, standpoint theorists believe social change requires the creation of knowledge that comes from those who are marginalized and oppressed, as opposed to those who oppress (Hartstock, 2004). Standpoint theory contends the perspectives of those who are oppressed are less skewed than the perspectives of the oppressors. As Hartstock (2004) explains, the ruling class is incapable of having a complete understanding of society because the societal structure was created to suit their own needs, ultimately limiting their knowledge and understanding. Characterized in Marxist theory as *false consciousness*, those who are a part of the dominant class cannot necessarily describe the social structure because they operate within it and take it for granted (Smith, 1999). Further highlighting a Marxist-inspired interpretation of power, FST position patriarchy and the male perspective as the dominant perspective. In contrast, FST understand those who self-identify as women as oppressed and the female perspective as marginalized (Moreton-Robinson, 2013). FST also recognize that there are certain women who are further marginalized due to the intersection of certain identities, such as age, class, sexual identity, and race, and aim to emphasize and privilege these subjugated experiences and perspectives.

Basic tenets of FST

FST raise feminist issues as well as guide theoretical, methodological, and political thought (Harding, 2004). In this process, FST challenge dominant androcentric and patriarchal paradigms and methodologies and help forge a feminist political consciousness (Houle, 2009; Moreton-Robinson, 2013). Furthermore, research using FST helps capture the knowledges and understandings that stem from women's movements, as well as push for a research methodology that can help articulate and differentiate the social values, interests, and agendas of the researcher (Harding, 1992). Here, I present three basic tenets of FST that guided my research methodology in the *Journey Women* project: (1) situated and context-specific knowledges; (2) multiple perspectives and multiple truths; and (3) strong objectivity.

Situated and context-specific knowledges

FST acknowledge science generally resonates with the experience that "Western men of the elite classes and races have of themselves and the world around them" (Harding, 1991, p. 48). Through this narrow race and class-based approach to research, women, and more specifically women who experience marginalization due to the intersection of multiple vectors of power (i.e., age, class, sexual identity, race, etc.), were rendered invisible (Smith, 1987). In response, Harding (1991) proposed we "redirect our analysis of women's situation and our agendas so that they are significantly closer to the more comprehensive ones advocated by women who suffer from more than what some women frequently see as simply gender oppression" (p. 193). In this regard, FST start with those living on the margins by privileging their positioned knowledge (Crasnow, 2009; Houle, 2009). Kourany (2009) offers a comprehensive description of how and why we must begin from the perspective of those who are oppressed:

> All knowledge is situated, positioned in a particular time and place; that where power is organized hierarchically – for example, by class or race or gender – persons can achieve only partial views of reality from the perspective of their own positions in the social hierarchy; that the view from the perspective of the less powerful is far less partial and distorted than the view from the perspective of the more powerful.
>
> (p. 210)

In short, FST acknowledge and privilege the lived experiences of research participants and their perspectives of these experiences. The belief that knowledge is situated and context-specific, and the corresponding epistemological assumption that countless histories exist, lead to the recognition that multiple knowledges exist. These knowledges are created from multiple perspectives and multiple truths, which I will now explore.

Multiple perspectives and multiple truths

FST moved feminist research into the deconstruction of traditional (male, white, and elite) understandings and experiences of gender by considering other positions of marginalization and oppression (Olesen, 2000), most notably by considering women's experiences in addition to other identity markers such as race, class, (dis)ability, and sexual identity (see Henderson & Gibson, 2013; Watson & Scraton, 2013). The focus on situated and context-specific knowledge complicates and problematizes not only Eurocentric and androcentric knowledge, but also the idea of one marginalized standpoint. For example, in recent years, we have seen the emergence of multiple African (Naidu, 2010) and Indigenous feminist standpoints (Moreton-Robinson, 2013). As Fox (2006) articulates:

> The identification of Indigenous peoples is complicated, since there is no precise definition that applies world wide, includes rural and urban contexts, or addresses the multiplicity of Indigenous peoples as distinct nations with various sovereign status, legal rights, and/or politically encapsulated within nation-state boundaries.
>
> (p. 403)

Just as there is no universal Indigenous identity, there is no universal Indigenous women's identity. These multiple identities lead to multiple locations of marginalization, which lead to multiple perspectives. Recognizing and understanding multiple perspectives requires a certain methodological approach. In the following section, I discuss Harding's (1992) notion of *strong objectivity* as a conceptual framework for privileging the perspectives that have be silenced and/or subjugated.

Strong objectivity

Harding's (1992) concept of *strong objectivity* problematizes the norms and methods of conventional science, as it asserts its processes are "too weak to permit researchers to systematically identify and eliminate from the result of research those social values, interests, and agendas that are shared by the ... scientific community" (p. 440). FST privilege strong objectivity because they acknowledge there are limitations to dominant conceptions of method and explanation, which lead to suppressed and distorted understandings (Harding, 1992, 2004; Rolin, 2009). To avoid confusion with dominant conceptualizations of objectivity, Harding (1993) considered changing the term to *strong reflexivity*. In this chapter, I will continue with the original concept of strong objectivity.

Identifying and clarifying the distorted lens of researchers requires uncovering the hierarchical structures that oppress those who are being researched within the researcher–researched relationship (Crasnow, 2009). Presumably, acknowledging positions of power, particularly as an obstacle to the production of scientific knowledge, enables the collection of data that is more representative of the lived-experiences of individuals who are marginalized (Rolin, 2009). Rolin (2009) and Harding (1991) highlight that the hierarchical relationship between researcher and research participants can impact what is shared or not shared by participants. Rolin (2009) explains, "relations ... can be used to dominate people ... [and] are likely to mobilize a complex set of motivations that prompt potential informants to either conceal or distort relevant evidence" (p. 219). She further articulates that this distortion can occur when: (1) research participants feel uncomfortable emotions, such as shame and fear, which leads to the suppression of information; (2) the capacity of research participants to communicate lived-experiences is limited, which is bound by the method(s) of data collection; and (3) the required trust between researchers and potential participants does not exist.

Uncovering the hierarchical structure that exists within the researcher–researched relationship necessitates an acceptance that knowledge cannot be separated from its producers and the society in which they live (Harding, 2004). Hence, FST involve uncovering the hierarchies that exist between the researcher and the research participants *and* co-creating collaborative and meaningful research methods that enable alternative knowledges and understandings to come to light. Through FST, the researcher–researched dynamic is examined, and action is taken to facilitate the creation of knowledge that honours the location and perspectives of research participants. In the latter part of this chapter, body mapping is presented as a method of inquiry that enables researchers to negotiate colonial methods of understanding. This arts-based form of representation is also presented as an example of a meaningful way to disseminate the artists' experiences of healing.

FST and leisure studies

In the 1980s and 1990s, FST was largely absent from most feminist leisure research. However, this omission does not necessarily negate the use of FST in early feminist leisure research. Indeed, FST have influenced leisure research, albeit slowly. Between the 1980s and 1990s, when FST were focusing on socially contextualized knowledges and doing research from the margins (Harding, 1991), Henderson (1994) suggests leisure research was focused on women-centred scholarship. This era of research continued to examine the difference between the female and (white, middle-class) male experience (Shaw, 1999), "but it also focused on examining a theoretical universal female experience" (Henderson, 1994, p. 125).

In the 1990s, leisure research moved towards acknowledging issues of power (Henderson, 1994; Scraton, 1994; Shaw, 1999). These new understandings were argued to transcend "the dualism of sex differences by presenting the complexity of powerlessness, which some women and other 'disenleisured' groups confront in their daily lives" (Henderson, 1994, p. 129). During this period, leisure research began to overlap more congruently with the basic tenets of FST (see Henderson & Bialeschki, 1991; Henderson, Bialeschki, Shaw, & Freysinger, 1996; Henderson & Gardner, 1996), but was still relatively behind other disciplines, particularly in its theoretical and methodological approach. Aitchison (2000) contends leisure focused on generating theory and research from within our own field. As such, cross-fertilization between other disciplines was limited, thereby limiting the enrichment of our own theoretical and methodological base by failing to capitalize on advances in other disciplines and areas of study (i.e., sociology, geography, cultural studies, and gender studies) (Coalter, 1997).

In the 21st century, the convergence of leisure studies with broader bodies of knowledge has allowed for the emergence of more critical explorations into the intersections of social justice and leisure experiences (e.g., Aitchison, 2000, 2003, 2005; Chesser, 2017; Klitzing, 2000, 2003; 2004; Yuen, 2008). As a result, scholars engaging in social justice research in our field are now able to merge various transformative approaches in their projects (Parry, Johnson, & Stewart, 2013; Stewart, 2014). Moreover, feminist leisure researchers are now better able to explore leisure in relation to social inequalities, power, ideology, and white hegemony (Arai & Kivel, 2009). Parry's (2007) decision to engage in mutual disclosure when interviewing breast cancer survivors, for example, can be understood as an act of *strong objectivity*. Though Parry (2007) does take up the language of *strong objectivity*, she took this course of action in hopes of facilitating opportunities for "the women to discuss their own stories and explain their own encounters grounding the knowledge gained in their lived experiences" (Parry, 2007, p. 55). As such, it is evident that certain tenets of FST have become implicit in our field.

Moving forward, our field would benefit from the *explicit* application of FST. In doing so, we cut across traditionally isolated strands of research within our own field (e.g., gender, race, ethnicity, heteronormativity, sexual identity – see Stewart, 2014), *and* venture out of the leisure research silo, addressing Aitchison's (2000) criticism of our field's inward focus. Furthermore, FST will lead to new understandings and knowledges, which may in turn create a political consciousness that inspires and activates social justice.

While FST have its advantages, it is not without its controversies. In the following section, I explore some of the tensions within FST. My experience with *Journey Women* is presented as an example of how these tensions can be negotiated.

Tensions or challenges within the theoretical perspective

In this section, I present three tensions and challenges of FST: (1) multiple perspectives, (2) essentialism; and (3) the lack of epistemological and ontological guidance. The first tension is acknowledged and reconciled, while the latter two challenges are acknowledged and argued to require further consideration. More specifically, I discuss decolonizing methodologies, a subset of Indigenous methodologies (Kovach, 2009), as an ontological and epistemological paradigm to ground the methodological framework of FST.

Multiple perspectives

A main critique of FST is their lack of clarity and focus. The issue of clarity and focus arises from FST's acknowledgement of multiple perspectives. However, as Hekman (1997) highlights, abandoning *the* feminist standpoint risks abandoning the point of feminist analysis and politics, which she argues to be "revealing the oppression of 'women' and arguing for a less repressive society" (p. 351). In other words, social change requires acknowledging multiple perspectives. This core tenet highlights ones of the ways in which FST is useful for advancing social justice issues (Kourany, 2009; Moreton-Robinson, 2013). Within the process of revealing difference and power structures, FST helps "to produce oppositional and shared consciousness of oppressed groups" (Harding, 2009, p. 3). Crasnow (2009) explains, "the resulting plurality is itself a resource rather than a liability" (p. 190). Multiple perspectives create multiples knowledges, which become valuable resources to social justice movements (Harding, 2004). The creation of shared consciousness has the potential to lead to the development of multiple strategies for social justice. Though these strategies may sometimes be in opposition, the widespread generation of critical ideas is considered essential to social transformation.

FST operates from the assumption that the perspectives of non-Indigenous women and Indigenous men can only offer us a partial understanding of the world. In this context, the *Journey Women* project offered a platform for Indigenous women to share their healing stories. This is important, as Amadahy (2006) states: "[a]ttitudes, teachings and practices in our Aboriginal communities ... negate, deny and discourage community support for women's voices" (p. 152). Embracing the stories of Indigenous women does not invalidate past research or other visions for change (Harding, 1991). Rather, it is an acknowledgement that differences in culture amongst women, especially in relation to experiences of colonization, bring about different approaches to change.

Essentialism

Another critique of FST is the perpetuation of *one* subjugated female experience (Flax, 1990; Hekman, 1997). Researchers have tried to overcome this critique by incorporating issues of intersectionality (Doucet & Mauthner, 2006; Hill-Collins, 2009; Olesen, 2000). However, much of the mainstream feminist theory remains within the Eurocentric conceptual framework (Parashar, 2000). While a substantial body of work continues to acknowledge and privilege women of colour, race continues to be conceptualized most often through a binary black–white paradigm (Hall, 2009). As Hall (2009) articulates:

> The insights of ... black feminist thought have been crucial to the development of my critical consciousness even as these theorists often displayed the same kinds of omissions and erasures (in this case, directed toward non-black women of color in general and indigenous women in particular) that they brilliantly critiqued within the work of white scholars.
>
> (p. 16)

While there are diverging opinions in Indigenous communities, there is a struggle to find a recognition of Indigenous perspectives within feminist research, and subsequently, a strong stance against the (white) feminist movement. Grey (2004) suggests the absence of Indigenous perspectives may explain why so few Indigenous women self-identify as feminist.

At the onset of *Journey Women*, it became clear to me that colonialism needed to be explored in explicit ways (see Green, 2007; Koshan, 2009). As such, I looked to decolonizing methodologies as a way of emphasizing colonized experiences. Employing FST alone does not necessarily bring colonization to the forefront. To simply regard identity for Indigenous women as one of sexism or marginalization ignores how "constant colonial incursions in Native spaces generate almost unimaginable levels of violence, which includes, but is not restricted to, sexist oppression" (Lawrence, 2003, p. 5). In the same regard, Indigenous feminism is first and foremost about understanding the current conditions marked by colonization (Maracle, 1996). The material and discursive impacts of colonization, such as sexual assault, domestic abuse, and substance-dependence, as well as racist representations, have become the norm in some Indigenous communities (Macdonald, 2017; Maracle, 1996). The application of Indigenous methodologies allows for this violence to be connected to the processes of colonization. As such, engaging FST with a decolonizing approach supports both feminist and colonized perspectives.

Lack of epistemological and ontological direction

While FST influence methodology, scholars have questioned if and how a standpoint approach influences the epistemological and ontological underpinnings of feminist research (Harding, 2009; Houle, 2009; Moreton-Robinson, 2013). As Houle (2009) contends, FST provide a methodological approach to research, but offer little guidance in terms of how we analyze the data, and what we do with the understanding and knowledge produced. She highlights this absence with the following questions: "Presumably the idea is not to begin with, extract from, but then leave outside, this stranger? Presumably not to begin at, but leave intact, that margin?" (p. 175). In other words, FST provide little insight for how to engage participants in the research process, and how to mobilize the new-found knowledge for social change. These challenges can be exemplified with FST's requirement for strong objectivity and a search for the limitations of dominant conceptions of method and explanation that suppress and distort our understandings. Action is supposed to be taken to mitigate the limitations, but precisely what kinds of action? Mediating this lack of methodological guidance from FST provides an example where merging FST with another critical theory such as Indigenous methodologies, which has stronger epistemological foundation, is beneficial.

In the *Journey Women* project, my concern related to privileging Western notions of explanation and understanding was guided, in part, by FST. As Saulteaux and Nêhiýaw scholar Kovach (2009) highlights, much of our knowledge has been created through a colonial lens – privileging written work and understanding experiences as separate, polarizing, and/or dichotomizing entities. With this in mind, my decision to use arts-based methods of analysis and representation was influenced by decolonizing methodologies, which strive to counter the colonial influence in the production of knowledge (Kovach, 2009).

While some scholars are moving forward with the idea of FST as resources for feminist epistemology (Crasnow, 2009; Rolin, 2009), I move towards integrating FST with other critical theories and methodologies, which are more explicitly connected to an ontological and epistemological paradigm. This integration resonates with Parry et al.'s (2013) suggestion that engaging in social justice research creates the potential for alternative perspectives, and inspires innovative ideas for social change.

Seeing things differently

> Turning old stories into something new.
> (Roberta, *Journey Woman*)

Roberta's quote calls attention to *Journey Women* as a project that transformed Indigenous women's stories of shame and trauma into stories of strength, courage, and resilience. Similarly, my own story as a leisure researcher was changed by engaging in this project. FST created a methodological foundation that led to a transformation in my own approaches to research. Specifically, I moved from privileging (1) theory-based to relational knowledge, and (2) rational to emotional ways of knowing. In the following section, I describe this transformation.

From privileging theory-based knowledge to relational knowledge

Western ways of knowing are grounded in rational, linear thought (Kovach, 2009). As Ngāti Awa and Ngāti Porou, Māori scholar Smith (1999) suggests, Western notions of understanding are based upon measuring, comparing, and evaluating. Classification, hierarchical ranking, and categorical systems of representation are examples of how colonized knowledge is produced and reproduced (Smith, 1999). The idea of relational knowledge stems from Opaskwayak Cree scholar Wilson (2001), who argues: "relationships are more important than reality" (p. 177). He explains "our systems of knowledge are built on the relationships that we have, not just with people or objects, but relationship that we have with the cosmos, with ideas, concepts, and everything around us" (p. 177). Through the *Journey Women* project, my knowledges became built upon various relationships including: the incarcerated Indigenous women I worked with while doing my PhD (a main inspiration for *Journey Women*); the stories, interviews, and body maps created by the artists; the fire that was lit every day of the workshop; the prayers; the drum; the collaborators of the *Journey Women* project (art therapist, artists, executive directors, Elders, counsellors, Indigenous research advisor); and books, articles, and other conventional academic forms of knowledge.

In accordance with FST, *Journey Women* was conceived on the margin – with Minwaashin Lodge and women who were a part of that organization. Collaborators helped guide the project's purpose, methods, analysis, and dissemination. FST also highlighted the need for me to ensure strong objectivity, ultimately contributing to a heightened personal awareness of the colonizing forces of academia. At the outset of this project, I was ready to engage in a reflexive journal, strive for transparency, and actively seek feedback from *Journey Women* collaborators. Little did I know this would be such a mind- and heart-opening experience, as the artists taught me to consider and remain accountable to "all my relations" (Wilson, 2001, p. 177). The process was tentative and slow, involved countless formal and informal conversations, meditation, and heartfelt vulnerability.

Following a preliminary analysis of the data with the artists (see Lu & Yuen, 2012a), I began using N-Vivo 10 to analyze the interviews in accordance with Strauss's (1987) open and axial coding process. In considering "all my relations," analyzing the data in this manner, where themes are further broken down or merged together, and quotations are used to illustrate the themes, no longer seemed appropriate. Pursing this conventional method of analysis went against the basic FST tenet of de-contextualizing the experiences and perspectives of the women. This issue of analysis led to a year-long period of paralysis in terms of conventional academic productivity, which was subsequently filled with relational engagement and newfound wisdom.

Eventually, with the guidance of *Journey Women* collaborators, I decided to use poetry to help analyze and represent the women's story of healing (see Sjollema & Yuen, 2017a). In short, FST created the methodological platform for the integration of my relational knowledge, which ended up guiding the epistemological trajectory of the project.

From privileging rational to emotional ways of knowing

Given one of the basic tenets of FST is privileging the situated knowledges of those who live on the margins, I was compelled to find ways that appropriately, adequately, and authentically represented the information that was shared during the *Journey Women* project. As such, art was used as the medium to convey emotional understanding, because of its ability to capture the emotional aspect and complexity of lived experiences, which is often removed from conventional methods of data analysis and representation (Sjollema & Yuen, 2017a). FST helped me see that the emotions of the artists' body maps, and the stories that emerged, were vital in helping me to understand the women's experiences of healing. As mentioned in the previous section, my engagement with strong objectivity contributed to the use of artistic mediums of analysis and representation in the *Journey Women* project, specifically poetry (Sjollema & Yuen, 2017a, 2017b) and collage (Yuen, 2016). Moreover, I facilitated *Journey Women* presentations at academic conferences that incorporated drama (Lu & Yuen, 2012b), stories, poems, and video clips (Lu, Yuen, & Della Pica, 2016; Yuen, 2016).

Alongside decolonizing methodologies, FST highlighted the importance of privileging emotions because of its recognition that knowledge is tied to power structures, particularly the colonial influence in the production of knowledge. As such, artistic mediums helped me move beyond Western notions of knowing with its fluid, metaphoric, symbolic, and interpretive modes of inquiry – which are more in line with Indigenous ways of knowing (Kovach, 2009). One image in a collage or one line in a poem can lead to the emergence of multivocal understandings. In other words, what begins as a single metaphor can produce multiple metaphors and understandings (see Yuen, 2016). For example, the first stanza in a poem that was created by myself and a research assistant to represent one artist's healing journey (full poem later on this section), "With women, warm and embracing," contains the two lines:

> to be given
> permission

The artist, Lisa, used these words to describe the workshop and art exhibit experience from the standpoint of a single mother. As she stated:

> My child care was taken care of [childcare subsidies were available], my food was taken care of for those three days [meals and snacks were offered during the workshop], I didn't have to pay for any of the materials, you know? I was just asked to come and be there and just be present.

When I shared these two lines of the poem with her, I expressed concern that readers might understand it to mean something related to her colonized past (as opposed to her experience as a single mother). Lisa agreed that her words could stem from her history of colonization and reiterated the meanings of her "mask of shame" in her body map. She had first shared this explanation while describing her body map during the workshop:

> When I became a teenager, my parents separated, and I was put through a lot of abuse as a teenager … My mother's side of the family, we do have Native heritage. But we were not allowed to talk about it. It's something we were told not to expose.

Lisa felt that she needed permission to participate in advocacy for multiple reasons. The original statement can be understood from the standpoint of a single mother; however, upon further reading, consideration, and discussions about the stanza, alternative understandings came to light – all of which were representative of her experience. Further, new understandings will arise as arts-based methods of representation are used to encourage readers to develop their own interpretations (Parry & Johnson, 2007). These understandings, which are arguably more meaningful to the reader, have the potential to spark action for social justice.

Advancing feminist social justice

Journey Women's arts-based methods of representation contain an emotional currency that contributed to the development of a political consciousness with the group during the body mapping workshop, as well as with the greater community during the public art exhibit. Understanding, seeing, and feeling though the body maps created a message that was accessible and provided a platform for advocacy, education, and public discourse (see Yuen, 2016). In the following section, I use poetry as a form of creative analytic practice (CAP) to represent the women's experiences of engaging social justice.

For this project, I engaged in CAP to capture and emphasize the artists' emotional experience of social justice. Berbary (2011) suggests CAP provides an opportunity to show rather then tell readers about complex experiences. CAP also "encourages involvement, inspires curiosity, creates inclusivity, and constructs depictions that remain in the thoughts of readers in ways that traditional representations sometimes do not" (Berbary, 2011, p. 194). My research assistant (who is a well-versed poet) and I created the poem below based on semi-structured conversations I had with the artists following their experiences of the workshop and art exhibit.

Even though the poems in the *Journey Women* project were created using direct quotes from the women, the poems were purposefully created to represent the artists' experiences of advocacy. According to Cannella and Manuelito (2008), decolonizing science deliberately refutes the "Eurocentric assumption (error) that some human beings have the power to 'know' others … but would rather acknowledge and focus on the complexities of our … conditions(s)" (p. 49). In this regard, the poem presented below is not meant to represent the "truth" about Indigenous women's experiences of social justice, but a moment of reflection in an ever-changing "*dance around the circle*."

As previously mentioned, CAP acknowledges multiple interpretations and encourages readers to form their own understandings (Parry & Johnson, 2007).

Here, I offer my own interpretation of Indigenous women's experiences of social justice and the premise on which the poem was created. As the title of the poem below reflects, social justice for *Journey Women* was a collective experience. Further, the process is not about "fighting" for social justice or fuelled by anger or hostility – provocative, perhaps, but always supportive and empowering. This being said, I also encourage you to form your own understandings, based on your own experiences, perspectives, emotions, and engagement with the poem.

With women, warm and embracing[3]
being with
the other women
they need to let it out
to be given
permission
to do it

Somebody:
strong and brave,
beautiful, creative

how empowering
we feel towards each other
nobody is putting you down
atmosphere's safe
familiar face
loving and embracing
women, warm
supporting and lifting us up

look at what we can do
with a little support

I felt a part
of something
chance to be seen
I'm ready and willing
I can share that
beautiful person
the courage to tell
to be an example

being
an Indian and a woman
and an artist and survivor
being strong and brave

As the *Journey Women* project continues to evolve, new understandings and processes for healing and decolonization will come to light. In the next section, I explore potential pathways for action within fourth wave feminisms.

Engaging with fourth wave feminisms

As you read this section, you may (and should) sense some tension. At times, I overuse the words *may* and *perhaps*, which serves a purpose and is intentional. Phrases such as noting the "requirement" of inspiring action and social justice, and "inserting" fourth wave feminism into the discussion are used when discussing Indigenous movements (Missing and Murdered Indigenous Women and Idle no More) and the *Journey Women* project. The reason for this tension is because I fear this chapter could be interpreted as "we are, yet again, trying to force a square peg in a round hole, or a round peg in a square hole." The framing of feminist research in a timeline and in sequential order (first, second, third, and now fourth wave) does not fit with Indigenous ways of knowing, which encompass fluidity, metaphor, symbolism, and interpretive communication (Kovach, 2009). Inserting Indigenous perspectives into a certain wave involves separating and polarizing pieces of work – a process characteristic of the Western tradition. Recognizing this tension, I continued to move forward with writing this chapter, because ideas and knowledge are not static, nor are they meant to be owned (Wilson, 2001). The tenets of fourth wave feminisms might have something to contribute to the *Journey Women* project and the potential is lost if there is no pause for consideration.

My experience with the artists involved in *Journey Women* suggests that their work was not about tapping into emotional synergy through technology (a major theme of fourth wave feminism) in hopes that their message would be transferred and mobilized amongst wider groups. Rather, upon answering my questions about their motivation to participate, the women were explicitly clear that they were speaking out through the art exhibit for themselves and other Indigenous women. Furthermore, when I asked the women if they were interested in participating in other forms of dissemination (i.e., conference presentations, co-authorship in articles and book chapters), the women clearly indicated they were choosing not to participate in some aspects of the project, namely, dissemination through written works in the academic sphere.

While the focus of *Journey Women* artists was inward, for themselves and other Indigenous women, it, admittedly, is my hope for *Journey Women*'s message to be shared within, as well as outside, Indigenous communities. For these reasons, I put research and dissemination funds towards the development of a *Journey Women* website (www.journeywomen.ca). We (*Journey Women* collaborators) are not entirely sure about the purpose of this website. Beyond dissemination, the purpose of this website remains to be seen. Nonetheless, the platform is there and maybe it will move to fit with the fourth wave rhetoric, or maybe not.

Technology and the roles of emotions

The consideration of fourth wave feminism reinforces the use of art for social change as its emotional currency contributes to the *affective intensity* of the fourth wave. Chamberlain (2016) uses the concept of affective temporality to highlight how social movements in the wave narratives are bound to emotional convergences, where feeling becomes transferred amongst wider groups, encouraging them to action. The role of affect is particularly powerful in fourth wave feminism, given its reliance on technology to fuel activism and inspire rapid mobilization (Chamberlain, 2016). As I will now discuss, it seems likely the emotions conveyed in photographs, songs, videos, and other art forms posted on Facebook, Twitter, YouTube, and other forms of communication via the internet, may have been powerful and catalytic in expanding the momentum and scope of two recent Indigenous movements in Canada: Missing and Murdered Indigenous Women and Girls (MMIW) and Idle no More.

MMIWG

The MMIWG movement can be traced back to 2002, when Amnesty International Canada, KAIROS, Elizabeth Fry Society, and United Anglican Church formed the National Coalition for our Stolen Sisters (Native Women's Association of Canada, n.d.). Since the creation of this coalition, reports such as *Stolen Sisters*[4] and *Sisters in Spirit*[5] have been published, a national round table on MMIWG has been established, the TRC's (2015b) calls to action have been shared, and a national inquiry into MMIWG was launched by the Canadian government in May 2017. In addition to traditional political actions, individuals began to create online "contact spaces," where "diverse activist-participants join together in political advocacy and community-building" – most often on sites like Facebook, Twitter, and Tumblr (Saramo, 2016, p. 210). #MMIWG, #Stolen Sisters, #ImNotNext, #AmINext were all fuelled by their visibility on these sites and carry messages aimed to educate, advocate, and mobilize action related to MMIWG.

The use of social media coincides with fourth wave feminists and their use of technology as a form of communication and mobilization (Chamberlain, 2016). For example, #AmINext was created by an Inuit woman named Holly Jarrett, whose cousin, Lorretta Saunders, was murdered in 2014 (Thompson, 2014). Jarrett's intention behind the campaign was to raise awareness and urge others to pressure the Canadian government for a public inquiry into MMIWG. Jarrett's hashtag became contextualized as many Indigenous women began posting pictures of themselves holding signs that read "#AmINext." That is, the overt political nature of these deeply personal posts appears to coincide with the socio-political-grassroots strategies that characterizes fourth wave feminism (Phillips & Cree, 2014).[6] When coupled with other forms of communication, such as newscasts and reports, social media has the potential to simultaneously support FST's tenet of situated and context-specific knowledges and facilitate the transformation of personal issues to political agendas.

Idle no More

Idle no More is another Indigenous movement that can be seen as an example of fourth wave feminism, as it gained momentum through various social media outlets. Founded in 2012 by four women (Jessica Gordon, Sylvia McAdam, Sheelah McLean, and Nina Wilson), Idle no More has become:

> One of the largest Indigenous mass movements in Canadian history … The National Day of Action on Dec. 10th, inspired thousands of people to action, committing themselves to ongoing resistance against neo-colonialism. In a few short months, Idle No More has become the center of media attention, drawing millions of people to our websites, twitter account and face book pages [sic] every day.
>
> (Idle no More, n.d., paras. 1–2)

In this context, Idle No More is an example of the instant, fast-paced, dialogue-inducing encounter that characterizes the fourth wave of feminism (Chamberlain, 2016). A notable moment early in this movement occurred when Chief Theresa Spence of the Attawapiskat First Nation went on a six-week hunger strike under the Idle no More banner and received nationwide media attention (CBC News, 2013). This hunger strike precipitated what Chamberlain (2016) calls "an explosion of the personal," as thousands of individual acts of Indigenous resistance soon followed (p. 463). In this way, Idle no More is characteristic of the fourth wave as it encompasses both online feminism and embodied activism.[7]

Intersectionality, globalization, and Indigenous women's issues

As emphasized by Munro (2013), intersectionality remains a key concern in the fourth wave. FST provide a strong methodological platform to help ensure that experiences of marginalization are understood beyond gender. Engaging in fourth wave feminism may contribute to increased knowledges about varying intersections of oppression as Indigenous communities around the world connect through the internet *and* simultaneously create global awareness, understandings, and action for social justice.

In the past, little attention has been given to Indigenous women's perspectives. Most often, issues related to land claims and self-government took priority over health and social issues, such as the overwhelmingly high rates of prostitution and violence against Indigenous women (Canadian Panel on Violence

Against Women, 1993). Until recently, the devastating numbers of missing and murdered Indigenous women in Canada were largely invisible. As the *Journey Women* project highlights, engaging FST within fourth wave feminism allows researchers to privilege Indigenous women's issues. By privileging an emotional discourse, FST can amplify feminist-Indigenous perspectives and activate global movements.

The centrality of emotion to movements like MMIWG and Idle No More compounds the importance of relationality and necessitates a process of social justice that recognizes one's liberation is always bound to the liberation of others. This pathway to justice resonates with a process described by Kanien'keha:ka scholar Alfred (2005) as "*Wasáse*, the Thunder Dance: a ceremony of unity, strength, and commitment to action" (p. 19). *Wasáse* is a spiritual revolution that offers an ethical and political vision for Indigenous peoples. He describes *Wasáse* as a "culturally rooted *social* movement that transforms the whole of society and a *political* action that seeks to remake the entire landscape of power and relationship to reflect truly a liberated post-imperial vision" (p. 27; emphasis in original).

As I learned through the *Journey Women* project, FST allow researchers to engage in ways of knowing (affect) that have the potential to contribute to the fourth wave of feminism, particularly in terms of using technology as a way of creating a collective emotional and political consciousness. For a brief moment, I ventured, very tentatively, to consider two Indigenous movements as possible examples of fourth wave feminism due to the traction gained using social media platforms. It is possible that *Journey Women* will begin to use social media platforms for dissemination and mobilization, and engaging with a fourth wave feminist perspective may offer some insight – or not. One thing is clear: *Journey Women* collaborators want to advocate *with women, warm and embracing*. FST offer a particular methodological approach to understand this experience, and the arts-based medium/method that was used in the project evoked emotional responses within the artists and their audience. Whether this project becomes a part of fourth wave feminism remains to be seen.

In the final section of this chapter, I continue the discussion around the dilemma associated with FST lack of epistemological direction. While incorporating decolonizing methodologies in the *Journey Women* project helped me to navigate issues related to data analysis and representation, I continue to have questions about my role as a researcher and, more specifically, what I should do, if anything, with the knowledge that was co-created with the artists.

Unfinished business

I wish to acknowledge that the art exhibit as a vehicle for social justice is my own interpretation of the experience. That is, it is my own observation that the art exhibit inspired and activated a desire to engage in decolonization by sharing Indigenous women's experiences of healing (acknowledging the impacts of colonization), while collectively celebrating their strength and courage. This observation is based on my own reactions to the exhibit, feedback from members of the public who attended, and the comments made during subsequent radio and television show interviews.

Finally, FST offered an appropriate methodology to understand Indigenous women's experiences of healing during data analysis for the *Journey Women* project. As I move forward with the project, however, I am left wondering about my role as researcher. FST do not offer a clear perspective for what I am to do with the understanding gained through the *Journey Women* project. As previously mentioned, the *Journey Women* artists' motivation to participate was largely influenced by a desire to share their stories of healing with other Indigenous women – *not* to educate the general public about colonization and be a part of a decolonizing movement. Comparable to experiences of Indigenous women in prison, the artists' experience required emotional labour and contributed to their healing (Yuen, 2011). Unlike the experiences of Indigenous women in prison, however, this experience was not to explicitly resist the oppressive structures related to their colonization (Yuen & Pedlar, 2009). Further discussion with *Journey Women* collaborators is required to explore if and how resistance happens.

While I have written about the methodology of the *Journey Women* project (Sjollema & Yuen, 2017a, 2017b; Yuen, 2016), I have not yet written about what impact the findings from the project might have on leisure studies. Some questions I continue to struggle with are as follows: If we decolonize our leisure practices, what would they look like? Should we leave "leisure" as a Western entity that does not fit within Indigenous discourses? What if the requirements of academia (which are still grounded within the dominant discourse) conflict with the (marginalized) understandings, values, and knowledges of our collaborators? Decolonizing methodologies continues to ground any action in decolonization, but still, what the decolonizing process looks like is not clear. One thing is certain. However. The answers lie in *all my relations*, which will require more time, reflection, discussions, and, in accordance with FST, it will require engaging in strong objectivity and honouring the perspectives of *Journey Women* collaborators.

Borrowing from Freire (2006), social justice requires both reflection and action. In addition to critically reflecting upon important ontological and epistemological assumptions, mobilization is necessary, whether it be through art exhibits, tweeting, Facebooking, YouTubing, blogging, political rallies, or academic dissemination. Engaging in FST will undoubtedly help our field explore and create meaningful approaches for action. I conclude this chapter with an excerpt from the poem "Seeking justice missing and murdered Native women," written by Algonquin-Huron-Métis scholar Monchalin (2014):

> Attend a vigil or say a prayer
> But please, don't just walk away or simply stare
> (p. 155)

Notes

1 *Indigenous* is a term used to represent the original people of the land. In Canada, *Native*, *Aboriginal*, and *Indigenous* are all terms that have replaced *Indian*, which encompasses people who identify as First Nations, Métis, and Inuit. While Indigenous is most used throughout this chapter, the application of other terms is based on the original source.
2 When discussing those who were involved in the *Journey Women* project, the conventional term *participants* is replaced with *women*, *collaborators*, and/or *artists*.
3 See Sjollema and Yuen (2017b) for an earlier version of this poem.
4 See www.amnesty.ca/sites/amnesty/files/amr200032004enstolensisters.pdf
5 See www.nwac.ca/wp-content/uploads/2015/05/Fact_Sheet_Missing_and_Murdered_Aboriginal_Women_and_Girls.pdf
6 While these posts may appear to reflect fourth wave feminisms, I am not necessarily assuming that individuals hashtagging their posts identify themselves as feminists.
7 Notably, neither Idle no More or MMIWG label themselves as feminist movements, or Indigenous feminist movements for that matter (see Green, 2007; Suzack, 2015).

References

Aitchison, C. (2000). Poststructural feminist theories of representing Others: A response to the "crisis" in leisure studies' discourse. *Leisure Studies, 19*(3) 127–144. doi:10.1080/02614360050023044

Aitchison, C. C. (2003). *Gender and leisure: Social and cultural perspectives*. London: Routledge.

Aitchison, C. C. (2005). Feminist and gender perspectives in tourism studies: The social-cultural nexus of critical and cultural theories. *Tourist Studies*, *5*(3), 207–224.

Alfred, T. (2005). *Wasáse: Indigenous pathways of action and freedom*. Peterborough, ON, Canada: Broadview Press.

Amadahy, Z. (2006). The healing power of women's voices. In K. Anderson & B. Lawrence (Eds.), *Strong women stories, Native vision and community survival* (3rd ed.) (pp. 144–155). Toronto, ON: Sumach Press.

Arai, S., & Kivel, B. D. (2009). Critical race theory and social justice perspectives on whiteness, difference(s) and (anti)racism: A fourth wave of race research in leisure studies. *Journal of Leisure Research*, *41*(4), 459–472.

Berbary, L. A. (2011). Post-structural writerly representation: Screenplay as creative analytic practice. *Qualitative Inquiry*, *17*(2), 186–196.

Canadian Panel on Violence Against Women. (1993). *Aboriginal women: From the final report of the Canadian panel on violence against women*. Ottawa, ON: Government of Canada.

Cannella, G. S., & Manuelito, K. D. (2008). Feminisms from unthought locations: Indigenous worldviews, marginalized feminisms, and revisioning an anticolonial social science. In N. K. Denzin, Y. S. Lincoln, & L. T. Smith (Eds.), *Handbook of critical and Indigenous methodologies* (pp. 45–59). Los Angeles: Sage.

CBC News. (2013, January 23). *Chief Theresa Spence to end hunger strike today*. Retrieved from www.cbc.ca/news/politics/chief-theresa-spence-to-end-hunger-strike-today-1.1341571

Chamberlain, P. (2016). Affective temporality: towards a fourth wave. *Gender and Education*, *28*(3), 458–464. doi:10.1080/09540253.2016.1169249

Chesser, S. (2017). Diapers and dissertations: An exploration of doctoral and postdoctoral trainee decision-making surrounding first-time parenthood. Retrieved from: uwspace.uwaterloo.ca/handle/10012/11148

Coalter, F. (1997). Leisure sciences and leisure studies: different concept, same crisis? *Leisure Sciences*, *19*(4), 255–268.

Crasnow, S. (2009). Is standpoint theory a resource for feminist epistemology? An introduction. *Hypatia*, *24*(4), 189–192. doi:10.1111/j.1527–2001.2009.01066.x

Doucet, A., & Mauthner, N. (2006). Feminist methodologies and epistemologies. In C. D. Bryant & D. L. Peck (Eds.), *Handbook of 21st century sociology* (pp. 26–32). Thousand Oaks, CA: Sage.

Duran, E., & Duran, B. (1995). *Native American postcolonial psychology*. Albany: State University of New York Press.

Flax, J. (1990). Postmodernism and gender relations in feminist theory. In L. Nicholson (Ed.), *Feminist/postmodernism* (pp. 39–62). New York, NY: Routledge.

Fox, K. (2006). Leisure and indigenous peoples. *Leisure Studies*, *25*(4), 403–409.

Freire, P. (2006). *Pedagogy of hope*. New York, NY: Continuum.

Green, J. (2007b). Taking account of Aboriginal feminism. In J. Green (Ed.), *Making Space for Indigenous feminism* (pp. 20–32). Winnipeg: Fernwood Publishing.

Grey, S. (2004). Decolonising feminism: Aboriginal women and the Global "sisterhood." *Enweyin*, *8*, 9–22.

Hall, L. K. (2009). Navigating our own "sea of islands": Remapping a theoretical space for Hawaiian women and Indigenous feminism. *Wicazo Sa Review*, *24*(2), 15–38.

Harding, S. (1991). *Whose science? Whose knowledge? Thinking for women's lives*. Ithaca, NY: Cornell University Press.

Harding, S. (1992). Rethinking standpoint epistemology: What is "strong objectivity"? *Centennial Review*, *36*(3), 437–470.

Harding, S. (Ed.). (1993). *The "racial" economy of science: Toward a democratic future*. Tuscaloosa: Indiana University Press.

Harding, S. (2004). Introduction: Standpoint theory as a site of political, philosophical, and scientific debate. In S. Harding (Ed.), *The feminist standpoint theory reader: Intellectual and political controversies*. New York, NY: Routledge.

Harding, S. (2009). Standpoint theories: Productively controversial. *Hypatia*, *24*(4), 192–200.

Hartstock, N. (2004). The feminist standpoint: Developing the ground for a specifically feminist historical materialism. In S. Harding (Ed.), *The feminist standpoint theory reader: Intellectual and political controversies* (pp 35–54). New York, NY: Routledge.

Hekman, S. (1997). Truth and method: Feminist standpoint theory revisited. *Signs*, *22*(2), 341–365.

Henderson, K. A. (1994). Perspectives on analyzing gender, women, and leisure. *Journal of Leisure Research*, *26*(2), 119–137.

Henderson, K. A., & Bialeschki, M. D. (1991). A sense of entitlement to leisure as constraint and empowerment for women. *Leisure Sciences*, *13*(1), 51–65.

Henderson, K. A., Bialeschki, M. D., Shaw, S. M., & Freysinger, V. J. (1996). *Both gains and gaps: Feminist perspectives on women's leisure*. State College: Venture Publishing, Inc.

Henderson, K. A., & Gardner, J. M. (1996). Claiming control: The recovering alcoholic woman and leisure. *Leisure Sciences*, *18*, 241–258.

Henderson, K. A., & Gibson, H. (2013). An integrative review of women, gender, and leisure: Increasing complexitie. *Journal of Leisure Research*, *45*(2), 115–135.

Hill-Collins, P. H. (2009). Defining Black feminist thought. In C. R. McCann & S. K. Kim (Eds.), *Feminist theory reader* (2nd ed.) (pp. 341–356). New York, NY: Routledge.

Houle, K. (2009). Making strange: Deconstruction and feminist standpoint theory. *Frontiers: A Journal of Women Studies*, *30*(1), 172–193.

Idle no More. (n.d.). *The story*. Retrieved from www.idlenomore.ca/story

King, S. J. (2008). What's queer about queer sociology now? A review essay. *Sociology of Sport Journal*, *25*, 419–442.

Klitzing, S. W. (2000). Leisure and women who are homeless: An exploratory study, Unpublished doctoral dissertation, University of Illiinois at Urbana-Champaign, Champaign, Ilinois.

Klitzing, S. W. (2003). Coping with chronic stress: Leisure and women who are homeless, *Leisure Sciences*, *25*(2–3), 163–181. doi:10.1080/01490400306564

Klitzing, S. W. (2004). Women living in a homeless shelter: Stress, coping and leisure. *Journal of Leisure Research*, *36*(4), 483–512.

Koshan, J. (2009). Making space for indigenous feminism (review). *Canadian Journal of Law and Society*, *24*(1), 134–136.

Kourany, J. A. (2009), The place of standpoint theory in feminist science studies. *Hypatia*, *24*(4), 209–218. doi:10.1111/j.1527–2001.2009.01069.x

Kovach, M. (2009). *Indigenous methodologies – Characters, conversations, and contexts*. Toronto, ON: University of Toronto Press.

Lawrence, B. (2003). Gender, race, and the regulation of native identity in Canada and the United States: An overview. *Hypatia*, *18*(2), 3–31.

Lu, L., & Yuen, F. (2012a). Journey Women: Art therapy in a decolonizing framework of practice. *The Arts in Psychotherapy*, *39*, 192–200.

Lu, L., & Yuen, F. (2012b). *Journey Women: Decolonization, social change and social justice*. Paper presented at International Conference on Gender, Health, and the Creative Art Therapies, Montreal, Quebec, May 5–6.

Lu, L., Yuen, F., & Della Pica, R. (2016). *Journeying through body-mapping: Decolonizing art therapy and research*. Paper presented at Ontario and Canadian Art Therapy Association Combined conference, Art therapy and Anti-Oppressive practice, Toronto, ON, October 15.

Macdonald, N. (2017). "It could have been me." *Maclean's*. Retrieved from site.macleans.ca/longform/almost-missing/

Maracle, L. (1996). *I am woman, a Native perspective on sociology and feminism*. Vancouver, BC: Press Gang Publishers.

Mohanty, C. T. (2003). Under western eyes: Feminist scholarship and colonial discourses. In. R. Lewis & S. Mills (Eds.), *Feminist postcolonial theory* (pp. 49–74). Edinburgh, UK: Edinburgh University Press.

Monchalin, L. (2014). Seeking justice for missing and murdered Native women. *Radical Criminology*, *4*, 149–154.

Moreton-Robinson, A. (2013). Towards an Australian Indigenous women's standpoint theory: A methodological tool. *Australian Feminist Studies*, *28*(78), 331–347.

Munro, E. (2013). Feminism: A fourth wave? *Political Insight*, *4*(2), 22–25.

Naidu, M. (2010). Wrestling with standpoint theory … some thoughts on standpoint and African feminism. *Agenda*, *24*(83), 24–35.

Native Women's Association of Canada (2015). *You are not alone: A toolkit for Aboriginal women escaping domestic violence*. Retrieved from www.nwac.ca/wpcontent/uploads/2015/05/Fact_Sheet_Missing_and_Murdered_Ab original_Women_and_Girls.pdf

Native Women's Association of Canada (n.d.). *Missing and murdered Indigenous women and girls a national crisis*. Retrieved from www.nwac.ca/mmiwg/

Olesen, V. L. (2000). Feminism and qualitative research at and into the millennium. In N. K. Denzin & Y. S. Lincoln (Eds.), *Handbook of qualitative research* (2nd ed.) (pp. 215–256). Thousand Oaks, CA: Sage Publications.

Parashar, A. (2000). Exclusions and the voices of the excluded. *Australian Journal of Legal Philosophy*, *25*(2), 323–332.

Parry, D. C. (2007). "There is life after breast cancer": Nine vignettes exploring dragon boat racing for breast cancer survivors. *Leisure Sciences*, *29*(1), 53–69.

Parry, D. C., & Johnson. C. W. (2007). Contextualizing leisure research to encompass complexity in lived leisure experience: The need for creative analytic practice. *Leisure Sciences*, *29*(2), 119–130.

Parry, D. C., Johnson, C. W., & Stewart, W. (2013). Leisure research for social justice: A response to Henderson. *Leisure Sciences*, *35*(1), 81–87.

Phillips, R., & Cree, V. E. (2014). What does the "Fourth Wave" mean for teaching feminism in twenty-first century social work? *Social Work Education*, *33*(7), 930–943. doi:10.1080/02615479.2014.885007

Razack, S. H. (1998). *Looking white people in the eye*. Toronto, ON: University of Toronto Press.

Rolin, K. (2009). Standpoint theory as a methodology for the study of power relations. *Hypatia*, *24*(4), 218–226. doi:10.1111/j.1527-2001.2009.01070.x

Saramo, S. (2016). Unsettling spaces: Grassroots responses to Canada's missing and murdered Indigenous women during the Harper government years. *Comparative American Studies: An International Journal*, *14*(3–4), 204–220. doi:10.1080/14775700.2016.1267311

Scraton, S. (1994). The changing world of women and leisure: "post-feminism" and "leisure." *Leisure Studies*, *13*(4), 249–261.

Shaw, S. (1999). Gender and leisure. In T. Burton & E. Jackson (Eds), *Leisure studies: Prospects for the 21st century* (pp. 271–281). State College, PA: Venture Publishing Inc.

Sinclair, R. (2007). Lost and found: Lessons from the sixties scoop. *First People's Child and Family Review*, *3*(1), 65–82.

Sjollema, S., & Yuen, F. (2017a). Evocative words and ethical crafting: Poetic representation in leisure research. *Leisure Sciences*, *39*(5), 109–125.

Sjollema, S., & Yuen, F. (2017b). Poetic representation, reflexivity and the recursive turn. In P. Shameshima, A. Fidyk, K. James., & C. Leggo (Eds.), *Poetic inquiry enchantment of place* (pp. 59–68). Wilmingon, DE: Vernon Press.

Smith, D. E. (1987). *The everyday world as problematic: A feminist sociology*. Toronto, ON: University of Toronto Press.

Smith, L. T. (1999). *Decolonizing methodologies*. New York, NY: Palgrave.

Spears, S. (2006). Strong spirit, fractured identity: An Ojibway adoptee's journey to wholeness. In K. Anderson & B. Lawrence (Eds.), *Strong women stories, Native vision and community survival* (3rd ed.) (pp. 81–94). Toronto, ON: Sumach Press.

Stewart, W. (2014) Leisure research to enhance social Justice, *Leisure Sciences*, *36*(4), 325–339. doi:10.1080/01490400.2014.916961

Strauss, A. L. (1987). Introduction. In *Analysis for social scientists* (pp. 22–39). Cambridge, NY: Cambridge University Press.

Suzack, C. (2015). Indigenous feminisms in Canada. *NORA – Nordic Journal of Feminist and Gender Research*, *23*(4), 261–274. doi:10.1080/08038740.2015.1104595

Thompson, A. (2014, September 13). *#AmINext aims to raise awareness about murdered aboriginal women*. CBC News. Retrieved from www.cbc.ca/news/canada/nova-scotia/aminext-aims-to-raise-awareness-about-murdered-aboriginal-women-1.2765405

Truth and Reconciliation Commission of Canada (2015a). *Summary of the final report of the Truth and Reconciliation Commission of Canada*. Retrieved from www.trc.ca/websites/trcinstitution/File/2015/Findings/Exec_Summary_2015_05_31_web_o.pdf

Truth and Reconciliation Commission of Canada (2015b). *Truth and Reconciliation Commission of Canada: Calls to action*. Retrieved from www.trc.ca/websites/trcinstitution/File/2015/Findings/Calls_to_Action_English2.pdf

"Wake up. The threat to our Indigenous women is Canada's problem" (2015, June 5). *Maclean's*. Retrieved from www.macleans.ca/news/canada/wake-up-the-threat-to-our-indigenous-women-is-canadas-problem/

Watson, B., & Scraton, S. J. (2013). Leisure studies and intersectionality. *Leisure Studies*, *329*(1), 35–47. doi:10.1080/02614367.2012.707677

Wesley-Esquimaux, C. (2006). The intergenerational transmission of historic trauma and grief. *Indigenous affairs*, 407. Retrieved from www.iwgia.org/iwgia_files_publications_files/IA_4_07.pdf#page=6

Wilson, S. (2001). What is indigenous research methodology? *Canadian Journal of Native Education*, *25*(2), 175–179.

Yuen, F. (2008). *Walking the Red Road: Aboriginal federally sentenced women's experiences in healing, empowerment, and re-creation*. Retrieved from uwspace.uwaterloo.ca/handle/10012/3590

Yuen, F. (2011). "I've never been so free in all my life": Healing through Aboriginal ceremonies in prison. *Leisure/Loisir*, special issue, *Leisure, Space, and Social Change*, *35*(2), 97–113.

Yuen, F. (2016). Collage: An arts-based method for analysis, representation, and social justice. *Journal of Leisure Research*, 48(4), 338–346.

Yuen, F., & Pedlar, A. (2009). Leisure as a context for Justice: Aboriginal women in prison and their experiences in ceremony. *Journal of Leisure Research*, special issue, *Critical Race Theory and Social Justice Perspectives on Whiteness, Difference(s) and (anti) racism in Leisure Studies*, *41*(4), 545–562.

Further reading

Crasnow, S. (2009). Is standpoint theory a resource for feminist epistemology? An introduction. *Hypatia*, *24*(4), 189–192. doi:10.1111/j.1527-2001.2009.01066.x

Doucet, A., & Mauthner, N. (2006). Feminist methodologies and epistemologies. In C. D. Bryant & D. L. Peck (Eds.), *Handbook of 21st century sociology* (pp. 26–32). Thousand Oaks, CA: Sage.

Green, J. (Ed.) (2007a). *Making space for Indigenous feminism*. Winnipeg: Fernwood Publishing.

Harding, S. (ed.). (2004). *The feminist standpoint theory reader: Intellectual and political controversies*. New York, NY: Routledge.

Kovach, M. (2009). *Indigenous methodologies – Characters, conversations, and contexts*. Toronto, ON: University of Toronto Press.

Chapter 7

Manning up and manning on

Masculinities, hegemonic masculinity, and leisure studies

Corey W. Johnson and Luc S. Cousineau

So, what is masculinity or masculinities? Connell (2005) described "masculinity" as those practices in which men (and sometimes women and trans* individuals) engage male social gender roles, with the effects being expressed through the body, personality, relations, and culture. In contemporary society, social structures, social relations, and social discourses communicate these understandings both overtly and covertly, and as humans we consume them both consciously and unconsciously and naively or critically across various contexts. Of course, one of these important contexts is leisure. As Kivel (1996) argues: "Leisure as a context for identity formation should not only focus on the individual, but should also focus on the cultural ideologies which shape and influence the individual"; hence, "the next step is to begin to understand how leisure contexts contribute to a hegemonic process which creates 'insiders' and 'outsiders'" (p. 204). One illustration is the vast number of advertisements we encounter during our leisurely consumption of media and how those displays of consumerism influence our gender norms.

On a continuous basis, men encounter elicit demonstrations of what it means to be masculine through the media, which cultivates and sustains stereotypic forms of gender and sexuality (Dunlap & Johnson, 2013; Johnson & Dunlap, 2011). Take Axe, a well-known brand of men's grooming products owned by the multinational consumer goods corporation Unilever. Since the 1990s, Unilever's marketing strategy for Axe has been simple and clear, "use Axe products, be a 'real' man, get women, and get laid." This strategy can be seen in the "Meet the Parents" Axe ad, which infers that most men cannot "achieve" idealized manhood without Axe products, and without that manhood men do not have enough redeeming qualities to "seduce women" and, ultimately, confirm their heterosexuality. The commercial begins with two parents opening the door exclaiming, "Welcome home," as they greet their son Travis and his girlfriend. Travis is marked as "less than manly" in a variety of ways. He is skinny, has unkept hair, no muscles, a high-pitched voice, and poor fashion sense. Consequently, his parents seem overwhelmingly happy and a bit surprised when Travis introduces his new girlfriend, as if it is the first time he has brought home a woman. As Travis introduces Cindy to his parents, they greet her happily, exclaiming that it is "nice to meet her as they have heard so much about her." She smiles as she holds on to Travis lovingly. As the parents welcome her into the house, they start to close the door as Travis half-heartedly laughs and says, "Oh mom, no." Reopening the door, he then introduces another woman, Shannon, to his parents. The parents both look baffled as another woman walks through the door and shakes their hand. Following Shannon's surprise entrance, Travis proceeds to introduce his parents to a host of additional women also waiting outside (i.e., Erin, Jessica, Sierra, Megan, Nicole, and Elizabeth). Travis smiles brightly, with a sense of both bravado and conquest. The look on the parents' faces moves from confusion to shock to disbelief. Travis looks back at his parents and gives a calculated laugh as a visual of the various scents of Axe deodorants and sprays fill the screen and a voice-over chimes in, "Axe, use in moderation." The message is very clear that Axe products make men masculine, which means heterosexual and sexually desirable. Uncritical consumers say things like, "It's just a commercial, what's the big deal?" Yet, the narrative told in this type of advertisement tells viewers that to successfully be a "real man," they must attract idealistically "beautiful women" and, the more woman they attract, the better men they will be. And, if, like most men, he cannot accomplish this aim on his own, he needs to buy Axe products to assist him.

What this example illustrates is that culture serves as both a cause and effect of masculine behaviour, and in Western society masculinity has taken shape in relation to securing and maintaining dominance. Masculine power is balanced by the general symbolism of difference whereby the masculine is valued over the feminine. While masculinity is grounded in difference, it is not a static characteristic or personal identity trait (Connell, 2005). Instead, masculinity is a fluid construct with a multitude of possibilities and manifestations (hence masculinities) that is organized within social relations and ultimately changes those social relations. According to Connell (2005), masculinity is not just an object of knowledge, but the interplay between the agency of the individual and the structure of the social institution.

In addition to recognizing the social construction of masculinity, it is also important to recognize that masculinity is based on its dialectical relationship to femininity (Connell, 2005). Therefore, it is necessary to situate masculinity in a historical and cultural context that enables scholars to discuss men's experiences and relationships in relation to the social structure. This conceptual framework illuminates how masculinity can be understood as an aspect of a specific culture's spaces, practices, and products. In this sense, although masculinity is performed in a variety of ways and can change across history and culture, most men often feel obligated – consciously or unconsciously – to perform masculinity situated amidst the current social and cultural climate. These dominant ideological norms of masculinities are referred to as hegemonic masculinity. Rose and Johnson (2017) suggest:

> Hegemonic masculinities refers to sets of practices in which dominant social positions of men are promoted at the subordinated social positions of

> non-masculine identities. Values and activities associated with hegemonic masculinity involve toughness, strength, conquest, domination, and heterosexuality, breadwinner, strong, stoic, emotionally detached, pragmatic, etc., even as these aspects are enacted and expressed in diverse ways.
>
> (p. 4)

Hegemonic masculinity, then, fosters access to power (greater financial influence, conscious and unconscious hiring and promotion decisions, decision-making authority, etc.) and legitimizes patriarchy. However, even within hegemonic masculinity, a hierarchy materializes as hegemonic ideals intersect with other privileged identity categories (e.g., heterosexual, white, wealthy), which exacerbate power and privilege. Therefore, hegemonic masculinity is a powerful process used to secure and maintain the current, dominant social order.

Hegemonic masculinity is an elaborate performance of social authority, and it is not easy to challenge openly. Men who eventually choose to challenge hegemonic masculinity are forced to confront a dilemma of difference (Johnson, 2013) and those on the outside are often easily dismissed. Sedgwick (1993) inspired much thinking about the dilemmas of difference related to hegemonic masculinity in her seminal and eloquent essay "Epistemology of the Closet." In it, she discussed how gay men are punished by hegemonic masculinity, merely for existing as gay in the assumed heterosexually hegemonic masculinity. She wrote:

> Heterosexist and masculinist ethical sanctions [find] ready camouflage. If the new common wisdom that hotly overt homophobes are men who are "insecure about their masculinity" supplements the implausible, necessary illusion that there could be a *secure* version of masculinity (known, presumably, by the coolness of its homophobic enforcement) and a stable, intelligible way for men to feel about other men in modern heterosexual capitalist patriarchy, what tighter turn could there be to the screw of an already off-center, always at fault, endlessly blackmailable male identity ready to be manipulated into any labor of channeled violence.
>
> (p. 56)

Hence, challenging hegemonic masculinity is not an easy feat, for gay men, poor men, effeminate men, or many "non-normative" men.

As men who also identify as feminists, our goals are to try (and we often fail) to combat patriarchy on an everyday basis! To do so, we must understand our own masculinities, the positive kinds and the toxic kinds (Ferber, 2000; O'Neil, 2010), and decide what we can do about them as activists, researchers, teachers, sons, husbands, brothers, friends, and socially just-oriented humans. To help prepare us for this theoretically informed, but action-oriented task, we will detail the historical and disciplinary roots of the study of masculinity, followed by the tensions and challenges we have encountered deploying this theoretical framework. Next, we detail three of our projects so that you can see the theory "in action," and how the study of masculinity fits into the emerging fourth wave. Finally, we end with a call to others, to consider so much unfinished business for understanding how masculinity and the critical research on men can offer as part of the solution for creating a more gender equitable world.

In an effort to understand a concept, it is important to understand how it came to be, how it has been transformed, and how it is being used most contemporarily. With this in mind, we use the following section to review the history of masculinity and, more importantly, its link to hegemonic masculinity.

Historical and disciplinary roots

In the early 20th century, Antonio Gramsci, a philosopher, politician, and later a founder and leader of the Communist Party in Italy, took up and translated the ancient Greek concept of hegemons through the writings of Karl Marx (Gramsci, 1971). A hegemon is a leader with domineering tendencies who creates norms, which are universally applicable, but generally serve the interests of those in power (Boswell, 2004; Wallerstein, 1983). Gramsci theorized the concept of hegemon beyond a leader to general society, arguing that hegemony (the process employed by hegemons) manifests in the relationships between those who have power (the dominant) and those who do not (the non-dominant) (Johnson, Barnett, & Hansen, 2014).

Hegemony requires no physical force and instead operates through indirect coercion (valued ideologies) and unconscious consent, such as an individual's desire to seek acceptance or be considered normal. A hegemonic system is dynamic, operating at a variety of levels to affect individuals and groups within a social hierarchy (Johnson et al., 2014). Halberstam (2011) argues there is not one single entity of influence for hegemony, but rather a matrix of connected ideals, which yield both individual and collective power. In this context,

> hegemony is the term for a multilayered system by which a dominant group achieves power not through coercion, but through the production of an interlocking system of ideas which persuades people of the rightness of any given set of often contradictory ideas and perspectives.
>
> (Halberstam, 2011, p. 17)

These overlapping and interconnected ideologies and social pressures create systems that reproduce an idealized target or norm. For example, even within gay male communities, idealized representations of masculinity and masculine bodies (such as muscular, young, hairless, white) dominate what is characterized as ideal and sought after, even if users already inhabit spaces of a marginalized masculinity. It is therefore both the ideal for the individual or group and the simultaneous means of policing the group, using the group's norms. However, these dominant ideologies are also continuously evolving at the same time as being already out of reach for many of the individuals to which they apply. Therefore, counter-movements against this idealization might lead to the development of sub-communities where badges of masculinity are valued in different ways (i.e. bears, leather men, drag queens, etc.).

The concept of hegemonic masculinity is regularly attributed to R. W. Connell's work throughout the 1980s and 1990s, with particular credit given to the theoretical work done to contextualize the concept in the book *Masculinities* (2005). In this work, Connell laid the foundation for the application of Gramsci's concept of hegemonic structures to the idea of masculinity and the performance/construction of masculinity ideals in the larger social setting. For Gramsci, and hence for Connell, the concept of hegemony "refers to the cultural dynamic by which a group claims and sustains a leading position in social life" (Connell, 2005, p. 77). Gramsci was not specific about the gendered nature of the concept as it is used by Connell, but Connell employs the concept to both explore and explain the nature and relationships between masculinities functioning in society: hegemony, subordination, complicity, and marginalization. These relational spaces between masculinities not only inform the interactions between those embodied by each representation, but also the nature of places occupied in the social hierarchy.

Before diving too deeply into the context and concept of hegemonic masculinity, it is also important to note that it comes along with a well-reasoned assertion that neither the nature of masculinities nor their place in the social order is fixed, and that masculinity itself is a pliable concept, or a moving target throughout history, which is also geographically and culturally malleable. In fact, Connell devotes an entire chapter of *Masculinities* to the historical exploration of the development of masculinity to illustrate that not only is the concept malleable over time, but that we have a remarkably short memory when deciding to call something "traditional." As an example, the male role as "breadwinner" did not emerge in Western society until the rise of mass industrialization and movement to urban living situations (i.e., Britain in the mid- to late-19th century). Connell does this for two reasons. The first is to help illustrate that the concept of a hegemonic masculinity as historically codified. To Connell (2005),

> hegemonic masculinity can be defined as the configuration of gender practice which embodies the currently accepted answers to the problem of the legitimacy of patriarchy, which guarantees (or is taken to guarantee) the dominant position of men and the subordination of women.
>
> (p. 77)

Simultaneously, Connell (2005) explains to the reader that "hegemony does not mean total control. It is not automatic, and may be disrupted – or even disrupt itself" (p. 37). Although we see the version of masculinity in this role as, indeed, hegemonic, what can fit in this space is susceptible to change and/or influence, and is at the mercy of changes in societal ideology.

So, what does that look like in our daily lives? Hegemonic masculinity is a pliable and movable concept where the practices by which men (and sometimes women) enact male social gender roles (i.e. breadwinner, strong, stoic, emotionally detached, pragmatic, etc.) to maintain patriarchy. This expression can manifest through the body, social/emotional action, or the engagement of the individual with social norms/pressures (e.g., big muscles, calm, no crying, financial independence, loves sex and has a lot of it). Social norms must then serve as both cause and effect of enacting masculinity and have manifested in Western society as a means of producing and maintaining dominance. Dominance, in this sense, is maintained not by physical power, but instead as codified through indirect coercion and unconscious consent of hegemony – or you must achieve those things to be a "good" man. Where the goal of hegemonic masculine action and social norms is domination, this power or access to it is contingent on the subjugation of the "other" – predominantly women, but also any other who is unable to meet the expectations of the hegemonic ideal, including Othered men (i.e., gay men, poor men, feminine men, etc.). Although hegemonic masculinity is organized and rewarded within social relations, the idealized pique (i.e., promiscuous, well-endowed, tall, educated, muscular, funny, wealthy, able-bodied, athletic, good drivers, etc.) can never be achievable for more than a small percentage of men (if any) and is ultimately unsustainable long term, keeping most men consciously or unconsciously insecure, inept, and in doubt.

In addition, Kimmel (2010) posits that the Othering in the context of hegemonic masculinity extends beyond creating a simple hierarchy, wherein certain identities are excluded from the hegemonic ideal. Othering also becomes the surface "against which heterosexual men project their identities, against whom they stack the decks so as to compete in a situation in which they will always win" (Kimmel, 2010, p. 27). Kimmel (2010) asserts that, not only does a hegemonic social structure subjugate, but it is also sexist and homophobic by its very nature. For example, Savin-Williams (1998) argued that, even though gay men are culturally defined and aligned with feminine interests, they have a great attraction to and desire for masculinity. In fact, he argues that gay men's same-sex attractions are often experienced as an obsession of wanting to be near men, with a desire for their masculinity. In a similar argument, Connell (2005) indicated that for gay men the point of reference for both personality and object choice is masculinity and that the choice of a man as a sexual object is not just the choice of a-body-with-penis, but of embodied masculinity. Both Savin-Willams (1998) and Connell (2005) argued that gay men cannot invent new objects of desire any more than heterosexual men can invent new objects of desire. Instead, gay men's desire is structured by the current gender order available to them. When attempting to redefine masculinity, their direction must include the effeminacy placed upon them by others, as well as those hegemonic masculine qualities they adopt. Thus, the research literature on gay men suggests that the subordination of gay men (which includes cultural exclusion, cultural abuse, legal violence, street violence, economic discrimination, and personal boycott) is facilitated by a gender order that positions gay men at the bottom of a gender hierarchy among men, symbolically expelling gay men from hegemonic masculinity and assimilating them to femininity. Nonetheless, Connell (2005) suggested that hegemony can be disrupted or even disrupt itself.

Collectively, the uptake of hegemonic masculinity has occurred across a variety of areas of study, and scholars have expanded on Connell's original conception through individual perspectives and social settings. However, this cross-applicability and malleability has also left the concept open to critique, and even Connell has revisited the concept to address some of these issues (Connell & Messerschmidt, 2005). At its core, Connell's concept of hegemonic masculinity is anchored by four main tenets, which inform both the theoretical employments of the concept, as well as its departures. Hegemonic masculinity is: (a) non-fixed and historically contextual; (b) performance or construction of masculinity and masculine traits which are then (c) ascribed to social, bodily, and ideological regimens, which police social, cultural, and physical value onto men, men's bodies, and opinions about men; and (d) by its nature creates Othering of those who are unable to meet these standards, while simultaneously providing a model against which to compare masculine performance. The following section will address some of the critiques levied at hegemonic masculinity and its application across areas of study.

Tensions or challenges within the theoretical perspective

In 2005, the same year that the second edition of *Masculinities* was published, Connell worked with James Messerschmidt to address some of the critical perspectives and commentary that were levied against the initial conceptualization of hegemonic masculinity (Connell & Messerschmidt, 2005). The aim of this collaboration was to redirect the use of hegemonic masculinity to better match Connell's original conceptualization of a representational structure that is movable and malleable, based on the social settings and social pressures exerted on those who embody that structure. Foremost, they defend both the use of masculinities and hegemony as useful concepts in the understanding and continued development of research and theory on social roles of individuals and the development/maintenance of those roles. Connell and Messerschmitt (2005) critiqued some of the evolution of the use of hegemonic masculinity as a concept, especially where it is applied in a binary-type understanding of gender or representational spaces. Owing to the inherent malleability of hegemony itself, they are quick to illustrate that the binary/dichotomous understanding is not true to the nature of hegemony or its intended application to masculinity. Their most thorough critique is reserved for work that inserts the concept of hegemonic masculinity into rigid typologies. Much like its application in a binary model of gender, the main tenets of Connell's Gramscian hegemonic masculinity are lost, with the consequence of it being oversimplified and by association improperly attributed to diverse and problematized collections of individuals. In this work, Connell and Messerschmidt (2005) also laud how the concept has been used to support the idea of multiple masculinities, which are not only interrelated and mappable one to another, but also contingent on one another for roles in the masculinities landscape. Each of these multiple masculinities is in a state of fluctuation relative to the its own boundary edges, as well as changing in relation to one another. Finally, Connell and Messerschmidt (2005) push for the development of a more complex model of gender hierarchy, one that is focused more on the intricacies of multiple representations and embodiments of masculinity and femininity and their interconnections.

Connell and Messerschmidt's (2005) work analyzing and critiquing hegemonic masculinity is complemented by other authors who provide contemporary theoretical challenges or proposed evolutions to the concept. Hearn (2004), as an example, argued the application of the term *hegemony*, with particular respect to hegemonic masculinity, is erroneous insofar as it does not adequately explain or represent hegemonic influence in the Gramscian sense. The crux of Hearn's (2004) argument is that, in the development of the hegemonic masculinity theoretical structure, men have not been sufficiently represented as gendered beings. That is, although men have been the subjects of the research, they have not been subjectively treated as gendered men, but are instead left as mostly essentialized beings. Therefore, Hearn (2004) proposed a move to a Critical Studies on Men (CSM) to better frame and understand discussions about men and masculinities, as well as their influences on gender and the social order.

Johanssen and Ottemo (2015) both praised the concept of hegemonic masculinity for its contributions and development in the literature over time while also providing a theorized direction for its further development. Johanssen and Ottemo (2015) suggested an evolution of the concept into a Ricoeurian utopic ideology; an idealized space with no fixed end, but instead an ever-moving goal to strive towards. This is a markedly positive spin on the existence and embracing of hegemonic masculinity and suggests that, rather than continuing a pejorative dialogue about hegemonic ideation as a source of oppression and subordination, it could be used as a positive benchmark for development and goal-setting.

Using the military as a context, Duncanson (2015) posited that the key to fostering gender equity is not the democratizing of gender relations, but instead more deliberate and direct change in the behavioural and social expectations of men to drive change toward inclusion. Duncanson's (2015) position relied on the presupposition that understanding our gender ideologies, produced by patriarchy, and particularly the influence and focus of hegemonic masculinity, is not only the driving force for change (or lack of change) but the only force that can create change in a postmodern cultural context. Duncanson (2015) called attention to the modifications in accepted American military masculinity as it has changed since World War II and Vietnam War era presentations. Currently, the peacekeeper or soldier-scholar are acceptable and attainable military masculinities, both of which contrast with the "defender-of-home" and "killer-of-evil" warrior manifestations of American military masculinity propagandized in the past.

The tensions with the discourse surrounding hegemonic masculinity, particularly in its early actualization into theory, exist in three main areas. The first is hegemonic masculinity as a representational structure; the representation of hegemonic masculinity in a binary application where one is, or is not, or has, or has not, the qualities of the hegemonic man. This was an oversimplification of the concept as it was presented by Connell (2005), and leads to a too-simplified understanding of the roles that masculinity and masculine ideology play in the lives of all people. Second is that, even with the application of the concept, men are not often understood as gendered beings, and are therefore lost in the same monolith of generalized understanding as pre-feminist women and women's issues were. Third is an assertion that understanding and working through hegemonic masculinity might be a way to positive progress; viewpoints juxtaposed to a view of hegemonic masculinity as inherently problematic. Through these critiques – theorization using hegemonic masculinity as a concept and a conceptual lens, and contemporary applications in research – we have begun to see things differently.

Seeing things differently: contemporary research with hegemonic masculinity

As we articulated earlier, to a historically unprecedented degree, masculinity in contemporary Western societies is available for scrutiny, interrogation, and thoughtful engagement by both individuals and social institutions; and yet a seemingly more self-aware masculinity is belied by centuries of cultural sediment, much of it reactionary, which continues to discipline the performance of masculinity, especially in its formative stages. After two decades, Connell's concept of hegemonic masculinity has gained significant traction. Work applying the concept proliferated in North America and Britain (see Kimmel & Messner, 2001; Whitehead & Barrett, 2001), but application of the concept was also taken up in Japan (Roberson & Suzuki, 2003), the Middle East (Ghoussoub & Sinclair-Webb, 2000), and other regions. During this time, hegemonic masculinity was also studied and applied in a variety of research contexts, including education (Martino & Pallotta-Chiarolli, 2003), health (Hurrelmann & Kolip, 2002), violence (Kaufman, 2001), and fathering (Kindler, 2002). Connell's original conceptualization of the hegemonic masculine as fluid in time and geography allowed for a variety of applications across disciplines and locations.

Authors like Hearn (2004) saw the pervasive influence of the hegemonic masculine in various literatures, from commercial mass media, advertising, division of labour, activities of the state, and criminalization of the "other" through laws against homosexuality. More contemporary uses of the concept, as in Halberstam (2011), expand on the policing of personal identities by preventing women from accessing power or by excluding them from masculine action (e.g., female masculinity). Similar to Halberstam (2011), Tyler and Fairbrother (2013) explored how rural, frontiersman masculinity has not only pervaded the modern urban understanding of what it means to be a "real man" (read: lumberjacks and cowboys) but has led to loss of life where the "stay and defend mentality" around personal property and family can influence public policy to the extent that men choose the defense of property (and sometimes death) over recommended evacuations during natural disasters – a hegemonic masculine remnant of frontiersmen, mythologized for their ability to "tame" nature.

Steve Garlick's (2010) work on internet pornography shows how hegemonic masculine ideals informed the development of the pornography industry but have subsequently been changed by the development of that industry, leading to changes in attitudes about sexual conquest, body morphology, representational dynamics, and the taboo nature of certain sex acts within hegemonic masculine ideology itself. Work exploring the roles the media have played on young men's representations of the self-online has shown that masculine identity online is manifested through stylized representations of the body and physique (Manago, 2013; Siibak, 2010). Light (2013), as well as Harvey, Ringrose, and Gill (2013), demonstrated that online peer network approval, as well as precise attitudinal and photographic representation of self, had significant effects on whether young men online were lauded or chastised for their own masculinity. Sweeney (2014) problematized a prominent juxtaposition for young men's masculinity where they must be both the party animal and the respectable man to meet a contemporary collegiate masculine ideal, and that this duality must manifest online and in person. In their interesting analysis of the UK television show *Playing it Straight*, Alderson (2014) highlighted how, within the context of the show, hiding homosexuality is rewarded and demonstrably stereotypically homosexual behaviour is devalued to the point of exclusion – an association with contemporary masculinity discourse, which continues to place the gay (homosexual) man in the category of "other" regardless of how or whether they manifest other hegemonic ideals. Also, Moisio, Arnould, and Gentry (2013) and Moisio and Beruchashvili (2016) have explored the role that domestic masculinity has played in the development of hegemonic masculine ideals and how "do-it-yourself" and masculinized spaces within the heterosexual home settings have been delimited by hegemonic masculinity. In this context, although the work on masculinities and hegemonic masculinities continues to evolve, its evolution has also begun to take shape in leisure studies.

Hegemonic masculinity in leisure studies

Most research on masculinity in leisure studies has been undertaken by Corey alone or with collaborators. Engaging with the "crisis of representation" presented to men as they engage with masculine ideologies, Johnson, Richmond, and Kivel (2008) had young men of different races explore how they engaged with the representational politics they faced with masculinity. Combining themes of race and media consumption as a leisure activity, Berbary and Johnson (2016) documented how drag kings (women performing as men) played with masculinity as a way of pointing out the fallacy of masculinity and disrupting patriarchy. Dunlap and Johnson (2013) and Johnson and Dunlap (2011) explored how straight men's and gay men's identities intersected with masculinity through their media exposure and consumption, and Kivel and Johnson (2009) explored constructions of masculinity and leisure as they are linked to media consumption. These projects, although several years apart and working with different populations of (mostly) men, served independently to highlight the continued influence of media and imagery on the perceptions and personifications of masculinity in men (and women acting as men), and led additional empirical support to previous work on the embodiment of misogynist attitudes in gay bars.

Using the country and western gay bar as a backdrop, Corey (Johnson, 2002, 2008; Johnson & Samdahl, 2005) explored how gay men enacted hegemonic masculine ideals within that leisure microcosm, even as they are feminized and reduced by the same hegemonic masculine ideologies outside of the gay bar setting. How patrons negotiated hegemonic masculinity in response to a weekly lesbian night in this predominantly gay male environment was telling about how the power of gendered social structures was largely unaffected by sexual preference. Revisiting race, but with a specific focus on leisure pursuits, Kivel, Johnson, and Scraton (2009) examined how individuals have been represented in terms of race in leisure literature, presenting a reconceptualization of leisure research, which accounts for individual experiences within the broader discourses of ideology and power. And, most recently, Rose and Johnson (2017), using critical ethnography, explored some of the ways in which masculinities served as both a rationale and an outcome of men facing homelessness living in the margins of an urban municipal public park.

In addition to Johnson and collaborators, Blanco and Robinett (2014) provide a contemporary application of Connell's concept of hegemonic masculinity. Their research examines the effect of hegemonic masculinity on leisure practices and public discussion of leisure practices of young men in the United States. Exploring how these young men engaged with and discussed their leisure, Blanco and Robinett (2014) found many were willing and active participants in leisure practices that were non-hegemonic in nature (e.g., bubble baths). They also noted the men's engagement with non-hegemonic activities were silenced in public, for fear of reprisal and reduction in masculine status. In contrast, the authors found "men who meet hegemonic expectations are not required to explain their behaviours" (p. 363).

Other scholars have examined leisure pursuits using hegemonic masculinity as their frame of analysis, but this work has not occurred within leisure studies, nor does it draw on leisure theory. These contributions include work on video games and gamers (cf. Chess & Shaw, 2015; Dill & Thill, 2007; Kirkland, 2009), youth sports (cf. Connell, 2008; Gottzén & Kremer-Sadlik, 2012;

Messner, 2011), and outdoor pursuits (cf. Brandth & Haugen, 2005; Humberstone, 2000; Humberstone & Pedersen, 2001).

Men's involvement in advancing feminist social justice

At the surface, the inclusion of masculinity and men into writing about feminist theory and ideology might seem counterintuitive. However, in a fourth wave of feminist thought, we believe that it is a necessary inclusion as a means of consciousness-raising and for a more socially just theoretical framework.

We recognize that our argument is not without problematic undercurrents, insofar as the historically dominant group (men) is arguing for inclusion. Our argument is not for the insertion of men and masculinities into feminist theory full stop, but instead the use of feminist theory with contemporary theories and understandings of masculinity to open up that concept up for discussion and use outside of a problematic "traditional maleness" as limiting – perpetuating marginalization, oppression, and violence. By including men and masculinity in feminist thought and discussion, the ownership of feminist theory and feminist practice is opened up to those who may have believed it was not a tool for their use and, since masculinity can belong to men, women, trans* and non-binary individuals, it can belong to us all. The allowance (or affordance) of men to engage fully with, and contribute to, feminist theorization would allow men to more wholly critique and/or engage with gender spaces and social roles, and provide new avenues for expression of self and development of social norms.

Despite our call for more men's participation in feminism, we would remind folks, as Corey (Johnson, 2013) has previously suggested, that;

> [M]en cannot appropriate the use of feminism for the study of gender (and masculinity) without consideration of the issues surrounding the privileged subjectivity as men … ensur[ing] that we are not responsible for creating and recreating androcentric biases, reinforcing male privilege, and/or erasing the important position of women in the creation and dissemination of new knowledge.
>
> (p. 248)

As men are embraced in feminist theorization, two additional avenues are opened to them beyond the social engagement with masculinity.

To begin, along with extending our theory base, men are more able to engage fully with activist labour within the feminist movement. Beyond the peripheral, male ally support provided in the past, the engagement of men as feminist activists, who are accepted and welcomed by the wider feminist landscape, allows for the development and maintenance of programs like the United Nations HeForShe campaign and IMPACT 10x10x10, where men work actively with feminist ideals to support and develop women's full social involvement. In this framework, ten male heads of state, ten male corporation leaders, and ten male university presidents have committed to becoming change leaders for gender equity. These efforts materialize in all sorts of initiatives, such as the head of state in Rwanda creating a network of One Stop Centers to give sexual assault victims immediate access to police, medical, and support services, or the CEO of Unilever (which coincidentally owns Axe body spray) launching an initiative to support skills training for over 168,000 female smallholder farmers in its supply chain (HeFor She.org, 2017).

At the University of Waterloo, where we both work, our President has "provided six scholarships, valued at up to $12,000 each over four years, to outstanding female students admitted to Year One of an undergraduate science, technology, engineering, or mathematics (STEM) degree program in which females are currently underrepresented" (HeForShe.org, 2017). Programs like this can benefit from a well-developed feminist activist grounding and use male feminists (in some places, celebrity male feminists) to present and propagate a socially and gender-conscious message in universities, political arenas, and on international stages, to allow men to better understand their roles in the development and maintenance, as well as dismantling, of patriarchy. The use of male celebrity feminists (e.g., HeForShe) is of particular interest, as it calls into question the motivations of those men. Regardless of their motivation, men's involvement invariably increases the notoriety and significance of these issues.

Second, accepting men and masculinities into a feminist space allows and gives men new and functional tools to critique other men; critiques which are functionally and affectively different when levied from more traditional women-centered/feminist spaces. For example, critiques levied by Jackson Katz, a former high school and college football star and gender violence activist, who gave a small TEDx talk (with around 100 audience members), has now been viewed on the internet over 1.8 million times.

In arguing that gender-based violence is inherently a men's issue, Katz's messaging has found purchase in "high-status homosocial male organizations and groups – such as fraternities, organized sports, and the military" (Messner, Greenberg, & Peretz, 2015, p. 3). For the past two decades, Katz has been actively involved in a gender-based violence prevention capacity with the U.S. military. In addition, the U.S. Air Force now requires all of its members to participate in a bystander intervention training developed by Katz (Messner et al., 2015). Benefiting from the same patriarchal powers they seek to dismantle, social and gendered criticism levied by men like Katz (read: straight, white, male, affluent, former athlete, educated) weighs differently than others; but also evokes critical attention from those who dispute their messaging (Kimmel, 1998, 2013). By facilitating this type of critique, a fourth wave of feminism, which includes men, may have the effect of more efficiently moving resources from men to women by using feminist men as leverage.

In more broadly sharing the ownership of masculinity, we, who strive to be feminist activists and facilitate men critiquing men, have the potential to make changes to leisure landscapes as they currently stand as well. Leisure contexts and behaviours are often structurally gendered, which means that we ascribe levels of acceptability along gendered lines to our own participation, and the participation of others. Although these ascriptions are malleable and socially contextual, they form important markers for some social understanding of appropriate (or inappropriate) leisure pursuits. This assigned (in)appropriateness may go beyond being oppressive to those who push the gendered boundaries and may become exclusionary for those who do not conform. In a Canadian sport context, for example, field hockey is generally understood as a women's game, and men who play not only face questions about the nature of the game and their reasons for playing, but they may also face queries about the nature of their uniforms, their perceived effeminate natures, and even heteronormative assumptions about their sexuality. For these reasons, among others, male participants in this sport face challenges beyond simple access to teams or playing time, and must manage socially oppressive behaviours associated with misappropriated ideas about their participation.

Men who sew face similar stigmatized leisure participation emerging from heteronormative assumptions about domesticity and traditionally domestic practices. Different from cooking (a traditionally feminized domestic task, which has been dominated by men commercially for centuries) and knitting (a traditionally feminized domestic task, which has been reclaimed by millennials as a new handmade-chic activity for both men and women), male domestic sewers remain anomalous and problematic for traditional norms. As a result, men can be seen as successful fashion designers, but not skilled home sewers. Both sewing and field hockey present leisure contexts where a developed feminist theory, which includes examinations of men and masculinity, has (as of yet) failed to properly explore. Although the heteronormative nature of these situations can, and should, be analyzed with existing feminist and gender theories, the leisure contexts and effects of masculinities and hegemonic gender understandings in these leisure spaces require the attention of leisure scientists and theorists moving forward. The application of contemporary masculinity and feminist theories to the existing spaces of leisure participation and understanding opens new avenues for exploratory and explanatory research about our leisure lives, and how those leisure lives affect and are affected by social pressures, norms, expectations, and deviations. It also allows leisure sciences to approach research in a more socially just way, expanding not only understandings of place and space, but also how those places and spaces are explored.

Engaging with fourth wave feminisms

The work of engaging with fourth wave feminism and masculinity is of critical importance, at least on the part of male authors and scholars who might dare to claim the moniker of feminist. It is not enough to simply claim to be a feminist scholar in name; it must emerge through the embodiment of feminist epistemological perspectives and engagement with issues of power, social justice, and role politics as they affect members of a society. As discussed in Chapter 1, these applications of feminist thought move across and between previous waves of feminist theory speaking to the blurred boundaries between waves and Maclaran's (2015) online actualization of third wave micropolitics.

A move away from the radically exclusive politics of some parts of second wave feminist thought, through the individualistic and reclamation nature of what might be called the third wave, opens up the possibility that not only can men be seen and accepted as full-fledged feminists, but that their contributions to the scholarship and social action inherent in the larger feminist movement can be useful, if not absolutely necessary. In this way, men's engagement with feminism and critiques of masculinity could be discussed as decidedly fourth wave on its own. This is perhaps well tied to the inclusion of an appreciation for skepticism in a fourth wave femtheory (Dean & Aune, 2015), which, although it does not welcome anti-feminist sentiment, does allow for theoretical considerations about how feminist practice can be applied, even by men. Further, fourth wave feminism appears like it will revisit and reinterpret previously made arguments about men in feminism and the roles they can play in addressing patriarchy. Although the globality and rapid mobilization afforded by the internet can serve to channel problematic discourses directly to feminist researchers/activists (Chess & Shaw, 2015), it has also permitted coordinated mobilization and widespread action promoting feminist causes, actualized (at least in part) by men (Earl & Kimport, 2011). Nuanced, well-researched, and supportive men's engagement with feminist theory and discourse has also allowed for the study of men as sexed and gendered entities to emerge, not in contrast to women and women's studies, but as a complement to these works engaged with power and gendered spaces.

For example, Luc's use of feminist theory and research practice has come through working with young adults to examine their engagement with gender and leadership, and their personal experiences navigating these difficult patriarchal spaces. In the co-ed, overnight summer camp setting, Cousineau and Roth (2012) explored how young adult staff members strongly expressed gendered leadership preference for males, even while engaged with "care work" at summer camps. These findings created an interesting juxtaposition between the highly gendered notion of "care work" as women's work and the expressed idea that leadership and camp management was better suited to male leaders.

Luc's current interest expands on this previous work using feminist theory to guide an exploration of the roles and influence of online men's activism and activist spaces on the offline lives of those engaged with it. Included in this online involvement is the participation in men's rights activist (MRA) groups, which emphasize a perceived devaluation of men's rights and roles within Western society by other groups, and pays particular attention to women's groups and feminism (Banet-Weiser & Miltner, 2016; Jordan, 2016; Schmitz & Kazyak, 2016). These MRA groups, which speak for the reclamation of men's social roles and promote the entitlement of men to social power and prestige (Jordan, 2016; Schmitz & Kazyak, 2016), encourage the deconstruction of women's and minority rights in favour of a hegemonic superiority for men. Their development and growth in anonymous and non-anonymous online communities is likely telling of hidden growth in offline sociopolitical spaces and we must ask: How do these ideas translate to offline spaces? And what effect do these ideologies have on institutional decision making outside of the internet?

This work builds on his previous work on discursive internet spaces (see Bergstrom, 2011; Bernstein et al., 2011; Knuttila, 2011; Springer, 2015), critiques of neoliberal social spaces (see: Brodie, 2008; Brown, 2005; Kennelly, 2014; Smith, 2005), and overt and tacit understandings of the internet and web as masculinized areas which render permissible certain types of behaviour and activity that are patently taboo offline (Cousineau, ongoing). Luc's research trajectory includes a digital ethnography (Cousineau, Oakes, & Johnson, in press, 2018; Pink et al., 2016) of "men's rights" internet communities and their translation to offline actions and activities. Digital ethnography focuses on the multiplicity of digital engagements, and the diverse ways that individuals engage with media – some of which are disconnected from the digital. Research in this area will help us understand how bloggers and ideologues like Daryush Valizadeh – aka Roosh V[1] – can develop sufficient following to have public meetings and merit international media coverage in countries where goals of gender equality are understood to be well established. This research trajectory can also help to shed light on the role that digital cultures play in the development of populist movements like Black Lives Matter, and how counter- and quasi-counter-movements materialize and propagate online, then transition to offline action.

And, despite Corey's contributions to the leisure studies literature on masculinity discussed earlier, he continues to employ a theoretical lens around masculinity, adopting and adapting to a fourth wave. He is currently working on a large study that looks at geo-social networking applications (GSNAs). GSNAs use cell phones and satellites to create computer-mediated communication whereby users exchange a series of electronic messages and participate in different relational activities via cyberspace that ultimately cultivate in-person meetings (dates, meet-ups, sex hook-ups, etc.). These online communications are radically and rapidly changing the nature of our cultural landscape, including gender identities, sexual practices, use of public space, commerce, and quality of life. Collectively, these projects advance a "hopeful" optimism that fourth wave feminism is "breaking" on the shores of leisure studies.

Unfinished business

Of course, there are limits to our approach. Our positionality is, and must be, different from many others who employ feminist thought and theory for social justice. Although not in and of itself a limitation, it renders the imbrication of theoretical perspectives more complex and demands that we are continually aware and sensitive to our own power. Our subject matter is challenging, not just to us, but to dominant social paradigms. These challenges are ones that we can meet with reading, careful consideration, thought, and again more reading. However, these are luxuries and privileges that are not always recognized by the public, and as such form and maintain the social places and spaces that police us. Because of this, our approach is sometimes subjugated, and our research diminished because of its criticality.

Despite these limits, we engage with masculinities and feminist theory as ways of working toward social justice goals: seeing masculinity issues as issues of power and subordination, largely by men toward women, as well as men toward other men – all perpetuating patriarchy. Feminism has provided us with a toolkit of theories and perspectives which has allowed us to see and experience our power-laden and gendered lives differently, and, to cast a critical gaze on spaces of power, privilege, and subjugation we are a part of, bound up in our masculinity – hegemonic or not. Through conversations such as the ones discussed throughout this chapter, we can begin to break down the idealistic hegemonic masculinities in society and begin to build up a shared sense of humanity that is inclusive to all. And, with the politics of hope (Johnson & Parry, 2015; Parry & Fullagar, 2013) as our torch, we think scholarship on masculinity, movements like HeForShe, the continued work of activist/scholars like Jackson Katz, and our own research endeavours, can make a difference.

Can this transformation work? Let's end as we began. In 2016, given the critiques levied at previous ad campaigns, by both scholars and consumers, Axe employed a marketing strategy that, instead of celebrating and reinforcing a monolithic, patriarchal, hegemonic masculinity, celebrated and offered representations of a variety of men, masculinities, personalities and body types, embracing what make them attractive and unique. This change in narrative offers a refreshing display of modern masculinity and self-positivity. Moreover, this new series of Axe ads displays characters that are relatable and inclusive. One such example is the "Find Your Magic" Axe ad, which begins on a loud city street with shots of large billboards displaying idealistic "fit" men and their six-pack abs. The camera then zooms into a car on the street with a woman and man sitting and laughing lovingly at each other. Suddenly, an off-screen male voice begins to narrate, "Come on, a six-pack? Who needs a six pack, when you got the nose." A camera then further zooms in on the man sitting in the car, who looks to be very tall and slim with a rather large nose. The man in the car continues to laugh with the woman beside him as he looks at the camera with a million-dollar smile. "Or a nose, when you got the suit," as what appears to be a cowboy dressed in a blue-striped suit walks confidently down a crowded street placing a cowboy hat on his head, as others walking by him stop and turn to look at him. "Now you don't need the suit, when you've got the moves," as the scene changes to a gym with people running on treadmills. The camera zooms in on one man running backwards on the treadmill as he dances to the beat of his music and smiles over at the girl running beside him. "Or moves, when you got the fire," as the scene changes to a man with flaming red hair in a bathroom hyping himself up by boxing and screaming. "Or fire, when you rock those heels," as it displays two men wearing colourful shirts and heels dancing down a runway while a panel of judges hold up a sign that says "10." "Or heels, when you ride those wheels," as it displays what appears to be a newly married couple on a dance floor. The man in the scene is sitting in a wheelchair with a woman on his lap, and they are spinning in circles with vibrant smiles on their faces. "Looks; man, who needs looks, when you got the books," as two younger boys are shown in a music store buying records and catching each other's attention. "Or books, when you got some balls," as it shows a younger man and woman who appear to be streaking with a flag wrapped around their naked bodies laughing at each other as they run from the police. "And who needs all that, when you get the door," as a younger man opens the door for a woman getting out of a yellow car. "When you got the dough, the brains, the touch, the 'awe'," as it first displays a man behind the counter of what appears to be a pizza parlour clapping his hands together as a cloud of flour appears; then a man standing in front of a chalkboard with a complicated math equation written down, throwing a piece of chalk towards the camera; then a woman laying on a bed grabbing a pillow in sexual delight; and finally a man with a long red beard and leather jacket, sitting on a couch with soft cute little kittens playing on his shoulder. "That's right, who needs the other thing, when you've got your thing, now work on it!" as the scene cuts back to the first man in the car with the him smiling toward the camera as the woman in the driver's seat puts the car in drive and begins to pull away. The ad concludes by re-showing some of the characters applying the Axe grooming products to themselves as the words "Find. Your. Magic" appear across the screen. This ad, then, works to represent men as diverse subjects, with many masculinities, as opposed to products sold to achieve the unachievable, limiting, constraining, violent, oppressive: hegemonic masculinity. Indeed, it puts forth the possibility of opening up masculinity to be more than "getting women and getting laid."

Advertisement campaigns such as this simultaneously highlight the importance of opening up the necessary dialogue surrounding masculinity and function to promote a society that is just, inclusive, and creates space for all of us to Man Up, and Man On!

Note

1 Roosh V, a self-proclaimed "pick-up artist," ignited a storm of controversy and media coverage when he planned a series of men's meet-ups in major Canadian cities seeking men who supported his messages of a return of men as the rulers and controllers of public and private life (Valizadeh, 2015c), keeping women outside of the workforce (Valizadeh, 2015b), advocating for legalized rape (Valizadeh, 2015a), and for men to treat every woman they meet like "a slut" (Valizadeh, 2013).

References

Alderson, D. (2014). Acting straight: Reality TV, gender self-consciousness and forms of capital. *New Formations: A Journal of Culture/Theory/Politics*, *83*(1), 7–24.

Banet-Weiser, S., & Miltner, K. M. (2016). #MasculinitySoFragile: Culture, structure, and networked misogyny. *Feminist Media Studies*, *16*(1), 171–174.

Berbary, L. A., & Johnson, C. W. (2016). En/activist drag: Kings reflect on queerness, queens, and questionable masculinities. *Leisure Sciences*, *27*(4), 1–14.

Bergstrom, K. (2011). "Don't feed the troll": Shutting down debate about community expectations on reddit. com. *First Monday*, *16*(8).

Bernstein, M. S., Monroy-Hernández, A., Harry, D., André, P., Panovich, K., & Vargas, G. G. (2011). 4chan and /b/: An analysis of anonymity and ephemerality in a large online community. *Proceedings of the Fifth International AAAI Conference on Weblogs and Social Media* (pp. 50–57). Available at https://eprints.soton.ac.uk/id/eprint/272345

Blanco, J., & Robinett, J. (2014). Leisure helps get the job done: Intersections of hegemonic masculinity and stress among college-aged males. *Journal of Leisure Research*, *46*(4), 361.

Boswell, T. (2004). American world empire or declining hegemony. *Journal of World-Systems Research*, *10*(2), 516–524.

Brandth, B., & Haugen, M. S. (2005). Doing rural masculinity – From logging to outfield tourism. *Journal of Gender Studies*, *14*(1), 13–22. doi:10.1080/0958923042000331452

Brodie, J. (2008). We are all equal now. *Feminist Theory*, *9*(2), 145–164. doi:10.1177/1464700108090408

Brown, W. (2005). Neoliberalism and the end of liberal democracy. In *Edgework: Critical essays on knowledge and politics* (pp. 37–59). Princeton, NJ: Princeton University Press.

Chess, S., & Shaw, A. (2015). A conspiracy of fishes, or, how we learned to stop worrying about #GamerGate and embrace hegemonic masculinity. *Journal of Broadcasting & Electronic Media*, *59*(1), 208–220.

Connell, R. W. (2005). *Masculinities* (2nd ed.). Berkeley: University of California Press.

Connell, R. (2008). Masculinity construction and sports in boys' education: A framework for thinking about the issue. *Sport, Education and Society*, *13*(2), 131–145. doi:10.1080/13573320801957053

Connell, R. W., & Messerschmidt, J. W. (2005). Hegemonic masculinity: Rethinking the concept. *Gender & Society*, *19*(6), 829–859.

Cousineau, L. S., Oakes, H., & Johnson, C. W. (2018, in press). Appnography: Digital ethnography for app-based culture. In D. C. Parry, C. W. Johnson, & S. Fullagar (Eds.), *Digital dilemmas: Transforming gender identities and power relations in everyday life*. Basingstoke: Palgrave Press.

Cousineau, L., & Roth, J. (2012). Pervasive patriarchal leadership ideology in seasonal residential summer camp staff. *Leadership*, *8*(4), 421–440.

Dean, J., & Aune, K. (2015). Feminism resurgent? Mapping contemporary feminist activisms in Europe. *Social Movement Studies*, *14*(4), 375–395.

Dill, K. E., & Thill, K. P. (2007). Video game characters and the socialization of gender roles: Young people's perceptions mirror sexist media depictions. *Sex Roles*, *57*(11–12), 851–864. doi:10.1007/s11199-007-9278-1

Duncanson, C. (2015). Hegemonic masculinity and the possibility of change in gender relations. *Men and Masculinities*, *18*(2), 231.

Dunlap, R., & Johnson, C. W. (2013). Consuming contradiction: Media, masculinity and (hetero)sexual identity. *Leisure/Loisir*, *37*(1), 69–84.

Earl, J., & Kimport, K. (2011). *Digitally enabled social change: Activism in the internet age*. Cambridge, MA: MIT Press.

Ferber, A. L. (2000). Racial warriors and weekend warriors: The construction of masculinity in mythopoetic and white supremacist discourse. *Men and Masculinities*, *3*(1), 30–56.

Garlick, S. (2010). Taking control of sex? hegemonic masculinity, technology, and internet pornography. *Men and Masculinities*, *12*(5), 597–614.

Ghoussoub, M., & Sinclair-Webb, E. (2000). In *Imagined masculinities: Male identity and culture in the modern middle east*. London: Saqi Books.

Gottzén, L., & Kremer-Sadlik, T. (2012). Fatherhood and youth sports: A balancing act between care and expectations. *Gender & Society*, *26*(4), 639–664. doi:10.1177/0891243212446370

Gramsci, A. (1971). *Selections from the prison notebooks of Antonio Gramsci* [*Quaderni del Carcere*, 6 vols. Rome: Editori Riuniti.] (Q. Hoare & G. N. Smith, Ed. and Trans.). New York: International Publishers.

Halberstam, J. (2011). Introduction: Low theory. In *The queer art of failure* (pp. 1–25). Durham, NC: Duke University Press.

Harvey, L., Ringrose, J., & Gill, R. (2013). Swagger, ratings and masculinity: Theorising the circulation of social and cultural value in teenage boys' digital peer networks. *Sociological Research Online*, *18*(4), 9.

Hearn, J. (2004). From hegemonic masculinity to the hegemony of men. *Feminist Theory*, *5*(1), 49–72.

HeForShe.org (2017). HeForShe official website. Retrieved from http://www.heforshe.org

Humberstone, B. (2000). The "outdoor industry" as social and educational phenomena: Gender and outdoor adventure/education. *Journal of Adventure Education & Outdoor Learning*, *1*(1), 21–35. doi:10.1080/14729670085200041

Humberstone, B., & Pedersen, K. (2001). Gender, class and outdoor traditions in the UK and Norway. *Sport, Education and Society*, *6*(1), 23–33. doi:10.1080/713696039

Hurrelmann, K., & Kolip, P. (2002). In *Geschlecht, Gesundheit und Krankheit: Manner und Frauen im Vergleich* [*Gender, health and illness: Men and women compared*] (K. Hurrelmann & P. Kolip, Eds.). Bern, Germany: Verlag Hans Huber.

Johansson, T., & Ottemo, A. (2015). Ruptures in hegemonic masculinity: The dialectic between ideology and utopia. *Journal of Gender Studies*, *24*(2), 192–206. doi:10.1080/09589236.2013.812514

Johnson, C. W. (2002). Gone country: Negotiating masculinity in a country-western gay bar. Doctoral dissertation, University of Georgia. Available from C. ProQuest Dissertations & Thesis Global.

Johnson, C. W. (2008). "Don't call him a cowboy": Masculinity, cowboy drag, and a costume change. *Journal of Leisure Research*, *40*(3), 385.

Johnson, C. W. (2013). Feminist masculinities: Inquiries into leisure, gender, and sexual identity. In V. J. Freysinger, S. M. Shaw, K. A. Henderson, & M. D. Bialeschki (Eds.), *Leisure, women, and gender* (pp. 245–257). State College, PA: Venture Publishing Inc.

Johnson, C. W., Barnett, J., & Hansen, A. W. (2014). Cultural hegemony. In *The encyclopedia of diversity and social justice*. New York, NY: Routledge.

Johnson, C. W., & Dunlap, R. (2011). "They were not drag queens, they were playboy models and bodybuilders": Media, masculinities and gay sexual identity. *Annals of Leisure Research, 14*(2–3), 209–223.

Johnson, C. W., & Parry D. C. (2015). *Fostering social justice through qualitative inquiry: A methodological guide*. London, UK: Left Coast Press.

Johnson, C. W., Richmond, L., & Kivel, B. D. (2008). "What a man ought to be, he is far from": Collective meanings of masculinity and race in media. *Leisure/Loisir, 32*(2), 303–330.

Johnson, C. W., & Samdahl, D. M. (2005). "The night they took over": Misogyny in a country-western gay bar. *Leisure Sciences, 27*(4), 331–348.

Jordan, A. (2016). Conceptualizing backlash: (UK) men's rights groups, anti-feminism, and postfeminism. *Canadian Journal of Women and the Law, 28*(1), 18–44.

Kaufman, M. (2001). The white ribbon campaign: Involving men and boys in ending global violence against women. In B. Pease & K. Pringle (Eds.), *A man's world? Changing men's practices in a globalized world* (pp. 38–51). London: Zed Books.

Kennelly, J. (2014). "It's this pain in my heart that won't let me stop": Gendered affect, webs of relations, and young women's activism. *Feminist Theory, 15*(3), 241–260. doi:10.1177/1464700114544611

Kimmel, M. S. (1998). Who's afraid of men doing feminism. In Tom Digby (Ed.), *Men doing feminism* (pp. 57–68). New York, NY: Routledge.

Kimmel, M. S. (2010). Masculinity as homophobia: Fear, shame, and silence in the construction of gender identity. In S. R. Harper & F. Harris III (Eds.), *College men and masculinities: Theory, research, and implications for practice* (pp. 23–31). San Francisco, CA: Jossey-Bass.

Kimmel, M. (2013). *Angry white men: American masculinity at the end of an era*. New York, NY: Nation Books.

Kimmel, M. S., & Messner, M. (2001). Boyhood, organized sports and the construction of masculinities. In *Men's lives* (5th ed.). Boston, MA: Allyn and Bacon.

Kindler, H. (2002). *Väter und Kinder [Fathers and children]*. Weinheim/Munich, Germany: Juventa.

Kirkland, E. (2009). Masculinity in video games: The gendered gameplay of *Silent Hill. Camera Obscura: Feminism, Culture, and Media Studies, 71*(24, 2), 161–183. doi:10.1215/02705346-2009-006

Kivel, B. D. (1996). In on the outside, out on the inside: Lesbian/gay/bisexual youth, identity, and leisure. Unpublished manuscript, University of Georgia.

Kivel, B. D., & Johnson, C. W. (2009). Consuming media, making men: Using collective memory work to understand leisure and the construction of masculinity. *Journal of Leisure Research, 41*(1), 109.

Kivel, B. D., Johnson, C. W., & Scraton, S. (2009). (Re) theorizing leisure, experience and race. *Journal of Leisure Research, 41*(4), 473.

Knuttila, L. (2011). User unknown: 4chan, anonymity and contingency. *First Monday, 16*(10).

Light, B. (2013). Networked masculinities and social networking sites: A call for the analysis of men and contemporary digital media. *Masculinities & Social Change, 2*(3), 245–265.

Maclaran, P. (2015). Feminism's fourth wave: A research agenda for marketing and consumer research. *Journal of Marketing Management, 31*(15–16), 1732–1738.

Manago, A. M. (2013). Negotiating a sexy masculinity on social networking sites. *Feminism & Psychology, 23*(4), 478–497.

Martino, W., & Pallotta-Chiarolli, M. (2003). In *Boys' stuff: Boys talking about what matters*. Crows Nest, NSW, Australia: Allen and Unwin.

Messner, M. (2011). Gender ideologies, youth sports, and the production of soft essentialism. *Sociology of Sport Journal*, *28*(2), 151–170.

Messner, M. A., Greenberg, M. A., & Peretz, T. (2015). *Some men: Feminist allies and the movement to end violence against women*. Oxford, UK: Oxford University Press.

Moisio, R., Arnould, E. J., & Gentry, J. W. (2013). Productive consumption in the class-mediated construction of domestic masculinity: Do-it-yourself (DIY) home improvement in men's identity work. *Journal of Consumer Research*, *40*(2), 298–316.

Moisio, R., Beruchashvili, M., Moisio, R., & Beruchashvili, M. (2016). Mancaves and masculinity. *Journal of Consumer Culture*, *16*(3), 656–676. doi:10.1177/1469540514553712

O'Neil, J. M. (2010). Is criticism of generic masculinity, essentialism, and positive-healthy-masculinity a problem for the psychology of men? *Psychology of Men & Masculinity*, *11*(2), 98–106. doi:10.1037/a0018917

Parry, D. C., & Fullagar, S. (2013). Feminist research in the contemporary era. *Journal of Leisure Research*, *45*(5), 571–582.

Pink, S., Horst, H., Postill, J., Hjorth, L., Lewis, T., & Tacchi, J. (2016). *Digital ethnography: Principles and practice*. Thousand Oaks, CA: Sage.

Roberson, J. E., & Suzuki, N. (2003). In *Men & masculinities in contemporary Japan*. London: Routledge.

Rose, J., & Johnson, C. W. (2017). Homelessness, masculinity and health. *Gender, place and culture*. doi.org/10.1080/0966369X.2017.1347559

Savin-Williams, R. C. (1998). Memories of childhood and early adolescent sexual feelings among gay and bisexual boys: A narrative approach. In M. S. Kimmel & M. A. Messner (Eds.), *Men's lives* (4th ed.) (pp. xxii, 600). Boston: Allyn and Bacon.

Schmitz, R. M., & Kazyak, E. (2016). Masculinities in cyberspace: An analysis of portrayals of manhood in men's rights activist websites. *Social Sciences*, *5*(2), 18. doi:10.3390/socsci5020018

Sedgwick, E. K. (1993). Epistemology of the closet. In H. Abelove, M. A. Barale, & D. M. Halperin (Eds.), *The lesbian and gay studies reader* (pp. 45–61). New York, NY: Routledge.

Siibak, A. (2010). Constructing masculinity on a social networking site the case-study of visual self-presentations of young men on the profile images of SNS rate. *Young*, *18*(4), 403–425.

Smith, M. (2005). Resisting and reinforcing neoliberalism: Lesbian and gay organising at the federal and local levels in Canada. *Policy & Politics*, *33*(1), 75–94.

Springer, N., J. (2015). Publics and counterpublics on the front page of the internet: The cultural practices, technological affordances, hybrid economics and politics of reddit's public sphere. PhD thesis. Available from ProQuest. Retrieved from http://noahspringer.com/wp-content/uploads/2015/12/Springer_Reddit_Dissertation.pdf

Sweeney, B. (2014). Party animals or responsible men: Social class, race, and masculinity on campus. *International Journal of Qualitative Studies in Education*, *27*(6), 801–818. doi: 10.1080/09518398.2014.901578

Tyler, M., & Fairbrother, P. (2013). Bushfires are "men's business": The importance of gender and rural hegemonic masculinity. *Journal of Rural Studies*, *30*, 110–119. doi:10.1016/j.jrurstud.2013.01.002

Valizadeh, D. (2013, November 28). *Act as if every girl were a slut*. Retrieved from www.returnofkings.com/21805/act-as-if-every-girl-is-a-slut

Valizadeh, D. (2015a, February 16). *How to stop rape*. Retrieved from www.rooshv.com/how-to-stop-rape

Valizadeh, D. (2015b, October 21). *Why women shouldn't work*. Retrieved from www.rooshv.com/why-women-shouldnt-work

Valizadeh, D. (2015c, September 21). *Women must have their behavior and decisions controlled by men*. Retrieved from www.rooshv.com/women-must-have-their-behavior-and-decisions-controlled-by-men

Wallerstein, I. (1983). The three instances of hegemony in the history of the capitalist world economy. *International Journal of Comparative Sociology*, *24*, 101.

Whitehead, S. M., & Barrett, F. (Eds.) (2001). *The masculinities reader*. New York, NY: John Wiley & Sons.

Further reading

Berbary, L. A., & Johnson, C. W. (2016). En/activist drag: Kings reflect on queerness, queens, and questionable masculinities. *Leisure Sciences: An Interdisciplinary Journal*, *39*(4), 305–318.

Johansson, T., & Ottemo, A. (2015). Ruptures in hegemonic masculinity: The dialectic between ideology and utopia. *Journal of Gender Studies*, *24*(2), 192–206. doi:10.1080/09589236.2013.812514

Johnson, C. W., & Samdahl, D. M. (2005). "The night they took over": Misogyny in a country-western gay bar. *Leisure Sciences*, *27*(4), 331–348.

Pascoe, C. J. (2012). *Dude, you're a fag: Masculinity and sexuality in high school – With a new preface*. Berkeley: University of California Press,

Rose, J., & Johnson, C. W. (in press, 2017). Homelessness, masculinity and health. *Gender and Society*. Manuscript submitted for publication.

Chapter 8

The fourth wave

What #MeToo can teach us about millennial mobilization, intersectionality, and men's accountability

Stephen M. A. Soucie, Diana C. Parry, and Luc S. Cousineau

As discussed in the introduction to this volume, feminist scholarship has an established history of creating ripples and pushing the field of leisure studies in new directions. Given over 30 years of critical inquiries from feminist researchers, scholars in leisure and all of its specializations now have access to an array of nuanced and robust understandings of the complex phenomena of leisure and gender, as well as how they can be studied and represented. Embracing this critical tradition, each chapter in this book functions to provide key insights into some of the innovative conversations and actions currently being taken up by leisure scholars operating within the emergent and dynamic fourth wave of feminism – even if their work may not be readily positioned as such. Taken together, the collection of chapters in this volume calls attention to both the possibilities and limitations of using technology to blur boundaries across waves or movements of feminist thought, and rapidly globalize local feminist agendas – specifically in relation to sexual violence against women.

Given that the #TimHunt incident in June 2015 provided the initial inspiration for this book, it would be remiss of us if we did not address the (re)emergence of the #MeToo movement in October 2017. Since the conceptualization of this project, several feminist-inspired hashtags have entered public consciousness (e.g., #ItsNeverOkay, #PinkTax, #AmINext, #ILookLikeAnEngineer, #SayHerName, and #ShoutYourAbortion). In late 2017, however, the digital environment was dominated by a single hashtag: #MeToo. For leisure scholars, then, an intersectional analysis of the #MeToo movement offers unique and timely lessons about the fourth wave of feminism. In this sense, we have chosen to use #MeToo as an heuristic tool to think about how to represent women's rapid, multivocal response to sexual violence in the current digital landscape, as well as men's role in fostering gender equity moving forward.

From a ripple to a tsunami: #MeToo

On October 5, 2017, the *New York Times* published an investigation by Jodi Kantor and Megan Twohey (2017) into nearly three decades of sexual harassment and assault allegations against Harvey Weinstein, a powerful film producer in Hollywood. In this article, actors Ashley Judd and Rose McGowan openly shared their experiences of sexual violence at the hands of Weinstein. A pivotal moment, this was the first instance of multiple women going on the record to address allegations against Weinstein that date back to 1990 (Victor, 2017). Three days later, on October 8, Weinstein was fired from the film production company he had co-founded, the Weinstein Company – after initially denying the allegations and taking a leave of absence. On October 10, the *New Yorker* published a 10-month investigation by Ronan Farrow (2017) that included interviews with 13 women who stated that Weinstein had sexually harassed or assaulted them. Though not personally impacted by Weinstein's actions, cultural icons like Kate Winslet and Judi Dench swiftly denounced his behaviour (Victor, 2017).

As Weinstein's demise began to dominate the news cycle, a broader conversation about a culture of male sexual predation in Hollywood and other industries began to emerge. On October 15, Alyssa Milano, an actor and activist, tweeted the statement shown in Figure 8.1.

Figure 8.1

Almost instantly, several high-profile women operating within the Hollywood industrial complex responded in solidarity with tweets of #MeToo, including Lady Gaga, Rosario Dawson, Evan Rachel Wood, Debra Messing, Anna Paquin, Patricia Arquette, and Gabrielle Union. Soon, wave after wave of women, and some men, inside and outside Hollywood began using the hashtag to share their experiences with sexual harassment and assault. Within four months of Milano's initial call to action, at least 100 men in positions of power across various industries were accused of sexual violence (USA Today, 2018).

To be sure, we have seen male actors replaced in roles (e.g., Kevin Spacey and Danny Masterson), male politicians stripped of office (e.g., Al Franken and John Conyers, Jr.), male sport coaches and owners removed from the game (e.g., Rich Rodriguez and Jerry Richardson), male chefs taken out of the kitchen (e.g., Mario Batali and Josh Besh), male investors blocked from the boardroom (e.g., John Lasseter and Gavin Baker), male magicians separated from the stage (e.g., David Blaine and David Copperfield), and male media personalities taken off the air (e.g., Matt Lauer and Charlie Rose). In this context, #MeToo is more than an ephemeral hashtag. It has become the largest cultural reckoning with sexual violence since women began to enter the workforce en masse in the 1980s.

Hashtag feminism

How is this wave of feminism distinct from previous waves? According to Cochrane (2013), the fourth wave is defined by technology; more specifically, the digital "tools that are allowing women to build a strong, popular, reactive movement online" (n.p.). In the mid-2000s, the emergence of blogging and citizen journalism functioned to provide visibility for women who had historically struggled to make it past traditional media gatekeepers. Everyday feminists quickly learned to harness this technology and advance the goals of previous waves (i.e., reproductive rights, equal pay, and workplace harassment) on a macro scale. By 2009, for example, Jessica Valenti's foundational website Feministing.com purported to have 600,000 readers per month (Solomon, 2009). As a multitude of similar online spaces began to develop, a new generation of young women and girls (millennials) became exposed to, and eventually began to create, feminist-inspired writing, videos, and memes. Undeniably, this shift in the digital landscape helped return feminism to the realm of public discourse.

In the last five years, we have seen the rise of social media platforms like Facebook, Twitter, Snapchat, and Instagram. These outlets provide feminists from across the globe with the tools to connect, build relationships, and organize. Digital activism in the form of hashtag campaigns, which can reach hundreds of thousands of people through the concentrated efforts of a few, is a contemporary example of how online technology is being taken up in the fourth wave. Feminist-inspired hashtags that have emerged since 2013 (e.g., #SolidarityIsForWhiteWomen, #NotYourAsianSidekick, #WhyIStayed, #Rape

CultureIsWhen, #EverydaySexism, and #YesAllWomen), and their associated campaigns, have provided space for those who are marginalized to share multi-vocal (humorous, angry, sad, and reflexive) responses to sexual violence, and find solidarity.

Through the pervasiveness and ingenuity of digital feminist activism, feminist thought has now re-emerged as a legitimate body of knowledge, taken seriously as a political and social perspective in Western society after a long period of being ignored. As a result, taking up a feminist identity is no longer reserved solely for Women's and Gender Studies students on college and university campuses, or activists in not-for-profits. In Canada, this is perhaps best exemplified by Prime Minister Justin Trudeau's public declaration of himself as a feminist and to share his decision to raise his children with similar values:

> I'm raising my daughter to be a feminist, yes, but [I'm] also raising my sons to be a feminist, and understanding power dynamics and imbalances, and the need to be there to stick up for friends, or individuals who are being victimized or marginalized or harassed or bullied. This is something we have to really focus on as a society.
>
> (Trudeau, 2017, n.p.)

Beyond simply a fringe or women's-only movement, the fourth wave of feminism is distinctly more popular and "men-friendly" than previous waves (Phillips & Cree, 2014, p. 941). Moreover, a brief survey of the #MeToo movement in Canada suggests feminist activism in the fourth wave is complicating the divisive online/offline binary perpetuated through the discourse of hashtag feminism.

Millennial mobilization: #MeToo in Canada

The #MeToo movement has triggered various forms of feminist activism across the world. To sketch some of the localized responses, we searched the Canadian Broadcast Corporation (CBC) website (cbc.ca) for the phrase "MeToo." Despite our prior acknowledgement of the movement as a global social phenomenon, we were still surprised by the number, and geographic distribution, of meaningful feminist-inspired actions taken up by individuals in their local communities. As previously discussed, #MeToo emerged in mid-October 2017. Since then, individuals from across Canada have taken the following concrete actions to address sexual violence in their local communities:

In late October 2017, Joanne Ogilvie, a survivor of sexual assault, chose to partner with the Young Women's Christian Association (YWCA) and host a community discussion in Regina, Saskatchewan, about sexual violence in the media and trauma (CBC News, 2017b). For those unable to attend in person, the event was live-streamed on the YWCA Regina Facebook page. Around the same time, the Union of British Columbia Performers (UBCP) organized a town hall to provide women in the local entertainment industry a safe space to discuss their experiences with sexual violence (Rahmani, 2017); and the Imago Theatre Company, a feminist theatre located in Montreal, Quebec, began offering a free 15-week all-woman mentorship program designed to empower young female artists (Indongo, 2017).

In November 2017, Downstage, a theatre company from Calgary, Alberta, hosted two "Intimacy for the Stage" workshops to teach performers, directors, coaches, and choreographers the importance of bystander intervention and seeking consent (Rieger, 2018). Similarly, Erin Kembel, owner of EMK Clothing in Winnipeg, Manitoba, donated 50 percent of the proceeds from all scarves sold in her store to Willow Place Shelter (CBC News, 2017a). At the shelter's request, Kimbrel also collected donations of pajamas for women and children.

In December 2017, several women worked together to organize a #MeToo march in Toronto, Ontario (McLaughlin, 2017). Two of the organizers – Aisling Chin-Yee, a Canadian film director, and Mia Kirshner, a Canadian actor – also created the #AfterMeToo campaign, which hosted a symposium in Toronto on December 5 and 6, 2017, to address sexual violence in Canada's entertainment industry (McLaughlin, 2017).

In January 2018, 29 Women's Marches were held across Canada. In Saint John, New Brunswick, Keri-Lynn Calp has organized the Women's March for the last two years, aiming to make it an annual event as long as is necessary (Trainor, 2018). After attending the 2017 Women's March in Saskatoon, Nancy Johnson took on organizing a similar march in her hometown of Thunder Bay, Ontario, for 2018 (CBC News, 2018). Both women cited the #MeToo movement as motivation to act. At the end of January 2018, the Red Gate Arts society, located in Vancouver, British Columbia (BC), hosted a town hall about consent and accountability in the BC entertainment industry (Hennig, 2018).

In February 2018, Sandra Pasmen, a visual artist from Kamloops, BC, hosted her first art exhibit, which featured a 47-piece collection that she created and centered around the theme of women's empowerment. All proceeds from the silent auction of the pieces were donated to the Family Tree Family Centre, a non-profit that provides support to mothers on the margins (Dickson, 2018). Responding to the momentum of the #MeToo movement, Women in Film and Television Atlantic is now working to establish a code of conduct for all workers (union and non-union) in the Atlantic entertainment industry (von Stackelberg, 2018).

Here, then, we can see a plethora of examples from both rural and urban Canadian communities that call attention to some of the ways in which #MeToo has become a consciousness-raising tool for women and girls to debate, organize, and build a strong, reactive, and popular movement. All of these examples are Canadian, and they are complemented by countless examples of the power of #MeToo to move activism between online and offline settings from the US, UK, Australia, and many other countries. In this context, exploring feminist activism within an online/offline binary is no longer productive. Instead, it is important for leisure scholars to acknowledge that in this wave "activism online is offline activism and offline activism is online activism" (Zimmerman, 2017, p. 59). Building on this lesson, what else can the #MeToo movement teach us about contemporary feminist praxes?

Interconnected does not mean intersectional

"When feminism does not explicitly oppose racism, and when antiracism does not incorporate opposition to patriarchy, race and gender politics often end up being antagonistic to each other and both interests lose" (Crenshaw, 1992, p. 405). For leisure scholars, the #MeToo movement is a reminder that, although we are more interconnected in this wave – we must continue to be intentional about centering intersectional perspectives. To be sure, Crenshaw's (1988) initial attempts at sketching how women of colour experience complex inequalities based on the intersection of race and gender remain deeply relevant to our field of study. Why? As Lorde (1984) deftly noted, "there is no such thing as a single-issue struggle because we do not live single-issue lives" (p. 163). Unfortunately, there has been "little direct engagement with intersectionality within leisure scholarship" (Watson & Scraton, 2013, p. 35). This is troubling, as Crenshaw's (1988) concept is useful for all researchers seeking to "analyze oppressive, privileged structures, diversity, and heterogeneity" (Zimmerman, 2017, p. 64). Taking up an intersectional analysis of #MeToo, as an example, allows for a critical examination into some of the ways in which this movement has been represented in the media and appropriated by mainstream (White) feminism.

Tarana Burke is the senior director of Girls for Gender Equality, a non-profit based in Brooklyn, New York, focused on empowering young women and girls of colour. In 1996, Burke was working as a youth camp director when a young female camper disclosed that an older man in her life had sexually assaulted her on multiple occasions. A survivor of sexual violence herself, Burke froze. Unsure of how to respond, she sent the camper to talk to another female counsellor. As the camper walked away, Burke recalls wanting to whisper, "me too" (Brockes, 2018, n.p.). In the two decades since, Burke has become a public educator and now uses this phrase as a consciousness-raising tool in girl-centeered programming to help encourage "empowerment through empathy" (Hill, 2017, n.p.) After growing up on the margins, Burke concentrates her efforts in working-poor and racialized communities, "where rape crisis centers and sexual assault workers weren't going" when she started her activism (Hill, 2017, n.p.).

After 20 years of offline use, mostly during workshops and community events, Burke's phrase went viral following Milano's call to action on Twitter. Alerted by friends and colleagues that Me Too was circulating widely online, Burke responded with the tweet shown in Figure 8.2.

Figure 8.2

Over the next two weeks, #MeToo was included in 1.7 million tweets from users in more than 85 countries (Park, 2017). During this same period, Facebook claims that 45 percent of U.S. users had at least one friend include the phrase "me too" in a post (Park, 2017). Rather than joy, Burke soon "felt a sense of dread, because something that was part of my life's work was going to be co-opted and taken from me and used for a purpose that I hadn't originally intended" (Garcia, 2017). More specifically, she was upset because:

> The celebrities who popularized the hashtag didn't take a moment to see if there was work already being done, but they also were trying to make a larger point … I don't fault them for that part, I don't think it was intentional but somehow sisters still managed to get diminished or erased in these situations. A slew of people raised their voices so that that didn't happen.
>
> (Hill, 2017, n.p.)

Twenty years ago, Burke founded the Me Too movement as a community-based response to sexual violence. Without warning, Burke's grassroots message became rapidly popularized by a White female celebrity and adopted by mainstream feminism. Here, then, we can see Burke articulating feelings of ambivalence in relation to negotiating the sudden visibility of Me Too with the historical erasure of black feminist thought by mainstream (White) feminism.

Upon learning about the Me Too movement started by Burke, Milano released a statement acknowledging that a friend had sent her the image embedded in the initial tweet and that she had circulated the phrase without knowing its origins (see Figure 8.3).

While Burke continues to be bombarded with ways to monetize Me Too (Brockes, 2018), she is not concerned about retaining ownership: "It is bigger than me and bigger than Alyssa Milano. Neither one of us should be centered in this work. This is about survivors" (Garcia, 2017). Given Burke's vision for the movement, it is interesting to note how #MeToo was first represented by the media. Deadline.com, for example, chose to title their initial article: "Alyssa Milano Launches 'Me Too' Hashtag to Raise Awareness of Sexual Assault and Harassment" (Ramos, 2017a). Following Burke's emergence, Deadline.com updated the title to read: "Alyssa Milano Tweets 'Me Too' Hashtag Inspired by Tarana Burke, Raising Awareness of Sexual Abuse" (Ramos, 2017b) Although Burke is made visible in this second version, the word "launches" is now missing – as well as the corresponding implication that Milano is the leader of the movement.

On October 19, 2017, Milano appeared on Good Morning America to position herself as a "vessel" rather than a "leader" of the burgeoning movement to end sexual violence (Kindelan, 2017). During this interview, Milano also took time to highlight the importance of recognizing and collaborating with existing community-based efforts – including Burke's Me Too movement. Without

Figure 8.3

question, Milano's early ally-ship helped solidify Burke's position as the "founder" of #MeToo. Operating in this role, Burke has since received several accolades. Most notably, Burke and other "silence breakers" were named *Time Magazine*'s Person of the Year in 2017. While Burke's image was relegated to the inside pages, white celebrities like Taylor Swift and Ashleigh Judd were featured prominently on the cover alondside the text: "The Silence Breakers – The Voices that Launched a Movement." It is here, then, that we once again see a desire from the media to erase Burke and frame Milano as a leader of the #MeToo movement.

Until recently, Burke had remained publicly quiet about her concerns with the representation of #MeToo leadership in the media. On February 21, 2018, Burke tweeted the messages shown in Figure 8.4.

Undeniably, the dominant media representation of #MeToo centers the leadership of Milano and erases Burke's two decades of work on the front lines,

Figure 8.4

supporting working-poor women of colour who have experienced sexual violence. At the same time, these tweets should not be interpreted as evidence of Burke's desire to be named a leader. Rather, as a woman of colour raised in a working-poor home, Burke spoke out to encourage others to reflect on how the representation of #MeToo in the media might be shaping both the legacy and future goals of the movement. Indeed, the real-world impact of Me Too extends beyond first months and the Hollywood Hills. Burke wants us to remember this important history and vision, as a global social phenomenon she brought to life from the margins ripples further and further away from its radical roots.

As leisure scholars, what can we do to ensure that we are not contributing to the erasure of women of colour like Burke? In 2017, Christen Smith, an anthropologist from the University of Texas at Austin, was attending a conference when she heard a speaker reading an excerpt from her book without giving her credit (Tiangco, 2018). After consulting with friends and colleagues, Smith decided to create T-shirts with the text "Cite Black Women" and take them to the 2017 National Women's Studies Association (NWSA) annual conference in Baltimore, Maryland. She quickly sold out. Following this conference, Smith made another batch and took them to the 2017 American Anthropological Association annual meeting in Washington, DC. She sold out again. At both conferences, she was inspired by the number of non-Black female academics from various cultural backgrounds wearing the T-shirt to "their panels and sessions and posting selfies on Twitter" (Inge, 2018, n.p.). Given the enthusiastic response, Smith decided to create Cite Black Women accounts on social media platforms like Facebook, Instagram, and Twitter.

On January 1, 2018, the Cite Black Women Facebook page released a series of posts detailing five resolutions for the new year: (1) Read Black women's work, (2) integrate Black women into the core of your syllabus; (3) acknowledge Black women's intellectual production; (4) make space for Black women to speak; and (5) give Black women the space and time to breathe. Radical and practical, these vows provide leisure scholars with actionable entry points into thinking deeply about who we make visible and who we erase in our activism, research, and teaching. Though we are more interconnected than ever before, the popularity of the Cite Black Women project is a reminder that we must be intentional about taking up a feminist praxis based on intersectionality. If not, just like #MeToo, we will continue to "discover" social phenomena that those on the margins (for example, indigenous women) have known about and organized against for years.

Men's accountability

Moving forward in the fourth wave, what lessons can leisure scholars learn from #MeToo about engaging men as allies in ending sexual violence? Matt Lauer, former co-host of the flagship *Today* show at the National Broadcasting Company (NBC), is among more than 100 men in positions of power across various industries that have been accused of sexual violence in the wake of #MeToo. In a memo issued to staff, Andrew Lack, NBC News Chairperson, claimed to have first learned about the allegations on Monday, November 27, 2017 (Bauder, 2017). Two days later, Lauer's contract with NBC was terminated on the grounds of "inappropriate sexual behaviour in the workplace" stemming from a "detailed complaint" filed by a colleague (Bauder, 2017). On the Wednesday morning of that week, only hours after learning about the allegations and Lauer's dismissal, Savannah Guthrie, co-host of the *Today* show, offered the following response live on-air: "We are grappling with a dilemma that so many people have faced these weeks. How do you reconcile your love for someone with the recognition that they have behaved badly? And I don't know the answer to that" (Rubin, 2017, n.p.). While we do not have an answer either, our activism is centered on the feminist praxis that we must begin this process by fostering a culture of accountability.

What does a culture of accountability look like in our community of (leisure) practice? In 2015, University of Waterloo (UW) President Feridun Hamdullahpur accepted an invitation from the UN Women's HeForShe campaign to participate in the IMPACT 10x10x10 framework alongside governments, businesses, and other universities (heforshe.org). Through this framework, Hamdullahpur and nine other university presidents from across the globe committed to developing innovative approaches to achieve gender equity, most notably through the engagement of men on campus. As Associate Vice-President Human Rights, Equity and Inclusion at UW, Diana (Parry) was selected to be the IMPACT 10x10x10 campus lead.

Fostering a culture of accountability at UW

Since 2016, Stephen has worked with Diana and UW's HeForShe campaign to facilitate a monthly healthy masculinity workshop across each faculty on campus. These small group conversations with 10–15 men function to foster moments of critical introspection rarely encouraged in most male-only spaces. To reduce defensiveness, current best practice suggests beginning these sessions by making the issue of sexual violence personally relevant to men (Flood, 2006). In this context, Stephen often opens the discussion by asking participants to consider some of the ways in which the dominant narrative of manhood has structured their lived experience: What does it mean to be a "real man"? What emotions are "real men" supposed to have? How are "real men" supposed to be different from women? While reflecting on these seldom-asked questions, participants are provided the space to connect their individual understandings with broader sociocultural narratives of masculinity. Through this critical exercise, men's individual tensions are revealed to be collective tensions. To be sure, most men are not comfortable with the dominant (and hegemonic) narrative of masculinity in our society. Unfortunately, perhaps through pluralistic ignorance (Prentice & Miller, 1993), most men feel as if they are the only ones uncomfortable when other men make sexist comments or jokes. Hence, they remain silent and allow women's oppression to continue uncontested.

From this consciousness-raising foundation, Stephen leads participants into a group discussion about men's responsibility to end sexual violence. We are not guilty because we are men, we are responsible. We have a responsibility to show up for difficult conversations. We have a responsibility to amplify the voices of those on the margins. We have a responsibility to mobilize our privilege. Though men's desire to become engaged as gender equity champions is often piqued during these sessions, there is no blueprint for what an individual should do once the workshop ends. What is currently missing from most anti-violence engagement strategies targeting men, then, is a mobilization component. To address this significant gap, Stephen (Soucie), Diana (Parry), and colleagues have begun to integrate the principles of design thinking into existing feminist pedagogy. Design thinking is best understood as an "orientation toward learning that encompasses active problem solving and believing in one's ability to create impactful change" (Carroll, 2014, p. 16). Rather than perpetrators or bystanders, we utilize design thinking to engage men as leaders and problem solvers. Through this unique approach, men at UW are learning the tools necessary to self-organize and address sexual violence on campus. These workshops are something that can be taken up, tweaked to reflect the social and cultural context of the geographical location, and offered at universities around the world.

The underlying motivations for engagement activities like the HeForShe campaign, or UW's masculinity workshops, are to engage men as part of the solution to issues like those discussed in this chapter. By engaging men in these ways, we hope that a pre-emptive tone can be set that prevents men from transitioning to a worldview that frames them as the victims in societal change, rather than important agents in progressive social development. The #MeToo movement provides both progressive narrative and counternarrative related to this positioning of men as either agents of change or victims. On the one hand, #MeToo allows men to acknowledge and engage with the difficult discussions around rampant sexism, patriarchal power, sexual behaviour, and privilege, which are at the core of why the movement has become so big and so loud. Even as some men try to distance themselves from those accused, and their accusers, with ill-conceived counterpoints like Russell Simmons' #notme (Bryant, 2018), others, like Dr. Michael Kehler of the University of Calgary, are using #MeToo as an anchor to discuss masculinity, personal interactions, and our culture of complacency around sexual violence (Weber, 2018). Men who are victims of sexual violence have also used #MeToo to expose their victimization, most famously actor Terry Crews.

On the other hand, men (and some women) are using the #MeToo movement as a sign that the social status quo, and the rightful place of men as powerful and in control, are under attack (Lynch & Paglia, 2017). In particular, Men's Rights Activists (MRA) have seized on elements of the #MeToo movement to highlight its possible ill-effects on men. Notwithstanding the belief in many MRA communities that feminism has already transitioned our social order to one that privileges women and disadvantages men, #MeToo offers MRAs the opportunity to position men as being robbed of their right to due process and judged only in a kangaroo court of public opinion (Lapidus & Park, 2018). For MRAs, the strength of #MeToo is an indication not of pervasive problems in the social order and how we address sex, sexuality, and power, but rather of a "witch hunt" meant to further disadvantage men and solidify the social and political stranglehold on power held by feminism (Mumford, 2018). The fear expressed by these advocates of men's rights at the possible loss of due process is steeped with irony, given that accusers (especially women, but men as well) are consistently devalued and dismissed when they report sexual assault to the police, and frequently suffer attacks of character and behaviour if those accusations ever make it to trial. Most don't (Sable, Danis, Mauzy, & Gallagher, 2006).

We firmly believe that the #MeToo movement can serve as a catalyst for deeper social change in our sexual and social relationships. Speaking to the roles of men as part of that positive change, small actions (like engaging in thoughtful discussion about sexual violence), and larger actions (like calling out friends, family, or even strangers for behaviours that victimize or subjugate), are necessary for the power of #MeToo to translate into tangible change for the future.

As scholars/academics/activists, our role is to take on these large and small actions, and consciously integrate the lessons learned through the exposure of the pervasiveness of sexual misconduct in society into our work. As leisure scholars, our work extends into the liminal spaces between isolated units of life, and we have a responsibility to interrogate how the paradigms of leisure, work, and power are changed by social movements like #MeToo. These discussions must also be taken up within the discrete sub-fields within leisure studies, and we would call on scholars from tourism, sport and sport management, therapeutic recreation, outdoor recreation, parks, and others within the broad umbrella of leisure research to take up this call. The work in each of these areas must move beyond basic notions of "add gender and stir," which does little to interrogate social structures and less still to promote positive social change, and must take on and resist traditional notions of power, gender, sexuality, and place. Some of this work is already being done in sport (Lebel, Pegoraro, & Harman, 2018), and tourism (Wearing, Small, & Foley, 2018), but it must continue and grow. These are also onto-epistemological questions. As Berbary (Chapter 2), Fullagar et al. (Chapter 3), and Watson (Chapter 4) demonstrate in this book, the value of challenging worldviews and preconceived notions of what is "correct" could lead us into a better future.

Concluding thoughts

Even while writing this book, we understand that the fourth wave of feminism is contested terrain, and the discussion and debate surrounding it is far from complete. The intended purpose of the book is not to espouse an all-encompassing conceptualization of a fourth wave, or to set it as a standard by which to judge all feminist work in leisure studies, but to encourage conversation about approaches and intentions in research as we engage with a rapidly changing world. This book is not meant to be an end, but a beginning.

References

Bauder, D. (2017, November 29). NBC fires Matt Lauer for "inappropriate sexual behaviour." Retrieved from www.theglobeandmail.com/news/world/nbc-terminates-matt-lauer-for-inappropriate-workplace-behaviour/article37122404/

Brockes, E. (2018, January 15). *Me Too founder Tarana Burke: You have to use your privilege to serve other people.* Retrieved from www.theguardian.com/world/2018/jan/15/me-too-founder-tarana-burke-women-sexual-assault

Bryant, K. (2018, January 9). Russell Simmons makes at least one good decision following sexual assault allegations. *Vanity Fair.* Retrieved from www.vanityfair.com/style/2018/01/russell-simmons-suspends-not-me-campaign

Carroll, M. P. (2014). Shoot for the moon! The mentors and the middle schoolers explore the intersection of design thinking and STEM. *Journal of Pre-College Engineering Education Research*, *4*(1), 14–30.

CBC News (2017a, October 29). *Get cozy to help domestic violence victims: Winnipeg designer raises money for shelter through scarf sales.* Retrieved from www.cbc.ca/news/canada/manitoba/emk-metoo-fundraiser-1.4375372

CBC News (2017b, October 24). *Prevalence of sexual assault stories in the media sparks discussion in Regina.* Retrieved from www.cbc.ca/news/canada/saskatchewan/post-sexual-assault-trauma-regina-1.4369426

CBC News (2018, January 19). Women's march to take to the streets in Thunder Bay, organizer says voices "still need to be heard." Retrieved from www.cbc.ca/news/canada/thunder-bay/thunder-bay-women-s-march-2018–1.4493772

Cochrane, K. (2013, December 10). *The fourth wave of feminism: Meet the rebel women.* Retrieved from www.theguardian.com/world/2013/dec/10/fourth-wave-feminism-rebel-women

Crenshaw, K. (1988). Demarginalizing the intersection of race and sex: A black feminist critique of antidiscrimination doctrine, feminist theory and antiracist politics. *University of Chicago Legal Forum*, *1*(8), 139–167.

Crenshaw, K. (1992). Race, gender, and sexual harassment. *Southern California Legal Revue*, *65*, 1467–1476.

Dickson, C. (2018, January 30). *If she only knew: Art show aims to empower women.* Retrieved from www.cbc.ca/news/canada/british-columbia/if-she-only-knew-art-show-1.4510732

Farrow, R. (2017, December 22). *From aggressive overtures to sexual assault: Harvey Weinstein's accusers tell their stories.* Retrieved from www.newyorker.com/news/news-desk/from-aggressive-overtures-to-sexual-assault-harvey-weinsteins-accusers-tell-their-stories

Flood, M. (2006). Changing men: Best practice in sexual violence education. *Women Against Violence: An Australian Feminist Journal*, *18*, 26–36.

Garcia, S. E. (2017, October 20). *The woman who created #MeToo long before hashtags.* Retrieved from www.nytimes.com/2017/10/20/us/me-too-movement-tarana-burke.html

Hennig, C. (2018, January 30). *Vancouvers art and entertainment industry launches conversation about consent*. Retrieved from www.cbc.ca/news/canada/british-columbia/town-hall-consent-red-gate-arts-society-1.4511186

Hill, Z. (2017, December 6). *Black woman Tarana Burke Founded The "Me Too" movement*. Retrieved from www.ebony.com/news-views/black-woman-me-too-movement-tarana-burke-alyssa-milano

Indongo, N. (2017, December 5). *Montreal feminist theatres mentorship program gives young women tools to find their voices*. Retrieved from www.cbc.ca/news/canada/montreal/imago-montreal-artista-metoo-1.4426575

Inge, S. (2018, January 23). *"Cite Black Women" campaign gains momentum*. Retrieved from www.timeshighereducation.com/news/cite-black-women-campaign-gains-momentum

Kantor, J., & Twohey, M. (2017, October 5). *Harvey Weinstein paid off sexual harassment accusers for decades*. Retrieved from www.nytimes.com/2017/10/05/us/harvey-weinstein-harassment-allegations.html

Kindelan, K. (2017, October 19). *Alyssa Milano on #MeToo campaign: We are going to be vocal until this stops*. Retrieved from abcnews.go.com/Entertainment/alyssa-milano-metoo-campaign-vocal-stops/story?id=50582023

Lapidus, L. & Park, S. (2018, February 15). The real meaning of due process in the #MeToo Era: President Trump should know that also fairness requires that those reporting violence and harassment be fully heard. *The Atlantic*, Retrieved from www.theatlantic.com/politics/archive/2018/02/due-process-metoo/553427/

Lebel, K., Pegoraro, A., & Harman, A. (2018). The impact of digital culture on women in sport. In D. C. Parry, C. W. Johnson, & S. Fullagar (Eds.), *Digital dilemmas: Transforming gender identities and power relations in everyday life*. Basingstoke, UK: Palgrave.

Lorde, A. (1984). Eye to eye: Black women, hatred, and anger. In *Sister outsider: Essays and speeches* (pp. 145–175). Trumansburg, NY: Crossing Press.

Lynch, L. (Host), & Paglia, C. (Guest). (2017). Modern feminism needs to "stop blaming men" says Camille Paglia [Radio series segment]. In K. Marley (Prod.), *The Current*. Toronto, Ontario: Canadian Broadcasting Company Radio.

McLaughlin, A. (2017, December 2). *Toronto's #MeToo march gives hundreds of sexual misconduct survivors space to stand together, heal*. Retrieved from www.cbc.ca/news/canada/toronto/toronto-me-too-march-1.4430207

Mumford, G. (2018, February 12). Michael Haneke: #MeToo has led to a witch hunt "coloured by a hatred of men." *Guardian*, Retrieved from www.theguardian.com/film/2018/feb/12/michael-haneke-metoo-witch-hunt-coloured-hatred-men

Park, A. (2017, October 24). *#MeToo reaches 85 countries with 1.7M tweets*. Retrieved from www.cbsnews.com/news/metoo-reaches-85-countries-with-1-7-million-tweets/

Phillips, R., & Cree, V. E. (2014). What does the "fourth wave" mean for teaching feminism in twenty-first century social work? *Social Work Education*, *33*(7), 930–943.

Prentice, D. A., & Miller, D. T. (1993). Pluralistic ignorance and alcohol use on campus: some consequences of misperceiving the social norm. *Journal of Personality and Social Psychology*, *64*(2), 243.

Rahmani, T. (2017, October 30). *"Almost everybody has a story": B.C. actors union to host sexual harassment forum*. Retrieved from www.cbc.ca/news/canada/british-columbia/almost-everybody-has-a-story-b-c-actors-union-to-host-sexual-harassment-forum-1.4372347

Ramos, D. (2017a, October 15). Alyssa Milano launches "Me Too" hashtag to raise awareness of sexual assault and harassment. *Deadline.com*. Retrieved from https://web.

archive.org/web/20171016080830/http://deadline.com/2017/10/alyssa-milano-me-too-hashtag-twitter-rose-mcgowan-sexual-harassment-awareness-1202188999/

Ramos, D. (2017b, October 15). Alyssa Milano tweets "Me Too" hashtag inspired by Tarana Burke, raising awareness of sexual abuse. *Deadline.com*. Retrieved from http://deadline.com/2017/10/alyssa-milano-me-too-hashtag-twitter-rose-mcgowan-sexual-harassment-awareness-1202188999/

Rieger, S. (2018, January 05). Calgary theatre community talks consent in wake of #MeToo movement. Retrieved from www.cbc.ca/news/canada/calgary/calgary-theatre-sexual-harassment-1.4474140

Rubin, R. (2017, November 29). Savannah Guthrie fights back tears announcing Matt Lauer's firing. *Variety*. Retrieved from http://variety.com/2017/tv/news/savannah-guthrie-announces-matt-lauer-firing-video-1202625849/

Sable, M. R., Danis, F., Mauzy, D. L., & Gallagher, S. K. (2006). Barriers to reporting sexual assault for women and men: Perspectives of college students. *Journal of American College Health*, 55(3), 157–162.

Solomon, D. (2009, November 14). Fourth-wave feminism. Retrieved from www.nytimes.com/2009/11/15/magazine/15fob-q4-t.html

Tiangco, K. (2018, January 28). *Black women's work isn't credited enough*. Retrieved from http://naturallymoi.com/2018/01/black-womens-work-isnt-credited-enough/

Trainor, S. (2018, January 10). *Women's March 2.0 rallies to be held in Saint John, Fredericton*. Retrieved from www.cbc.ca/news/canada/new-brunswick/womens-march-2018-new-brunswick-1.4480667

Trudeau, J. (2017). Prime Minister Justin Trudeau talks housing, sexual assault and Canada's future. Interviewer: Matt Galloway. Maytree Conference at the Rotman School of Business, University of Toronto, Toronto, Canada.

USA Today. (2018, January 30). *After Weinstein: More than 100 high-powered men accused of sexual misconduct*. Retrieved from www.usatoday.com/story/news/2017/11/22/weinstein-aftermath-all-men-accused-sexual-misconduct/884778001/

Victor, D. (2017, October 18). *How the Harvey Weinstein story has unfolded*. Retrieved from www.nytimes.com/2017/10/18/business/harvey-weinstein.html

von Stackelberg, M. (2018, January 28). *Local film industry working on sexual harassment policy*. Retrieved from www.cbc.ca/news/canada/nova-scotia/women-in-film-workshop-1.4507798

Watson, B., & Scraton, S. J. (2013). Leisure studies and intersectionality. *Leisure Studies*, 32(1), 35–47.

Wearing, S., Small, J., & Foley, C. (2018). Gender and the Body in Leisure and Tourism. In L. Mansfield, J. Caudwell, B. Wheaton, & B. Watson (Eds.), *The Palgrave handbook of feminism and sport, leisure and physical education*. London: Palgrave Macmillan.

Weber, B. (2018, February 28). Boys to men: Calgary lecture series examines masculinity in #MeToo movement. *Calgary Herald*, Retrieved from http://calgaryherald.com/news/local-news/boys-to-men-calgary-lecture-series-examines-masculinity-in-metoo-movement

Zimmerman, T. (2017). #Intersectionality: The fourth wave feminist Twitter community. *Atlantis: Critical Studies in Gender, Culture & Social Justice*, 38(1), 54–70.

Index

affect: theories of 34, 43
agency/structure 4, 37, 126–127, 130–136
agential realism 38; *see also* Barad, Karen; new materialism

Barad, Karen 38; *see also* agential realism; new materialism
biopower 91–95; *see also* Puar, Jasbir
Brah, Avtar 62; *see also* difference; identity; intersectionality
Butler, Judith 18–20, 83–85; *see also* Queer theory

Connell, R.W. 129–136; *see also* hegemonic masculinities
contextualisation 60; *see also* intersectionality
creative class 91
Crenshaw, Kimberle 7, 59; *see also* difference; identity; intersectionality
Creolisation theory 61, 62, 64; *see also* intersectionality

deconstruction 23–24; *see also* post theories
Deleuze, Gilles 15, 40; *see also* affect, theories of; new materialism
difference 3, 61–62, 127–128
diffraction 27–29, 39; *see also* post theories; new materialism
digital feminist activism 1, 6–7, 9, 46, 60, 70, 95–96, 149–152

feminist leisure lens 71
fourth wave feminism 3, 5–9, 70, 151–158; *see also* digital feminist activism

gendered subjectivity 4, 17–18, 137
globalization 7–8
Gramsci, Antonio 129–134; *see also* hegemonic masculinities
Grenfell Tower 58, 60, 62, 63, 64, 73
Guttari, Felix 40; *see also* affect, theories of; new materialism

hegemonic femininities 73
hegemonic masculinities 71–72, 90, 127–135, 159–160
hegemony 130
heteronormative 128, 139
hockey: Edmonton Oilers 90–94; Pride Tape 79, 90–94
homophobia 90–91, 128
homonationalism 87–89
homonormative 87, 139
Humanism 13–30
Humanist Man, the 15–17

identity 61, 126–128, 135
interdisciplinary 68
intersectionality: interconnectedness 7; thinking intersectionally 58; leisure and 85–86; queer theory and 85–86; intersectional analysis 90–94, 154–158

Katz, Jackson 138; *see also* men's role in feminism

leisure, and: embodiment 66; media 126–127, 142–143; hegemonic masculinity 135–137; resistance 18–80, 25–27, 43, 158; poststructural feminism 13–14, 23–24; sexuality 86; space 65; Whiteness 67, 87

masculinities *see* hegemonic masculinities

men's rights activists 140–141, 160–161
men's role in feminism 128, 137–141, 158–161; *see also* Katz, Jackson

neoliberalism 49, 90–94
new materialism: Deleuzian onto-epistemologies 15; matter 38; representationalism 39; *see also* agential realism; Barad, Karen; Deleuze, Gilles; Guttari, Felix
new media ecology 44

Othering 131–132

palimpsest 14; *see also* post theories
post-feminism 4–5, 43
post theories: postmodernism 13; poststructuralism 13–30, 36; postcolonialism 13, 61; posthumanism 13; *see also* Queer theory
psychoanalytic theory 94
Puar, Jasbir 87–88; *see also* biopower

Queer theory: charmed circle 82, 87; Critically Queer 84–85; decolonizing sexuality 95–96; Gender Trouble 83–85; gay and lesbian studies 83; queer 79; performativity 15, 18–20, 24–25, 38, 84; queer liberalism 85; queer of colour theorists 87; sex wars 82; *see also* Butler, Judith; Rubin, Gayle; Rifkin, Mark; Sedgwick, Eve; post theories

relationality 42
Rifkin, Mark 91–94; *see also* Queer theory; settler colonialism; settler homonationalism
Rubin, Gayle 81–82, 87; *see also* Queer theory

Sedgwick, Eve 128; *see also* Queer theory
settler colonialism 89–90; *see also* post theories; Queer theory
settler homonationalism 89–90
sexual violence 1, 8, 154–158
Spivak, Gayatri Chakravorty *see* strategic essentialism; post theories
strategic essentialism 61; *see also* post theories

waves of feminism: possibilities and limitations 2–3; first wave 3; second wave 3; third wave 3–4; *see also* fourth wave feminism
Web 2.0 34
White epistemic certainty 68